SHADOWRUN:
DENIABLE ASSETS

MEL ODOM

SHADOWRUN: DENIABLE ASSETS
Cover art by Victor Manuel Leza Moreno
Design by Matt Heerdt

Published by Catalyst Game Labs,
an imprint of InMediaRes Productions, LLC
PMB 202 • 303 91st Ave NE • E502 • Lake Stevens, WA 98258

ACKNOWLEDGEMENTS

For Loren Coleman and John Helfers,
who invited me back into the shadows and
made me welcome.

DEDICATION

For my son Chandler, who ran the deep shadows
of Hong Kong with me!

CHAPTER ONE

"You don't talk a lot."

Mr. Johnson's voice was tight. Mr. Johnson wasn't his name, of course. Every corp contact or person that hired a shadowrunner used that cover name, or one similarly innocuous.

Hawke looked at the man. "Compared to whom?"

Mr. Johnson stared at him for a moment. "For someone in your business. I just thought you'd talk more."

Hawke sighed and shifted on the booth seat. He was nearly two meters tall barefoot and weighed about 120 kilos. The leg-room in Tang's Rice and Noodle Bar hadn't been designed with him in mind, but he was better off than the trolls. Hawke shaved his head and kept his face clean. Rangy and athletic, he stood out in a street full of skells, but his hooded duster blunted the hard lines and shadowed his face. His swarthy skin color came from his Cuban mother, but his green eyes were a gift from his Irish father.

Mr. Johnson was a typical youngblood corp exec. He was in his thirties, which meant he'd never rise much above his current station, and one day he'd be cannon fodder for the megacorp he served. He didn't have any kind of edge to him, and seemed more defensive than proactive. He had a good manicure, but he'd ragged his nails recently. Crusty blood lined the nail beds of the index and middle fingers on his left hand.

The man's smooth-shaven face and gelled black hair reflected the neon gleam penetrating the front window of Tang's in Santa Fe's Old Town District. His stylish suit was well cared for, but it was heavy with body armor and hung wrong as he sat in the booth. It had been cut to conceal the protection while standing, further marking him as disposable. A guy didn't pull down the big cred while standing—unless he had a pistol in his fist.

Tang's was a low-rent place, but had plenty of space for its clientele to spread out among the booths and tables. Security was at a minimum, but the hidden high-tech and the experienced wait staff could sniff out a Lone Star SWAT team a mile away. By the time the cops arrived, every runner in the place would have vanished in the maze of alleys around the joint.

Southwest turquoises and yellows warred with Japanese reds and blacks in the color scheme, barely holding back the dark night outside the window overlooking the street. Two female bartenders kept drinks flowing, along with endless chatter, but Hawke knew both women were heavily cybered. They moved like they were articulated with ball bearings. The vidcams were equipped with Saeder-Krupp 20mm miniguns. Seasoned fragrances rolled from the kitchen in the back of the house.

The high menu prices included the security, and were well worth the investment.

"Despite this." Hawke tapped the innocuous Mitsuhama Computer Technologies white noise generator sitting on the table. "We're not here to talk. You're here to offer me a run. I'm here to decide whether I want it. If there's not enough cred involved, I walk away. If I don't like the run, I walk away. If the run is something I don't think I can do, I walk away."

In the darkness slashed by neon, Mr. Johnson hung on every word.

"If I think you're setting me up," Hawke said in that same flat, matter-of-fact voice, "I kill you and I walk away."

Mr. Johnson leaned back.

"Is there anything else you'd like to discuss?" Hawke asked.

"Not really," Mr. Johnson said, then shook his head. "No."

"Okay."

Mr. Johnson reached into his jacket too fast, caught himself, and moved slower. "I've got a credstick I was instructed to give you."

"Sure." Hawke kept the Raecor Sting holdout pistol concealed in his big hand. The small weapon fired flechettes that could destroy the man's face or throat across the table.

His hand trembling slightly, showing how new he was to the assignment, Mr. Johnson laid the credstick on the table. "It's got five thousand nuyen on it. Just for listening to me. Like we agreed."

"All right." The upfront payment was one of the main reasons Hawke had agreed to the meet. Showing up and walking away for that much cred was a null-brainer.

"Don't you want to check it?" Mr. Johnson waved at the slot

set up in the table.

"No." Slotting the credstick might confirm the available balance, but it might also alert any neighborhood chipheads looking for their next Better-Than-Life download that he had an open credstick on him, not one attached to a System Identification Number. Since he didn't have an official SIN, most of Hawke's work tended to be cred and carry.

"You trust me."

"No. If the cred's not there, I find you again. And then we don't have a nice meeting."

Mr. Johnson hooked a finger into his shirt collar and pulled.

"The run," Hawke reminded him. He was growing restless. Any meeting with a Mr. Johnson that took longer than two minutes was a minute and a half too long. They hooked up just to swap info and cred, not life stories.

"There's someone down in Aztlan we'd like you to . . . recruit," Mr. Johnson said.

"This person willing to be recruited?"

"I don't know."

"Snatching someone against their will costs more." Hawke had "liberated" corp assets in the past. Often those assets were human or metahuman. Some wanted to change corps, others didn't. Hawke tried to stay away from the "recruitments" involving unwilling participants, because handling outside pressure was hard enough without dealing with internal pressure as well.

Mr. Johnson slid a datachip in a protective case across the tabletop to Hawke. "Everything you need to know is there."

Hawke made no move to take it. "Is the recruit corp-connected?"

"My understanding is that the recruit is subcontracted and working on a special project somewhere in Aztlan. I don't know the exact location."

"How special is the project?"

"The corp the recruit is working for has no idea of the project's real worth." Mr. Johnson let out a tense breath. "That's all I know."

Hawke believed the man. A disposable Mr. Johnson wouldn't be given any substantial information. Hawke picked up the datachip and snugged it into a special case designed to negate GPS tracking and RFID pings. For all intents and purposes, to anyone following the datachip through the Matrix, it had just dropped into a black hole.

Unless they had better Matrix-ware than he did.

"Are you taking the assignment?" Mr. Johnson asked.

Hawke slipped the case into his pocket and rose, towering over the smaller man. "Is there a comm address where I can reach you in the data?"

"Yes, but—"

"Then I'll let you know." Movement reflected in the window alerted Hawke that three men were converging on him. Recognizing one of them immediately, he knew he was looking at trouble.

CHAPTER TWO

Slowly, Hawke turned to face the three new arrivals.

"*Hoi*, Hawke," Deckard said with a cold smile. The expression pulled his broad face into a grim rictus that exposed the huge canine teeth jutting up from his massive lower jaw. "Long time, no see."

Standing nearly two and a half meters tall, Deckard was huge. Corded muscle coiled over his broad troll body and his cyber additions on his arms and face picked up the neon gleam. Silver hoops hung from his pointed ears. His massive horns curved back over his head, flanking the scarlet mohawk between them. His beard was scarlet now as well. Natural dermal bone deposits created a bumpy landscape on his harsh face.

He wore a tight, sleeveless, armored leather jacket to show off his bulging biceps and his cyberware. Ridged armored pants encased his legs and slid down into heavy combat boots. He carried a matched set of Ares Predator IVs holstered at his hips like an Old West gunslinger.

Two other similarly clad and equipped trolls stood on either side of Deckard.

"Do we have biz?" Hawke asked in a quiet voice.

"Not you and me," Deckard replied, looming over him. "The biz we had between us is over. You made that clear."

Hawke waited, because the troll made no move to stand aside.

"I came to make you a deal, Mr. Johnson," Deckard said, still focusing on Hawke.

"I—I don't know you." Mr. Johnson looked sick and nervous. He cowered back in his seat.

Deckard grinned. "No reason you should. Hawke don't give a lot of credit to the chummers he works with. Claims all the glory for himself. But he ain't always the one that gets things done."

The glory Hawke recognized was staying alive in the shadows without hitting too many megacorp radars. There were jobs
a runner claimed, and there were ones that he walked away from
if he didn't want to get skragged. Deckard didn't understand that
concept. For the troll, it was all about the cred. Greed overrode
good sense too often.

"I worked with Hawke," Deckard said. "Provided firepower on
some of the runs he took on. Pulled his fat out of the fire on a few
occasions. Fact is, I'm better than him. Whoever you're represent-
ing, you're better off hiring me."

Hawke felt Mr. Johnson's eyes on him, but he didn't turn
around. Deckard was dangerous.

"I'm not authorized to talk with anyone else regarding this
matter," Mr. Johnson said. "Hawke was mentioned by name. My
employers want him."

Deckard scowled at that. "Good thing you gave Hawke that
open credstick and the datachip then, isn't it? I have those, we're
in biz. You can tell your corp overseers that you upgraded the service, maybe get yourself a promotion. We'll renegotiate the price
when I'm ready."

Hawke smiled at that and brought his wired reflexes online. The neural boosters and adrenaline stimulators implanted
throughout his body ignited, and the world around him suddenly
slowed down.

"Hawke?" Mr. Johnson asked, his voice echoing a little
strangely now that it sounded so slow, and Hawke could hear the
distinct intonations. "What's the meaning of this?"

"Deckard's trying to hijack my run," Hawke said. "We worked
together a few times."

"We were *partners*," the troll growled.

"I don't do partners." Hawke had to work hard to keep his
speech slowed to normal speed. His fight or flight instinct was on
full alert, hammering at his mind and body. He was so jacked up
now he could barely stay on top of it. He was chaos incarnate, just
waiting to explode.

"Hawke dissed me," Deckard said. "Thought he could use me
and lose me like a joytoy after the ride was over." He glared at the
big man. "Well, we see how that worked out, don't we?"

"Our biz was finished," Hawke said. "We could have done
more biz in the future."

"Really? Were you planning on pulling me into this?"

"I don't know what this is." Hawke knew he should have departed Santa Fe after finishing the runs with Deckard. The troll had gotten too proprietary, wanted to lead instead of be led. Hawke had no intention of letting that happen.

"What *this* is," Deckard said, "is mine. Hand over the credstick and the datachip. I'll let you walk away."

"You can't do that," Mr. Johnson said, rising from the table to stand by Hawke.

Hawke didn't respond, but he was surprised and a little respectful of the guy's reaction. It also meant whoever was employing him was powerful—and cutthroat.

Mr. Johnson frowned at the troll. "The corp I represent won't do biz like that. They'll scuttle this assignment."

Deckard shrugged. "Don't make any difference to me. I get the info on that datachip, I bet there's another corp out there willing to pay to play. Or maybe just to find out what's on that chip."

Several of Tang's patrons had stealthily slipped away from them. Hawke knew the miniguns were trained on their table, too.

"Or maybe," Hawke said quietly, "the corp behind Mr. Johnson will put a contract out on you and your little buddies."

The two trolls backing Deckard looked at each other. Street samurai weren't always the brightest in the bunch, tending to deal in brawn and more brawn. Just like Deckard. Only Deckard had a few conniving bones and some larcenous marrow thrown in as well.

"Biz is biz," Deckard said. "They want it, they'll deal with me."

And that probably was the bottom line. A corp needed someone to run through the shadows, and they couldn't get caught with dirty hands. The corp might just walk away from the whole thing, and the datachip didn't have anything on it to tie them to the run.

Everyone could possibly get away clean.

Except for Hawke. Deckard would let people know that he'd backed down, and word would get out. And the shadows carried word—rumor, truth, whatever—at cybersonic speed.

"Give me the datachip," Deckard demanded.

Hawke reached into his jacket with his left hand, taking out the datachip with his forefinger and thumb. He still held the palmed Raecor Sting in his left hand as well, and manipulated the chip with practiced dexterity. Deckard saw the protective case and focused on it.

Hawke squeezed the Sting, and tiny, razor-sharp flechettes pinged out through the abbreviated barrel between his second and third fingers.

CHAPTER THREE

The initial burst of metal slivers destroyed Deckard's right eye. That one was—*had been*—still organic. The razored shards reduced the orb to a gelatinous mass of blood and ocular fluids that streamed down the troll's uneven cheek.

Deckard screamed and clapped a hand to his ruined eye. He staggered back a couple steps, bumping into the trolls behind him. Both of them already had weapons in their fists.

Hawke spun and grabbed Mr. Johnson by his jacket lapels. Hoisting the man off his feet, he threw him through the transplas window. Hawke followed as the miniguns inside the restaurant opened fire on the table.

His cloaked duster was guaranteed up to 20mm rounds, but that just prevented penetration. The hydrostatic shock—the impact of bullets actually striking an organic target—still passed through and could damage flesh. Bone could break as well.

Mr. Johnson hit the sidewalk in front of Tang's and immediately tried to get up. Cursing the man's stupidity, Hawke pushed off the windowsill toward him, scattering more glass shards. At least one of the minigun rounds or a bullet from an Ares Predator IV slammed between his shoulder blades as he leaped forward, knocking the wind out of him.

Hawke landed on Mr. Johnson, hammering the man to the ground, and croaked with his remaining breath, "Stay down or they'll kill you!" He hoped Deckard and the trolls had gotten caught in the minigun crossfire.

The street in front of Tang's emptied quickly. Some of the pedestrians had weapons, but none wanted to buy into a three-troll gunfight. Hawke was thankful for that.

Deckard and a remaining troll leaped through the smashed window and rolled to safety. Both of them got to their knees and raised large handguns. Hawke yanked Mr. Johnson to his feet as both trolls took aim. Time worked against all of them now. Lone Star had undoubtedly been alerted, and cruisers were en route.

Everything around Hawke moved as though mired in quicksand. Mr. Johnson wasn't able to keep up with his rapid steps that kept them just ahead of Deckard and the other troll's marksmanship. Hawke half-carried the man, shoving him forward and helping him stay on his feet as well.

They turned the corner and plunged into the relative safety of the dark alley. Hawke shoved Mr. Johnson forward. "Go!"

Terrified, the man ran for his life down the alley.

Hawke paused just inside the entrance, out of sight of Deckard and his partner. The trolls' feet slammed heavily against the sidewalk. At full wired speed now, Hawke reached into his jacket pocket and took out a small flash-bang grenade, armed it, and curled it inside the crook of his left pinkie.

Reaching behind him, Hawke freed the two katars he wore holstered across his back. The punching daggers elongated as sections guided by electronic memory clicked into place. Both weapons had H-patterned handgrips and were forty centimeters long when extended. The punching end came to an armor-piercing needle point and the base flared out to eleven centimeters wide. The gleaming monofilament edges sliced easily through flesh, bone, and most armor. Opponents bled out rapidly when he sank a dagger in to the hilt and withdrew it.

Mr. Johnson's receding footsteps drummed rapidly against the alley floor, but a trained ear would notice there was only one person running away now. Hawke would have realized that immediately, and known an ambush was waiting. He hoped Deckard and his companion, fearing their big score was getting away, wouldn't be so attentive.

Deckard rounded the corner first and had both pistols in front of him. Moonlight silvered his cybered eye as he tracked Mr. Johnson, but he seemed slow compared to Hawke.

With a quick flick of his wrist, Hawke tossed the flash-bang against the opposite alley wall. As the second troll joined Deckard, both of them registered the movement through the air and opened fire.

Although Hawke had planned on the impact with the wall to set off the flash-bang, one of the trolls' bullets did the job instead. The grenade went off prematurely, and he hadn't quite managed to turn away. The blinding strobes and thunderous detonation partially robbed him of his vision and most of his hearing.

Deckard and his companion got pole-axed by the maelstrom of light and sound. Evidently both had cybered hearing and vision. For a frozen moment, they stood in paralyzed agony.

Hawke shot forward, intending to take Deckard out of the action first. Instead, the second troll caught a glimpse or a sound of him approaching and started shooting again. The rapid-fire explosions echoed through the narrow alley.

Collapsing into a soccer tackle, Hawke managed to slide under the bullets cutting the air only centimeters over his head. The asphalt grated against his legs and hip as he tackled the troll. It felt like hitting a tree trunk, and the troll didn't budge more than was necessary to point his pistols down at Hawke.

Fighting street samurais at point-blank range was suicidally stupid. Besides the exterior armor, many also had subdermal layers tucked into their flesh to protect vulnerable spots. They were huge and heavy and hard to injure.

Unless someone knew what he was doing.

Hawke did. He rolled free and twisted to backslash across the troll's ankles. The katar's monofilament blade sliced through his opponent's hamstrings, and he lost control over his foundation.

"He's on me, Deckard! The drekker just cut my feet!" The troll fired into the asphalt, but Hawke was already gone. The bullets blasted small craters in the rough surface.

Deckard turned blindly, one eye ruined and the other still in synaptic shock from the light show, and fired at his companion, apparently hoping to tag Hawke. The bullets tore into the other troll. Most bounced off the metahuman's armor or subdermal plating, but a few ripped through unprotected flesh as well.

The troll squalled in pain and fear and tried to move. When he did, his maimed feet betrayed him, and he went down in a rush of falling meat.

With his right katar, Hawke slashed the troll's throat. The monofilament blade raked through the reinforced cartilage over the larynx. Thick blood sprayed out into the alley. The unmistakable smell filled Hawke's nostrils, and he switched to breathing through his mouth.

The squalling was replaced by a thick, strangled gurgle as the troll bled out.

"Cobb!" Deckard bellowed as he backed away and reloaded his pistols. "Cobb!"

Curling into a ball, Hawke got his feet under him and stood. He moved soundlessly and vectored in on Deckard from the side. The street sam turned, evidently catching sight or sound of his approach. He thrust his pistols out and started firing again.

Hawke ducked beneath the pistol on the right and let it slide past his shoulder. He used his left katar to shove the other pistol away. Then he twisted his shoulder and hip, putting all his weight into a straight punch to Deckard's chest.

For a moment the armor held, then the subdermal ceramic reinforcement over the sternum held, but in the end Hawke's blow sliced into the street samurai's heart.

The troll stood frozen in agony and shock. He looked down in disbelief with his good eye.

"Frag you, Hawke," Deckard snarled through bloody spittle.

"This didn't have to be personal. It was just biz."

"Everything's personal, you double-crossing drekker."

In case Deckard had a back-up heart and some kind of shut-down relay for the injured one, Hawke withdrew his right katar and launched a powerful uppercut with the left. The blade ripped through the subdermal armor at the troll's throat and speared into his brain.

The troll's corpse sagged and dropped. By the time CrashCart or one of the other emergency medical services arrived, the re-suscitation window would be closed. Deckard would just be an organ donor and cyber scrapheap waiting for scavengers.

A lot of shadowrunners ended up that way. Running wasn't a forgiving business, and the learning curve was lethal.

Hawke sprinted after Mr. Johnson as Lone Star sirens warbled over the sprawl.

CHAPTER FOUR

Mr. Johnson was out of shape, and had barely made it past the far end of the alley. Hawke easily caught up to the man and grabbed him by the elbow. At the sudden restraint, Mr. Johnson yelled and tried to pull away.

"Throttle down," Hawke advised. "They're dealt with."

Since the third troll hadn't put in an appearance, Hawke felt safe assuming Deckard's companion had gone down under the minigun fire. But that didn't slow him in keeping his charge moving down the street.

"I won't tell anyone." Pale and shaking, Mr. Johnson staggered at Hawke's side. "I swear."

At first, Hawke wasn't certain how to handle the man. A lot of Mr. Johnsons were often every bit as dangerous as whatever clandestine thing they were contracting for. Too many of them tried to eliminate shadowrunners they'd hired in order to sever any links to themselves.

Cars whizzed by on the street. Groups of people flowed from the bars, bodegas, and Stuffer Shacks on both sides of them, pooling and spooling in the shadows and neon. A Santa Fe Lone Star heavy cruiser slid to a stop in front of Tang's. The manager and the cooks knelt in the street with their hands clasped behind their heads. The Johnson started following their lead.

"Get up." Rolling his eyes, Hawke pulled at Mr. Johnson's collar to keep him on his feet. "Let's get you out of here."

"What about the trolls?"

"Fragged. They won't be following us. Lone Star's another problem." Hawke pushed the man ahead of him. "Did you drive?"

"No. I took a cab from the airport."

So Mr. Johnson wasn't local. Hawke filed the info away. "What about a hotel?"

The man shook his head. "This was a turnaround. Either we had a deal or we didn't. I wasn't going to be staying."

Hawke kept walking quickly down the sidewalk. He held Mr. Johnson's upper right arm tightly, and kept him in lockstep with him.

"Thanks for saving me back there."

Hawke nodded, but didn't mention that he'd had no choice. Letting Mr. Johnson get killed or jacked would have been bad for biz. Furthermore, if Mr. Johnson had been captured by Lone Star, even more drek could burn along Hawke's backtrail.

"What about the restaurant's video? I could be recognized."

"Got a record?"

"No." Mr. Johnson looked affronted. "No record. But I've got a profile at my corp."

Glancing at the man, Hawke wondered if that was actually the truth, or if Mr. Johnson was paranoid or inflating his ego. Whoever had sent him wouldn't have sent someone that could be easily identified.

"You won't get recognized from anything at Tang's." Hawke accessed his Personal Area Network and tagged breaking scream-sheets about the action at the restaurant. The scanty details mentioned no names and rolled the blurry footage from Tang's. "Did you see the way the employees filed out into the street on their knees? That's so they won't accidentally be shot."

"But the video—"

"Clear enough to show no Tang employee was involved in the dust-up, but not clear enough to allow any guests to be identified. That's part of why the charges are so high there. Plus, I had a white noise generator equipped with a video-mask. Everything at our table will show up distorted. I don't want to be identified either."

"Oh."

Two blocks down, Hawke guided Mr. Johnson into an alley. At the other end, he slotted a credstick to open the gates of a private parking area patrolled by sec-drones. Hawke threw pass-words at the sec-drones, then linked with the burgundy colored Shin-Hyung sedan he was currently driving.

He'd had the vehicle's rear spoiler removed to blend in with traffic. None of the performance had been sacrificed, and several offensive and defensive systems had been added. Keeping a car was expensive. Keeping the same car was expensive and dangerous, and maybe borderline foolish. The investments in this one were solely for personal protection while on the street.

"Where are we going?" Mr. Johnson stepped back as the remote controlled Shin-Hyung glided to a stop in front of them. Neon-green ground effects lit up his feet as the doors opened.

"The airport." Hawke settled into the driver's seat, which immediately embraced him and strapped him in. Inside the car, safe within the armor and weapons array, he relaxed a little more. "You need to get out of town."

Mr. Johnson hurried around the car and got into the passenger seat. The windshield glowed blue and scanned him with a bar of light from head to toe.

Hawke's PAN seized the information that the car's intel systems gleaned from the cyberware snooping his passenger. The upload filled a ghost-thin overlay in his vision. The scan picked up the stores Mr. Johnson had gotten his clothing, shoes, wallet, and accessories from. It also detected the kind of cologne and deodorant he wore.

Nothing in Mr. Johnson's body had been cybered or remodeled. He'd had his appendix taken out, but nothing had been put in its place. Seatbelts wrapped the man up, and would have doubled as personal restraints at a word.

UNKNOWN PASSENGER flashed across Hawke's PAN overlay.

Hawke initiated the passcodes to shut down the vehicle's self-defense array as he powered through the open parking gates and down the alley. In seconds he was out on the street, rolling through the sprawl toward the airport, zipping past the bustling stores and bars.

Mr. Johnson twitched uncomfortably. "What am I supposed to do?"

Hawke checked the radar overlay on his PAN. The car's systems showed they were alone and attracting no undue attention. Out of habit and in spite of the tech, he checked the rear-view and side mirrors.

"Get out of Santa Fe. Go home. Stay safe."

Mr. Johnson nervously licked his lips. "What about the run?"

"If it's a go, I'll be in touch."

CHAPTER FIVE

"Lemme see yer face."

The demand came from a stainless steel box beside the heavy sec-gates enclosing the salvage yard outside the Santa Fe sprawl. This far out, only the yard's sec lights punched holes in the night.

Hawke rolled his heavily-tinted window down and turned his face toward the camera mounted on the box. To the casual observer, it looked like two camera lenses were inset in the device. However, he knew one of them covered the barrel of an Enfield AS-7 assault shotgun. If the retina scan wasn't recognized, the shotgun took off the interloper's head.

"Come ahead, chummer." The mechanical voice squawked through an old school speaker box.

The massive gates parted as Hawke thumbed the window back up. The sedan rolled across the steel bridge that could retract and drop a car between heartbeats if the salvage yard owner so desired. Spikes waited at the end of the four-meter drop, and napalm flushed the area almost immediately afterward.

Krank liked his solitude, and protected it vigorously.

Drones and wild pigs provided roving security between tall stacks of wrecked cars and heavy equipment. The drones were armed and programmed to attack and take evasive action. According to Krank, the pigs were Arkansas razorbacks, trained to kill and eat intruders.

A small drone flitted into position in front of Hawke's windshield and hovered for a moment. It didn't linger long enough for him to spot what kind of weapon it carried.

A short distance farther on, one of the pigs—weighing at least three hundred kilos— brushed up against the sports car hard enough to rock it.

Hawke opened the comm to the main building. "If that mutated slab of bacon dents my car, I'm gonna slit its throat and donate its carcass to the nearest homeless squat."

"You just leave Alice alone." The voice on the other end of the connection was deep and musical. *"She's with child. Gonna gimme a whole new litter of guard pigs. 'Sides, that was just a love tap. If she'd meant anything by it, she'd've knocked you over."*

Two stories tall and covered with cheap metal, the main warehouse looked flimsy. But like the box at the front gate, looks were deceptive. The structure could take direct hits from miniguns, and even a cannon. The long rectangle had a few round windows that could be used as gun ports.

As Hawke neared the building, the large doors parted and he drove inside. When he was through, they slid closed behind him.

The spacious warehouse was occupied only by a few cars, trucks, and motorcycles. Parking space was provided at one end, and the other was a motor pool, where block and tackles hung over three grease pits.

The air inside was cool, despite the outside heat. Krank pulled down a lot of cred with the operation, especially so close to the Aztlan border, so he could afford AC for the entire space.

Hawke pulled the car into the parking area, switched off the engine, set the security systems, and got out. He walked toward the grease pit, his boots clicking against the pavement. The sound echoed over the whine of a drill coming from one of the grease pits.

Krank stood in the bottom. The dwarf wasn't quite four feet tall, and looked almost that broad. A shaggy gray-brown beard framed his heavy-featured face. The stump of a cigar jutted from the corner of his downturned mouth. He wore coveralls and an equipment belt. Goggles protected his eyes, and kept him hooked into the sec-video streaming through his PAN.

Hawke knelt at the edge of the pit and glanced at the Rover SUV. Most of the body panels had been removed to allow the mounting of bulletproof armor.

Krank glanced up at him. "Got in a bit of a dust-up, did you?"

Hawke just stared down at the man.

Krank pointed an oily, gloved finger at him. "Took a couple heavy rounds in the chest. Good thing your armor held, chummer."

Hawke slipped a hand inside his shirt and stuck fingers through the bullet holes. "Yeah."

"The car?"

"Slick as a gut. No damage."

Krank nodded, then took the cigar from his mouth and spat on the grease-caked floor. "Got anybody looking for you?"

"Lone Star, probably."

The dwarf dismissed that threat with a roll of his shoulders. "Null sheen. They don't find you at first, they won't come looking unless somebody's payin' 'em to. Who tried to put those holes in you?"

"The other was personal biz. I took care of it." Hawke still didn't like the idea of telling Krank so much, but the dwarf ran a tight operation.

"I like you, Hawke." Krank turned his attention back to the vehicle he was working on. "But nobody gets a free pass. Don't bring anything down on me, or you'll pay for it. Still heading out today?"

Hawke nodded, then stood and headed to the rooms on the second floor. The metal steps that zig-zagged up the wall looked dangerous. The long series of steps shivered beneath his weight.

The rooms up here were expensive, but worth it. In addition to the best privacy cred could buy, Krank also provided quick underground escape routes that wound under the harsh terrain outside the salvage yard. Years ago, the warehouse had been used for smuggling goods to and from Aztlan, and while Krank didn't traffic across the border any more, the tunnels remained in place and accessible—for the right price, of course.

Equipped with a bed, small kitchen area, and a bath, the room didn't offer first-class accommodations. But the Matrix jackpoints were guaranteed clean and untraceable.

Hawke dropped his gear on the bed and took out the datachip Mr. Johnson had given him. He slotted it and sat down to look at the run's parameters.

CHAPTER SIX

Seventeen hours later, Hawke stood in a no-name border town cantina located between Aztlan and Texas. He drank beer and ate tortillas while watching a trideo presentation of the smuggler's run up from Aztlan. Drones relayed the trideo to outlaw channels that paid for access. In some places the event was considered a sport; in others it was a training ground where young wannabes studied the drivers and machinery.

Hawke sat at a table with Doggle, an ork rigger who was a savant at blueprinting engines, but lacked the touch for wheelwork. The man's face was hard and lean, scarred by both his work and close-in fighting. Both lower canines had been capped in blue silver, and curled up over his upper lip. Thick, black hair hung in wild disarray, but didn't cover his pointed ears. Scuffmarks and grease stained his leather two-piece uniform.

The bartender took Hawke's order for another brew and drew one in a tall glass. He set a fresh bowl of salsa in front of him as well.

"In for the race?" he asked while slotted the proffered credstick.

"Yeah."

The bartender tilted his head toward an elf sitting at a corner table. "Crief's still taking action. The racers are twenty minutes out, and the local sec teams have been alerted. It's anybody's race."

Hawke nodded as he rolled a tortilla stuffed with salsa and popped it into his mouth.

"Nobody knows who called the Aztlan sec teams." Doggle's voice was low and rough. His eyes never left the trid viewer. "They got helos closing in, too. Whoever left word also told 'em this was a grudge smuggling run."

"Any local favorites?" Hawke sipped his brew.

"Outside of Flicker?"

"Yeah."

Doggle shook his big head. "Got a guy along from out of town. Supposed to be a real screamstar. Gets covered regularly on holo and in the screamsheets."

"For illegal smuggling runs?"

A grin split Doggle's face. "Illegal generally don't make something unpopular."

Hawke filled another tortilla and watched the racers. He recognized Flicker's dirt-covered beige and olive Thundercloud Morgan ATV squirting dirt and rock out from all four tires. The vehicle went suddenly airborne and sailed for a long distance before touching back down again. For a moment the driver fought the car, and Hawke held his breath as Flicker regained control.

A Tata Hotspur off-road racing truck followed the Morgan's path, going airborne as well. The larger vehicle sailed directly for the Morgan as Flicker fought for traction.

"Son of a slitch!" The wail ripped free of the younger men gathered around the tables. "Gunther's trying to take Flicker out!"

Roars of anger quickly filled the small bar.

The Hotspur landed within centimeters of Flicker's vehicle as she veered away. She juked the Morgan to the right, and the Hotspur's front tires caught up to her in seconds, burning at her rear bumper.

"He's trying to spin her out," Doggle rasped, then added inflammatory invective.

"Bad blood between 'em?" Hawke sipped his beer and watched the action. His eye roved over the crowd, looking for anyone taking undue interest in the race. Gunther's supporters probably didn't end with his pit team.

"Couple years' worth." Doggle spat on the sawdust-covered floor. "Gunther got one of Flicker's friends killed down Baja way."

"She doesn't have many friends."

"Could have more. She just chooses not to."

"Friends end up costing too much."

Doggle snorted. "She get that drek from you?"

"Nope. We're simpatico when it comes to that."

Doggle turned his dark eyes on Hawke. "Yet when you need a driver, here you are."

"Sometimes." Hawke returned the ork's stare full measure.

"Sometimes I'm here. Sometimes I'm not."

"She ever turn you down?"

Hawke pondered that for a moment, then shook his head. "No."

On the screen, Flicker's Thundercloud pulled to the left and barreled up an incline that looked too steep for the vehicle. Just as gravity and the loose soil started to play out under the ATV's churning tires and pull it back down, a pressurized blast kicked out the back of the Thundercloud. The additional boost propelled it up and over the grade.

A ragged cheer tore through the throats of the onlookers as Flicker's Thundercloud landed on top of the plateau on all four wheels. The tires chewed through the soft sand and found traction again, hurling the vehicle north toward Texas.

A helo opened up with miniguns and strafed the red dirt landscape. The wind carried whirling red dust clouds through the air and momentarily blurred the image transmitted from Low Earth Orbit satellites.

A nanosecond later, something wickedly fast jetted from Flicker's vehicle and vectored in on the helo. When the missile struck the aircraft, yellow-green foam covered the Plexiglas nose and slithered over the rest of the aircraft. Its engine failed, and it started down in an almost gentle decline.

"She coulda killed them." Doggle shook his shaggy head. "Chose not to, so Aztlan wouldn't take it personal."

Gunther fired a trio of missiles at another pursuit helo.

A chorus of curses raged from the crowd as they watched the missiles streak toward the helo. "Gunther's going for a kill! Aztlan's gonna be all over us!"

"I take it Gunther doesn't play by the same rules." Impassive, Hawke watched the doomed aircraft.

"No." Doggle hunched forward.

An instant before the missiles made contact with the helo, they blew up. The concussion fractured the aircraft's Plexiglas nose and caused the pilot to draw back as thunder and flames filled the night sky, but the helo remained whole.

A cheer rose from the throats of the cantina crowd.

"Flicker's got wiz jamming gear aboard that Thundercloud." Doggle grinned. "I helped her install it. These runs, they're just a game to her. Nobody's supposed to get hurt."

"Unless she gets caught."

"They haven't caught her yet." Doggle emptied his glass and signaled for another.

Hawke pushed the plate of tortillas over to the ork. Doggle hesitated, then helped himself to the food. His black eyes bored into Hawke's. "The most danger she's ever in is when she's with you."

Hawke thought that was an unfair assessment, but didn't say anything. He wasn't the only shadowrunner that hired Flicker.

"When you get her into this, whatever it is, just make sure you can get her back out."

Hawke nodded. "Always the plan."

CHAPTER SEVEN

Flicker strode into the cantina and drew instant acclamation from the crowd. She was dressed in black road leathers that fit her slender curves like a second skin. Her crash helmet dangled by its strap from her fingers. Lights pulsed inside it, keeping her in constant contact with her vehicle.

Her skin was almost as black as her leathers. Short-cropped black hair hung to the nape of her slender neck, parted a little by her elven ears. Her aquamarine eyes caught Hawke's gaze for a moment, then roved on. Her smile was bright and genuine, filled with adrenaline still buzzing through her. He remained in his chair, letting her choose the time and place.

Amid the crowd's adulation, Flicker strode to the bar and accepted a celebratory glass of foaming champagne. The trideo viewer repeated the race from start to finish on a loop.

Hawke waited and watched. Doggle sat beside him like a proud father.

A few minutes later, a big man with a sullen expression shoved the door open and entered. Cyberware gleamed along the left side of his face, covering the eye and the chin. His entire left arm was a cyberlimb he hadn't bothered to hide with cosmetic work.

He looked around for just a moment, then focused on Flicker. As he strode toward her, his big boots thumping against the wooden floor, Flicker's fan club reluctantly parted.

Hawke glanced at Doggle. "Gunther?"

The ork nodded.

Hawke started to get up, but Doggle laid a hand on his arm.

"Wait. This's been building for a while. Let her handle it."

Irritably, Hawke sat back down. Then he pushed his feelings aside and went neutral, digging into that pile of non-feeling he'd developed since taking up a life in the shadows. Feelings got chummers dead quick.

Flicker stood at the bar and sipped her champagne as she watched Gunther advance on her.

"Slitch! You slotted me up!" Gunther's voice rolled over the crowd.

"No, I didn't." Flicker's aquamarine eyes remained cool and distant. "I saved us from all the trouble you almost rained down. Killing Aztlan sec on these runs isn't allowed. You do that, you'll bring the wrath of the corps. They'll turn these fun runs into something lethal. Then there won't be any profit for anyone."

"I tried to save you from that helo. He had you in his sights."

"Not me. You were afraid he was locking on you." Flicker sipped her drink again, her eyes never leaving Gunther's face.

"Call me a coward again and I'll kill you." Gunther leaned in, emphasizing the fact that he was a head taller than her. His right hand slid along the bar toward her.

Hawke slid his hand to the butt of the Ares Predator IV at his back. Doggle touched his elbow and kept him from drawing. Glancing at the ork, Hawke spotted the Colt Manhunter already in Doggle's hand.

In a move so fast that Hawke almost couldn't track it, Flicker produced a thin stiletto and pinned Gunther's hand to the bar. The big man howled in pain and tried to yank his hand back, but that only made the agony worse. Blood spurted and covered him from wrist to fingertips.

Another blade gleamed in Flicker's hand as if it had suddenly materialized there. She laid the point against Gunther's left nostril hard enough to slice flesh.

"I move even a few centimeters and you're dead." Flicker's voice was cold, controlled.

Gunther froze.

Flicker leaned in, showing she wasn't afraid, and trusting her skills to pull her back if he did move. "I don't ever want to see you again." Her voice was just above a whisper. "If I do, I'll kill you. Do you understand?"

Obstinately, Gunter didn't reply. Flicker pressed the blade a little harder, and blood ran down his upper lip to trickle over his mouth.

"Yeah," he finally said.

Flicker stepped back, then took the knife away from his face and pulled the other out of the bar and his hand. She stood there, petite and unafraid, watching him.

Gunther walked to the tavern door, but he couldn't leave without comment. "Your time's comin', slitch. One a these days, you're gonna get what's comin' to you."

Four of the bar's regulars got up and escorted the big man through the door. Gunther pushed and shoved through them, but didn't try to resist.

After finishing her drink and accepting a lot of congratulations, Flicker came over to Hawke's table and sat down. She filled a tortilla with beans and salsa and ate.

"Work?" Her left eyebrow arched.

"Yeah. The pay's good."

Flicker smiled sourly. "Means the danger is lousy."

Hawke grinned. "Yeah. But it's a one-shot deal. In and out of Aztlan."

"What's the run?"

"Recruitment."

"Who's the recruit?"

"Archeology student."

Flicker chewed and thought for a moment. "What's so wiz about this archeology student?"

"I wasn't told."

"Does she want out?"

Hawke shrugged.

Flicker's face hardened. "I don't work kidnappings."

"I haven't started."

"Good to know. Then why are we going down there?"

Hawke took in a breath and let it out. "Curious, I guess. And if Mr. Johnson's willing to pay for the recruit, I thought maybe there'd be some biz there we could do on the side."

"The recruit's a girl, I take it."

Concealing a grimace, Hawke nodded.

"For a tough guy, you got a big soft spot. You want to know how much trouble this *archeology student* is in, and you've got enough cred to go take a look."

"I'm betting we can find a way to make it pay."

Flicker wiped her hands. "Anyone going to try to hang onto her?"

"Not that I know of. Maybe the other university people at the dig."

Blowing out a disgusted breath, Flicker leaned back in her

chair and wrapped her arms around herself. "Sounds like a milk run. I hate when it sounds this easy."

"Sometimes it is."

"Want to place a small wager?"

Hawke grinned. "No."

"Coward." Flicker leaned forward again. "Tell me about your archeology student."

CHAPTER EIGHT

Perspiration poured from Rachel Gordon, even while standing in the shadows of the tall trees surrounding the dig site.

The team had set up deep in the jungle, well away from any regular routes. A monitor lizard sat on a bare expanse atop a nearby hill, so still it looked like a yard ornament. Every now and again it would flick its tongue out or turn its head slightly. A floral scent rode the slight breeze, but it barely cut through the fecund smell of rotting vegetation.

The three other archeology students chosen for the fieldwork sat on small boulders lining an old erosion scar leading down from the hilltop. The shade was deeper there and there was more of a breeze. Clad in khakis, they talked among themselves, mostly complaining about the heat and the insects. They didn't socialize with Rachel, but she was fine with that. She'd always been a private person.

Despite the lack of amenities and the primitive campsite farther down the hill, Rachel loved being in the jungle much more than being in a lab or a classroom. Searching for artifacts was much better than looking at exhibits of them.

Finding an artifact would be best of all.

She lifted her canteen and drank the sterilized water, grimacing at the chemical taste that made it almost unpalatable. But she forced herself to drink to remain hydrated against the constant heat and humidity of the jungle.

She wore lightweight khaki shorts, shirt, and a vest that were durable against the brush and harsh terrain while remaining cool in the heat. She took down her strawberry blond hair, then tied it back into a bun that she crammed under her NeoNET ball cap.

She walked back to the dig site and peered over the edge of

the large hole that had been excavated over the last eight days. Below, native Guatemalan laborers excavated the site using shovels and buckets, working slowly and steadily. Dressed in bandannas and trousers they'd hacked off at the knees, some were barechested, while others wore shirts with the sleeves ripped off, they looked, well, strange to Rachel. They were all human; not an elf, ork, dwarf, or troll among them. And none were cybered, not even a little.

"Doesn't feel much like Boston, does it, Miss Gordon?" Professor Madison Fredericks joined her at the lip of the dig. He was a lean, nut-brown stick of a man in his late fifties. Dressed in stained khakis, a fedora, and sporting a white beard, he looked every centimeter the adventuring professor.

"No. It doesn't."

"You'll get used to this in time."

Rachel didn't want to think that would ever happen. Everything was so new and so exciting, much more than the trideos she'd learned from. Or even from the intoxicating lectures Fredericks had delivered in class. Those had made him her favorite professor.

Fredericks knelt down and his knees cracked under the strain. "How are you feeling?"

Rachel smiled at the older man. She was slender and tall for a woman. Workers here had mistaken her for the professor's daughter. She was twenty-three, and this dig counted toward her master's degree.

"If that's your stealthy way of asking if I've had any more *episodes* . . ." She didn't know what else to call the fragmentary glimpses of the strange world that had haunted her dreams lately.

Fredericks rubbed his jaw ruefully and grinned. "It is."

"No. I haven't, but I have been feeling somewhat queasy." The feeling had started this morning. She'd thought it was the heat at first, but it hadn't passed, just remained a steady pulse at the edge of her awareness.

Anxious, he looked at her. "You're not getting sick, are you? This heat, or perhaps something you ate?"

She shook her head. "No. I've been careful about water and the sun. I've only eaten what I've prepared myself."

"Good girl."

Sometimes it bothered her when he treated her like a child rather than a university student. However, she wouldn't say anything about it. That wasn't her way. As an orphan and foster child, she'd learned to accept what she was given.

"Maybe . . . we should try the hypnosis again?" Fredericks didn't sound entirely convinced, but he was getting antsy for the dig to prove itself.

Rachel folded her arms across her chest. "Not right now. This isn't . . . it isn't anything strong. Not like those other instances."

"All right." Fredericks managed to hide some of his impatience. "We've only got nine more days on this permit. I don't know if I can negotiate an extension."

"I know." Rachel let out a deep breath. That so wasn't her fault. She hadn't asked Professor Fredericks to take an interest in her *episodes*, or to try to find out the truth of them. He'd gotten sucked into them all on his own.

"Maybe we should branch out over the next couple of days." He straightened up and peered around at the jungle. "Spread our luck."

"No. What we're looking for, whatever it is that I've . . . seen, it's here." Rachel nodded at the hole.

"You're *that* certain?"

"Yes." That was the one thing she knew about whatever it was she was experiencing. They were on top of it. And they were getting closer.

Fredericks sighed and rubbed his beard. She knew he wasn't as confident, and might even be a little scared that she was wrong. "I hope you're right, Rachel. I can't begin to express to you the amount of favors I had to pull in to make this excavation happen."

A fact he'd reminded her of every single day of the dig, from the time they'd first arrived in the jungle to when they'd started digging to . . . now. "Still, there might be a few more favors I could call in, if necessary." Fredericks drank from his own canteen, a trickle of water dribbling through his beard. He capped the canteen and wiped the spill away. "I see you're properly supportive of our gracious benefactors."

Rachel knew he referred to her hat. She'd felt foolish in the fedora he'd brought for her. The baseball cap suited her better.

"*Gracious* benefactors?" She shook her head and tried not to scowl with displeasure.

"Certainly." Fredericks put his canteen away. "Possibly not as gracious as they could be."

"Condescending would be a better description."

Fredericks smiled mirthlessly. "You're so young. So naïve.

Most people don't care about the past, Miss Gordon. I know you've been told this. I mention it several times in my classes."

At that moment, a sharp pain lanced through Rachel's midsection. Nausea swam through her brain, and she staggered away from the edge of the hole to avoid falling in.

"Are you all right?" Fredericks was instantly by her side, holding her arm.

"I . . . will . . . be." Rachel barely squeezed the words out. Already, the sensation lessened.

One of the laborers' shovels clanked against stone, but the impact echoed in an empty space underground.

"*Señor.*" An older man, one of the leaders, waved excitedly at Fredericks. "*Señor* Professor. We have found something."

Fredericks released her and went immediately to peer into the hole, joined by the three other students. He swore in wonderment as Rachel staggered back over to join them.

A stone trapezoid lay partially exposed at the bottom of the hole. Strange writing scrolled across it. Guessing the size of the thing was impossible, as the shadows within the cave made depth perception difficult. The stone might be three meters or a dozen across.

"What is that?" one of the other students asked.

"That looks like the same language you've seen in your episodes." Fredericks waved the laborers back from the stone.

"It is." Rachel wiped her mouth with the back of her hand. She'd never seen the language before the professor had shown her the mystery artifacts in the university's collection. But somehow she'd recognized it. She still didn't have an explanation for that.

"Can you read it?"

"Some of it. It says: 'Beware the . . . shadow . . . being? No, not exactly . . . beware the Shadow . . . man?'" Even though she wasn't certain of the upper and lowercase inflections of the symbols, she knew instinctively that the last word was capitalized.

Fear vibrated through her. If this was true, if this really was an unknown crypt, did it mean the rest of her dreams—no, *nightmares*—were true as well?

Suddenly a chill wind seemed to gust up from the fetid jungle, raising goose bumps on her skin.

CHAPTER NINE

"Carefully! Move it carefully!" Professor Fredericks commanded the laborers, his loud, strident voice rising out of the hole.

The men used a primitive block and tackle to lift the large stone from the earth. They'd spent the last thirty minutes digging it free of the ground. The other archeology students stood on the opposite side of the hole from the block and tackle assembly.

The stone sat on top of a strange rock formation shaped like the mouth of a jar. As Rachel captured trideo of its removal, she couldn't help thinking they were uncovering a long forgotten crypt. A small part of her mind cringed at the expectation of some *thing* climbing out of it, boiling out in a horrid rush of spidery legs, like one of the creatures from her nightmares.

Stone grated as it moved and the thick rasp echoed below the earth. Whatever the stone covered, it was large. And empty.

"Easy!" Fredericks dodged the stone as it rose, swinging in the ropes tied around it. "Don't break that cover!"

Because it's valuable? Or because we may need it to trap whatever's waiting inside? Rachel didn't know which to think. The latter thought worried her.

In a few more minutes, the cover had been lifted out of the hole and rested on the ground. Fredericks had to use the short rope ladder to haul himself up from the dig.

"Rachel, come over here." The professor walked over to the cover and began studying it. He took a brush from his pocket and gently swept away loose dirt. He used dental tools to remove stubborn dirt, revealing more and more of the symbols.

Rachel captured more images, but her mind stayed busy interpreting the symbols carved into the stone trapezoid. Tension knotted within her.

"Can you read this?" Fredericks gestured at the cover with the brush.

"Yes. *This is the final resting place of—*" Rachel hesitated. Names were often difficult to translate.

"Skip it."

"Someone—*he who served the Shadowman in life, and now serves him in death.*"

"Shadowman again?" Puzzlement filled Fredericks's gaunt features. "You're sure?"

"Yes." Rachel didn't know why he would ask that. She was the one who hadn't believed in the myths and legends that had brought them down to Aztlan. "Do you know what that refers to?"

"Unfortunately, no." The professor touched the cover reverently. "I've never even heard of this 'Shadowman' before."

A vision from her dreams spiraled up from Rachel's subconscious. Even since she was a little girl, she had always dreamed of a deep jungle like this one, of being lost in a landscape that looked very much like the Guatemalan forest she stood in now, and feeling like she was being watched, like something was going to leap out at her at any moment. Those dreams had haunted her since she'd been a small child. Dealing with the terrors of foster care had paled in comparison.

But since she'd started translating the unknown language back at the university, her dreams had turned darker—much darker. The most recent one scared the drek out of her. She was running through a jungle the likes of which she had never seen before. The huge trees and weird plant and animal life didn't look even remotely familiar. But even more terrifying was what was pursuing her. She was never able to get a glimpse of it, but she knew it was big, and wanted nothing more than to tear her to pieces. As far and fast as she ran, she could never get away from it. And then, having run to exhaustion, she turned around just in time to see whatever it was burst out of the jungle, all teeth and claws, straight at her. She always woke up, drenched in sweat, before she could see what wanted to rend her limb from limb.

Could this 'Shadowman' be what's been chasing me through my dreams all these years? Now, it seemed those dreams had guided her here. But for every step forward she took, more questions came to light. "What does all of this mean? Why can I understand this language, and you can't?"

Fredericks returned to her and held her shoulders. She felt him trembling in his excitement. "Don't question your gift, Miss Gordon. You can read this language when no one else in the world can. That's a cause for jubilation, not reservation."

You're not the one who's had the nightmares all her life. Or the one who translated the document that led us here.

"Come on. Let's see what else we've discovered." After directing the other three students to stay on the surface in case of trouble, Fredericks grabbed an equipment pack and headed back into the hole.

After hesitating a moment, Rachel grabbed her own pack, a fresh canteen, and followed. The fetid stench of dead things filled her nostrils the moment she climbed into the hole. The rough and ragged walls held scars left by primitive tools. Light from above quickly faded, and she switched on her flashlight, adding her beam to the professor's and those of the men in front of her. The incline was sharp enough and uneven in several spots so that she dragged her free hand along the wall for support. She managed the climb down and saw Fredericks standing beside the opening. The professor spoke calmly into his commlink, dictating notes on what he saw.

Warily, Rachel peered into the opening, half-expecting the Shadowman's servant to slither out and grab her. Then a hand fell on her shoulder and she almost screamed.

The man wore black battle armor from head to toe, making him look like an insect, except for the lack of appendages. The helmet and mask revealed nothing of his features.

"Pardon me, Miss Gordon." His voice was inflected, an Eastern European accent, she was fairly certain. He'd introduced himself as Lieutenant Doyle. No first name, and she was pretty sure Doyle wasn't his name either. "Please step back and allow us to do our jobs."

Rachel moved back as two more black-suited figures dropped into the dig. Like the first man, they carried submachine guns and sidearms. The sec team had been provided by NeoNET. The professor hadn't been pleased to have them added to his expedition, but he hadn't been given any choice.

The man looked at her again as he held his primary weapon at the ready. "Please use LED vision equipment inside the underground vault if we deem it safe. We don't want to be blinded down there."

"Sure." Rachel knew she had to respond because the sec team

and Professor Fredericks wouldn't leave her alone until she did.

When the security team had joined the dig team in Guatemala City, Rachel had been afraid of the men and women. They weren't like the Lone Star guards hired to protect the university. A dangerous edge clung to these people.

"Let's do this." Doyle held his submachine gun in one hand and peered down into the opening.

"Be careful." Professor Fredericks's voice boomed inside the hole. "Whatever's down there, I don't want it harmed and, preferably left undisturbed."

"Understood, Professor. If something attacks us though, all bets are off."

What could possibly attack? Rachel stared at the opening. Whatever the place was, it had been undisturbed for millennia. Nothing she knew of could live that long.

The sec man stuck a leg over the edge of the opening, then dropped through. Rachel watched, fully expecting a mass of bloody bones to get vomited back out of the hole.

When that didn't happen to the first man, or the next two, or to Professor Fredericks, she slipped on a pair of LED-equipped goggles and clambered into the hole after them.

CHAPTER TEN

Rachel made the short drop easily, and stood within the group of sec men and Professor Fredericks. She took some solace in the bristling security and professionalism surrounding her, but the sense of being hunted that had haunted her dreams since childhood wouldn't be stilled. She felt it now, the sense of unease it created prickling at the base of her skull.

"We got us a cave." Doyle scoured the walls. "Big cave."

The cavern was primarily a naturally-created space, but several areas had been hacked out of the walls, creating stone closets big enough for a person to stand in. Judging from the broken debris in some of them, statues had once occupied those spaces. Most looked human, but there were some that had scaled skin, fine downy features, and fur. Rachel thought maybe this place was part museum and part mausoleum.

"Not just a cave, Lieutenant Doyle." Professor Fredericks leaned forward and pointed. "At least two. There's a passageway ahead."

Doyle swiveled his head to follow the line of the professor's finger. On the far side of the large space, the cavern dipped down and continued at an angle. There, Rachel spotted the opening of a passageway, or perhaps another cavern. More writing covered the walls there. The tension ratcheted up even higher inside her.

"All right." Doyle sounded agreeable, like this was nothing but a walk in the park. "We have a passageway. You sure you don't have any maps of this area, Professor?"

"None." Fredericks gazed around as he answered. He bent and picked up a forearm that ended in a clawed hand with dried webbing between the fingers. "All of this is new to me. Miss Gordon and I didn't know what to expect from this dig."

Rachel balked a little at the lie; Fredericks had expected a lot. Probably more than he'd even told her. But she kept quiet. Unease coiled more tightly within her. She wanted to climb back out of here, but part of her also wanted to know what lay ahead in the darkness.

"You get lucky, maybe you'll find something they'll name after you." Doyle started forward, his boots crunching on the remnants of the statues as he strode for the other side of the cavern.

Fredericks didn't reply.

Rachel followed the two men as they walked toward the passageway, recording the carvings that covered the walls as she walked. Most of the images were pictographs, crude stick drawings instead of the detailed symbols that had covered the cave's seal. In that moment, she realized that's what had covered the cave's entrance: a seal.

But was it supposed to keep things out?

Or keep things within?

Another chill ghosted through her as she studied the walls. Among the stick figures, one rose above the rest, a pictogram of a man larger than the others, above the throng, like he was floating—or flying. Rachel peered closer. Were the others . . . worshipping this floating man? And barely visible in the walls, were those . . . wings?

Fredericks joined her, his LED headlamp playing over the nearest wall. "Can you read the symbols?"

"I can. They're prayers."

"That's how I interpreted them. But prayers about what?"

"They're all honoring the Shadowman." Rachel pointed to several places on the wall. "The symbols for his name appear often."

Fredericks put his narrow face close to the wall. "Some type of long-lost cult, maybe? Darkness worshippers?"

Rachel played her beam over the wall. "Toward the end of whatever civilization lived in this area, maybe. There were others before. The ones who made the pictographs, perhaps. Many people lived here at different times."

Fredericks approached the wall and laid a tentative hand on the pictographs. His fingers traced the deeply carved images. "Thousands of years ago. Just think of it. Primitive people worshipping some sort of powerful being. A religious cult we're just now discovering."

And what if that thing *was still in the cavern system?*

That was the part that truly creeped Rachel out. She'd been ecstatic to be one of the students chosen for this expedition. She'd learned the forgotten language faster than anyone else in class. But she hadn't had the cred to finance the trip. Until he'd arranged a grant for her.

The idea of traveling to a foreign country had been amazing by itself. The possibility of encountering some kind of long lost creature, which she hadn't believed could exist, despite the amount of magic loose in the world these days, wasn't so wiz.

Fredericks looked at her, his eyes positively glowing with excitement. "I've got a feeling about this, Ms. Gordon. This is big. Something like this is what archeologists pursue their whole lives. Most seldom find it." He paused as he looked around. "But I believe we've found something extraordinary here."

"Are we ready to see what you've found?" Doyle stood waiting, his weapon cradled in his arms.

"Yes. Of course." Fredericks stepped toward the sec man.

"All right." Doyle nodded to one of the other mercenaries. "Send out the drone, Childers."

The man reached into his cargo pants pocket and produced a slender tube as long as his hand. As he held it in his palm, blue lights flared to life along its length. Delicate-looking, translucent wings sprang out, giving the device the appearance of a mechanical butterfly. Then thin legs unfolded, and the tube leaped into the air.

"That's Bernice." Childers pointed at the departing drone. He sounded young and cheerful. "She's our eyes and ears when we're in potentially hostile territory."

The drone disappeared down the dark passageway. The sec man stood still, but the fingers of one gloved hand moved rhythmically. Rachel assumed Childers was controlling the drone, seeing what it saw. After a moment, he stepped forward.

Doyle moved forward slowly, trailing the rigger. "Do you know what we're looking for, Professor Fredericks?"

"No. This is purely exploration, gentlemen."

"Is there any reason to believe anyone else has been down here lately?"

"After the way that entrance was sealed?" Fredericks's skepticism was thick enough to cut. "I wouldn't think so. Not without leaving a trace of their passage."

"That might not be the only entrance."

The possibility had crossed Rachel's mind as well. She trailed after Fredericks without the same level of enthusiasm he was showing. He was looking for a prize. She was afraid her nightmare was about to come true.

"How did you find out about the entrance your people dug up?" Doyle skirted a large boulder and followed Childers around a curving wall. The slope remained steady, winding down into the earth.

"Research." Fredericks paused to shoot trideo of more carved art on the wall.

We followed a dream. Rachel held her tongue, still not believing she'd been able to pick the spot for the dig so precisely.

They walked down a set of crumbling stairs into the next passageway. The drone glowed faintly blue in the distance. More pictographs and symbols covered the walls as they continued their descent.

Doyle walked easily, always balanced. "Is there any chance someone else might have gotten hold of the same research?"

"No."

Something *clicked* under Doyle's foot, the gentle scrape too mechanical to be merely a dislodged stone. Fear shattered inside Rachel, but even as she opened her mouth, it was already too late to yell a warning.

CHAPTER ELEVEN

A spear-wielding skeleton burst from a narrow recess in the wall. The thing had been carefully hidden among the pictographs, and had looked two-dimensional, even in the bright LED beams.

With superhuman quickness, Doyle dodged aside, blocking Professor Fredericks back with his body even as he turned his submachine gun on the skeleton warrior and fired. The silenced rounds smashed the bones into fragments that spun and fell to the floor. A few splinters bounced off Rachel's face and upraised palms with little force. Ricochets pinged down the passageway.

The sec man rigger controlling the drone grabbed Rachel and took her to the ground. The air whooshed out of her. He stank of sweat and armor.

The other sec man squatted down with his SMG to his shoulder. "Hold steady." Doyle kept his weapon pointed at the scattered remains of the skeleton.

Rachel half-expected the thing to rise up again and renew its attack. Things like that had happened in her nightmares, but she'd never witnessed it in the real world. Now that they were in the cave, though, the real world seemed far away.

Childers released Rachel and stood, taking his weight off her. She drew in breath with a wince.

"Sorry, ma'am." His tone was contrite but distant. His weapon never wavered from the remains of the skeleton, and his head roved to check all around them. "Was that thing spelled?"

Doyle kicked through the loose pile of bones. "Inanimate. Some kind of trap. I felt a counterweight shift underfoot when I stepped on it. Couldn't move fast enough to avoid setting it off." He looked at the third man. "Did you sense anything, Beaumont?"

The man shook his head. "Nothing magical about it." He hesitated. "But there's been a lot of magic in this place." He ran his fingers over the carvings like they were delicate and might break. "You can feel it."

Doyle shook his head and cursed with real feeling. "I hate magic. And I hate this fragging low-tech stuff, too. Gimme a street sam or a merc any day. At least then I know what I'm up against." Shaking his head, he continued sweeping forward.

Reluctantly, Rachel followed him, trailing the professor. The cave air turned colder around her.

"How far have we come?" Professor Fredericks keep examining the walls, his LED lights bobbing crazily as he looked up and down. The pictographs and symbols continued down the passageway.

Rachel wrapped her arms around herself and wished she'd brought a jacket. The outerwear would have been unbearable topside, but she wanted it now.

"Half a klick." Doyle kicked a meter-long, bright orange centipede out of their path. The meaty *smack* of the boot's impact filled Rachel's ears.

The creature plopped against the wall, fell, then rolled over and scuttled away on its many legs. Several more centipedes roamed the passageway around them. Doyle continued kicking his way through them.

Rachel had kept watch for other signs of mammalian life, bats and other rodents, but hadn't seen any. Plenty of spiders shared space with other crawling things that lived in the earth.

She couldn't help wondering if animals with higher intelligence stayed away from the cave and passageway on purpose. Or if there simply wasn't a way in. Or maybe those higher intelligences could sense the *wrongness* about the place—the same wrongness she was feeling now. None of those thoughts was particularly restful.

"Bernice has found another cave a short distance ahead." The rigger merc nodded down the tunnel and to the right.

Doyle called a halt. "How far?"

"Hundred twenty-three point nine-two meters."

"Anything moving?"

"Nothing Bernice has tracked." Childers shook his head. "Place looks crazy, though."

Rachel wished the armor didn't hide his face. If she could only see his features, things might not seem so bad.

Professor Fredericks rocked impatiently. "What do you mean? What do you see?"

"Statues and stuff." The man shrugged. "Some kind of gathering place."

"Well, Miss Gordon, it appears your instincts regarding this place were very good." Professor Fredericks grinned. He looked a little nervous, but his hopes for a spectacular find were evident.

Despite her fears, Rachel's excitement grew, but she didn't say anything.

The professor tried to proceed, but Doyle held him back with a hand against his chest. "Wait, sir. Beaumont, do you sense anything?"

Beaumont was quiet for a moment. Rachel thought she saw the air shimmer around the man for a moment, but she couldn't be sure.

After another moment, he shook his head. "I can feel the magic, stronger than here, but it isn't coming from anything definite. It's just stronger."

Doyle dropped his arm from the professor. "Single file. I got point. Beaumont, you watch out for the professor. Childers, stay with Miss Gordon."

As soon as she stepped into the room, Rachel felt the *wrongness,* and it was stronger than ever. Danger was hiding here, but she couldn't identify it. Her heart rate jacked up as adrenaline flooded her system, with every instinct telling her to flee this place right now.

"What is all *this?*" Doyle asked, actually sounding impressed for once.

"I have no idea . . ." Fredericks replied, his mouth hanging open as he stared all around.

"Me either," Beaumont said. "Trophy room? Effigies of the creatures the Shadowman defeated or killed?"

"Maybe . . . but effigies of *what?*" the merc leader asked.

No one had an answer for him, not even Rachel.

As Childers had stated, the room held a number of strange statues. Most of them were two and half and three meters tall, but Rachel just knew they weren't life-sized. The monsters they represented were much larger. Even though the artists that had created the images had been skilled, she knew they hadn't completely captured the ferocity of the inhuman beings.

Every one of the creatures was misshapen and terrifying. Some had too many arms, legs, or mouths. Some had too many heads. Gemstones glowed a rainbow of colors over the bodies of the things cast in black and blue stone. For an insane moment, they looked like game pieces, but Rachel knew the creatures had once—*maybe still*—lived.

What's more, she feared them. Even though she had never seen them before right now, somehow she instinctively knew they were the enemy.

She tried to bolt, but Childers wrapped a big arm around her. No matter how she moved, she couldn't get away from the sec man. His grip was firm and certain, almost bordering on painful.

"Easy." Childers held her. Pain flashed through her hands as she beat her fists ineffectually against his armor.

Doyle stepped toward them. "What's wrong with her?"

Professor Fredericks wandered away, drawn by the contents of the room. "I don't know."

"Has she acted like this before?"

"No."

I have! You've seen me! Every time I came out of my nightmare! Rachel wanted to scream the truth at him—at all of them—but couldn't. She'd been terrified before, but this time she had no control over her body. That was a first.

Childers reached up and captured her wrists. "Take it easy. Relax. Nobody's going to hurt you. You're going to hurt yourself."

Being restrained only made the panic clamoring inside Rachel worse. She threw her head at Childers, attempting to bite, and kicked at him, but only injured herself. Her lip split and she tasted blood, while her foot now throbbed inside its hiking boot.

Childers gripped her tighter. "I think we're going to have to slap-patch her. Get her to calm down. She's going to get hurt."

Rachel heaved and struggled against the rigger's implacable hold, but couldn't break free. Doyle reached into a chest pouch and took out a slap-patch. She couldn't let him put it on her.

If he did, she'd be trapped in her nightmare . . . and dead soon after.

CHAPTER TWELVE

"This is who we came for?" Flicker didn't sound amused. *"A beetle-head?"*

Crouching in the jungle a short distance from the dig site, Hawke grimaced at the relayed image playing on his commlink. Flicker had tied in video from a miniature drone she'd piloted into the cavern and passageway. The drone now clung to the wall near a spider's web, and had a clear view of events unfolding in the second cave. The web's strands, arrayed in front of the camera lens, looked wispy and huge.

"She's not a beetle-head."

"You mean Mr. Johnson's notes didn't mention that?"

Watching Rachel Gordon struggle, Hawke had to admit the young woman was acting like a Better-Than-Life chip-user going through a serious meltdown. But usually those people were burn-outs, ruptured psyches dragging the remains of their meat bodies around 'til they got their next fix. Up to now, Rachel had looked healthy and mentally stable.

Until she'd entered the second cave.

"And we both know a Johnson wouldn't lie." Flicker's tone dripped derision.

Hawke ignored her tone. "Is your little friend picking up anything else in the cave?"

Flicker was silent for just an instant. *"No."*

"No odors or auditory stimulus?"

Flicker consulted her readouts. *"None."*

"Then whatever's triggering her reaction is astral in nature."

"If you wanted to be sure of that, you should have brought a mage."

"Out here, I figured it'd be an easy grab and go. Rapid transit back to the border, and a hand-off with Mr. Johnson."

"The sec men upped that ante."

Hawke shifted in the shadows. His chameleon suit concealed him in the shadows, as long as he didn't move too quickly and no one got too close. The onboard sensor suite altered the suit's polymers to reflect the surroundings from proper perspectives to fool the naked eye. Cybered vision was harder to fool, but the brain still interpreted the feed. The problem was the heat down here seemed like a living thing that had crawled into the suit with him.

"The sec men are a problem, but I'm not worried about them." Sweat rolled down Hawke's back. The chameleon suit didn't come with a cooling system, because that would have made it pop out on a thermographic scan.

"I know the Johnson's offering a lot of cred for this job, but we can't spend it if we're dead. It's not too late to pull out." Flicker sounded neutral, playing devil's advocate. *"We can eat our expenses on this one and be back across the border in a few hours. I'll even split the loss with you. Won't take us long to find something else."*

Hawke magnified his view of the gem-encrusted statues. "I've never seen anything like this."

"I've never seen the inside of a dragon's stomach either, but I know I'm not that curious about it."

Hawke showed her a crooked smile. "No sense of adventure?"

"Adventure and curiosity don't offer big payouts. A guy named Katar Hawke told me that once upon a time."

Hawke grinned in spite of himself. Normally his curiosity never got high enough to get him killed. It wasn't that high now, but they were still on the sidelines. Watching cost nothing at this point.

"Incoming." Flicker's voice was suddenly quiet and deadly serious.

"Where?" Slowly, Hawke eased to a standing position, giving the camouflage suit time to wiz the surroundings and keep him concealed. He unlimbered the Nitama Optimum II assault rifle he'd chosen as his lead weapon.

During the Japanese occupation of San Francisco, General Saito's Imperial Marines had made the rifle immediately recognizable in the screamsheets and trideo. Its magazine carried thirty rounds, and the shotgun mounted underneath held five. The combination offered a lot of sudden firepower when necessary.

"I just marked ground troops approaching this location."

Hawke accessed Flicker's new feed through his comm and caught the overhead view from the aerial drone she'd put into the sky before they'd approached the campsite last night. At least two-dozen bogeys showed up on the screen. As Hawke watched, the drone's Identify Friend/Foe system lit up three more. They moved like seasoned pros, stalking through the jungle like big cats.

"Who are they?" Hawke watched the men as they converged on the dig. The native laborers had hunkered down in the shade and started talking.

"You know what I know. We're in Aztlan. Aztechnology usually stays close to anything going on in their territory."

"They granted the excavation permits."

"And they're probably keeping an eye on things, too." Flicker sounded irritated. *"Let the professor invest his time and cred, and prove his find first. If someone else is willing to do the grunt work, why not let them, and then step in and take whatever's here?"*

Hawke shifted on his feet, readying himself. "If Aztechnology is after whatever is here, it's gotta be something worth having."

"They've got a lot of troops in the field, not to mention a couple helos in the air. Taking whatever it is—and that's a problem right there—would be hard. They look like they're ready to geek anyone that gets in the way."

The comm video shifted and pulled back. This time Flicker's high-flying drone watching their backs and the surrounding terrain threw orange warning circles around two Aguilar-GX attack helicopters. Both hovered above the treetops behind the line of advancing men, close enough to be called into immediate assistance. Attention drawn by the thunder of the rotors, the dig crew looked up at the helos.

"GXs." Flicker cursed, sounding impressed at the same time. *"Whatever this is, Aztechnology isn't holding back on the firepower."*

"Gimme an ETA on the ground units. The helos won't sweep in until the groundpounders are in position."

Flicker looked at him and lifted a skeptical eyebrow. *"You're still thinking about doing this? Have you been mentally wiped?"*

Hawke kept calm and thought it through. "If Aztechnology goes big on this op, do you really think we're going to slide out of here without being noticed? If we're getting fragged on this thing, I'd rather go down looking for the win."

"They'll bury you in the same hole."

"Are you in or out?"

Flicker was silent for a moment, but made up her mind quickly. Time was working against them. Hawke knew she liked working with him because he stuck even when the going got rough.

"Present rate of ground travel puts them at the dig site in two minutes thirteen seconds." Her voice was professional, free of the anxiety that had been there a moment earlier.

"If you get the opportunity and things go totally south on this, get clear."

"I will. You knew that going in."

"See if your drone inside the cave can find another way out of there, just in case I can't come back out the way I'm going in." Hawke brought his assault rifle up across his chest, activated his wired reflexes, and sprinted out of the jungle.

CHAPTER THIRTEEN

Seated in her specially-modified ATV, Flicker watched the action unfold. Wired directly into the vehicle, the onboard components augmented her senses and made her feel more alive than any time in the meat world. These days, she seldom went anywhere without being wired into a drone through her PAN, mostly because she didn't like a single perspective.

The ATV stood three meters tall, four meters wide, and ten meters long. Covered in ablative armor and bristling with weapons and tech, it was a beast, but it was Flicker's beast, designed to meet her every demand. The ATV's skin contained camouflage nanites that helped blend it into urban or, as now, jungle environments. With the tech cloaking on, it was hard to detect from even a few meters away.

Getting the vehicle into Guatemala near the dig site had been difficult, but between them Hawke and Flicker had managed to pay off all the right people and sneak by all the wrong ones.

Right now she listened to several distinct levels of noise, tracking the encrypted radio buzz coming from the Aztlan sec men, Hawke's hurried breathing inside the camouflage suit, and the idle conversation of the laborers wondering what was in the hole the professor and the pretty *señorita* had discovered.

Her vision multi-tasked as well, picking up signals from the onboard systems as well as the drone in the cave and the airborne drones she had in the area. She cycled through the various perspectives and visual spectrums, hitting infrared and thermographic inside the cave as well as the telescopic views offered by the flying drones. She was inside the ATV as well as outside it.

When she'd gotten her first cyber implants and started driving, the sensory impressions from her body as well as the vehicles, then the added layers of the drones, had almost overloaded her mind. But she'd adapted. Now she could study them all separately or spin them all together and make sense of what she was seeing. When she wasn't jacked into a vehicle, she felt like she'd gone partially blind and deaf.

And she moved so slowly.

Now she was a tiger, coiled and ready for action.

Hawke broke cover and the laborers saw him. On unassisted video, Flicker only picked him up as a shimmering blur sprinting across the open country. Even the thermographic spectrum failed to tag him. Video acuity, aided by motion sensors, locked onto him and recognized him for what he was.

The Azzies would have that as well.

One of the GX helos lifted slightly.

Flicker blanketed the motion detector sensors the GX aimed at Hawke by agitating the intervening space with microwaves.

"You've been spotted. They're locking onto you."

Hawke didn't reply, saving his breath for running. A few laborers noticed the blur streaking across the open country. Whispers of angry spirits and awakened demons reached the ATV's audio pickups. Some of the men picked up shovels and axes. All of them retreated from the hole, fear tightening their faces.

Desperately, Flicker searched through the background geological material she'd dug into on the area. "In and out, my eye. You're one step away from getting fragged."

The ATV fed chems through her meat body and kept her chilled out. For the moment she was cold and hard and powerful, totally the ATV. She was wide and low to the ground, sitting on six oversized tires, waiting to be unleashed.

A few of the dig sec men started lifting their weapons. Flicker broke into their unit PAN and blasted them with a warning about the approaching Aztechnology troops.

"Who is this?"

"Stay off this freq!"

"Why would Aztechnology be here now?"

Dispassionately, Flicker watched the Azzies close on the sec men. They didn't bother declaring their identities or their intentions. They just opened fire.

Bullets and flechettes chewed through the trees and brush. Shredded vegetation drifted to the ground as the laborers and the remaining mercs dropped like felled timbers. Unarmored, the laborers practically exploded, bursting into bits and pieces across the terrain.

Flicker brought up her weapons array, but calmly held her fire. The time to cut and run without getting involved passed in a heartbeat.

Hawke threw himself the last few meters toward the hole. *"What intel do you have on that tunnel?"* His groan carried over the comm when he hit the ground.

"Nothing. It's new to the data I have."

"Gimme something I can use, Flicker."

Using one of the overhead drones, Flicker watched Hawke plunge into the hole, and couldn't help thinking it looked like an open grave. She flipped through the survey maps of the area she'd lifted from government, corporate, and military databases.

"There's an underground river that runs parallel to the tunnel farther in." Flicker took the incoming information from the cave drone and overlaid it onto the geo-maps.

"Drowning isn't a viable option."

The line of Azzie troops burst through the trees and arrived at the dig.

"You're about to have company down there."

Hawke cursed, but kept going.

Flicker plunged into his vidstream and saw the world as he saw it. He raced across the initial cave toward the passageway where the professor, the girl, and the three sec men had gone. His breath huffed in her ears.

"Close the door behind me."

"You don't know if you can get out the other way."

"I know we can't shoot our way through an Azzie attack team."

Flicker "felt" the hard jabs of a snooper prog banging into their comm freq. She fended it off automatically, shifting smoothly through the channels, and taking Hawke's comm with her. That wouldn't last long, though.

"Understood." It was times like this that Flicker wished she wasn't tweaked into hyperfocus by the chem suite. She knew her voice was cold and distant, not the voice of a friend. "Closing the door."

CHAPTER FOURTEEN

Flicker armed a quartet of missiles—two fragmentation and two high-explosive rounds—in the ATV's cannons. She ordered four anti-vehicle rounds into the second rotation, auto-locked those targets, and opened fire.

The initial salvo of rounds sped through the air in a low trajectory. The GX helos spotted them and tried to jam her signals as they warned the ground troops.

The Azzie troops hit the dirt, but the frag rounds blew up in the midst of them. Razor-sharp metal chewed into exposed flesh, and sometimes through the armored soldiers' Kevlar.

One of the helos managed to intercept an HE round and explode it in mid-air. The resulting blast ripped branches from trees and spread smoke and fire across the sky in long, curving tentacles.

The other HE round hit the dig site dead center. A huge spray of dirt and rock vomited out of the hole, filling the general vicinity with smoke and dust. A few seconds later, everything that went up came down again, burying the cave entrance under tons of dirt and rock.

Okay. Now let's just stay alive. Flicker fired her second salvo. She'd aimed one at the first GX helo and three at the second.

The single AV round exploded meters from the helo, but the second attack helo only managed to take out two of the AV rounds. The third slipped through the jammers like a greased eel and slammed into the GX.

The Azzie helo turned into a flaming fireball, a bit of luck Flicker hadn't been counting on. Fiery debris rained over the jungle.

The surviving helo targeted Flicker's general vicinity and fired its cannons. Machine gunners flipped out of the cargo doors, snug in their restraints, and opened up as well, flaying the jungle surrounding her vehicle.

Movemovemove! Flicker dumped six thermal smoke canisters from the ATV and trusted the hot particles contained in the rush of green vapor to obscure the helo's thermographic vision. She coaxed the engine to life and sped away through the jungle. Small trees and brush went down under the oversized tires.

She raced within cover as missiles struck the area where she'd just been. Shrapnel bounced off the ATV's reinforced sides, and the run-flat tires remained intact. She paralleled the tunnel as much as she could, twisting and skidding through the jungle while trying to go as fast as she could.

The remaining helo concerned her the most. If they were going to get away, it had to go down.

The blast concussion rushing down the tunnel knocked Hawke off his feet. He rolled and banged against the passageway walls as the shaft of sunlight behind him winked out. The rolling smoke cloud that overtook him blanked his infrared video. As he shifted to low-light vision, he forced himself to his feet and took a firmer grip on his rifle.

The amplified view was only slightly better than being blind. He paused against the passageway, rifle to shoulder, and waited for any Aztechnology troops to make an appearance. Likely some of them had made it into the hole before the blast closed it.

He pulled up Flicker's video feeds, splitting them between the oculars of the chameleon suit. Relief washed through him as he saw her tense face.

"How hot are you rolling?" Finally convinced that no one had made it into the cave, Hawke turned and ran along the passageway. His muscles felt loose and ready, and the disorientation he'd gotten from the blast was already fading. Also, the sooner he left the dust cloud, the better.

"Blistering. Caught a piece of luck. One of the helos went down."

"Can you get clear?"

"Not working on that right now."

"Staying with this isn't smart."

"This from the guy who jumped into the rabbit's hole after we knew things were about to get slotted."

"I needed a big score." Hawke stumbled in the darkness as he tried to adjust for the thermographic vision's inaccurate depth perception.

"You? You're the guy who always plans for a rainy day."

"I've had a lot of 'em lately."

"What—"

Hawke cut her off. "You're the queen of multi-tasking, not me. We'll talk later. Right now you need to get out of here."

"You came to me, omae, remember? Partly because you knew I had the skills and the hardware. But partly because you also know I won't leave you between a rock and a hard spot."

Guilt surged through Hawke, as heavy as the darkness and the stone and earth surrounding him. He *had* known Flicker wouldn't desert him—not as long as there was even a slight chance they could pull this off.

"This one's over." Hawke made his voice hard. "Get out now."

"I'm working on something. You just stay in one piece down there."

Hawke saved his breath. Once Flicker got her head set, she was set. He adjusted the chameleon suit's enclosed ventilation, adding more oxygen to the mix to keep his head clear. As soon as he cleared the dust cloud, he switched back to infrared and lengthened his stride.

CHAPTER FIFTEEN

The nightmare danced in Rachel's head as she fought against the sec men. *Runrunrunhidehidehide!* For a moment, she was back in the alien jungle, fleeing for her life. Behind her, something howled, almost powerful enough to rupture her eardrums, and the fetid stink of its breath filled her nostrils. The coppery taste of her own blood coated her mouth.

"Miss Gordon." One of the sec men leaned in close to her. She wasn't sure which one it was. "You have to calm down—" He tried to sound forceful as he attempted to get a slap-patch on her, but she jerked free. He stopped and spread his arms in frustration. "Professor. I need help over here."

Rachel spun away and cowered against one of the walls. The statues loomed around her, seeming to move toward her.

"I don't know what's wrong with her." Fredericks glanced over his shoulder at Rachel. "This is more your area than mine, I should think."

"The camp's been hit, professor." Doyle unlimbered his rifle and took a position covering the passage leading back to the dig site.

"Hit?" That caught Fredericks's attention.

"Attacked by Aztechnology."

Rachel tried to gain control of her breathing and force away the nightmare. If she was going to live, she knew she had to be able to think.

"That's absurd." Fredericks frowned, like a favorite student had just let him down.

His objection rang hollow. All of them had heard the blast preceding the cave-in that had sealed the opening to the surface. Rachel tried not to think about being trapped underground, or of any of the things that might be waiting in the darkness.

"Aztechnology has no reason to attack us," Fredericks said.

Doyle peered down the passageway. "You said you had all the permissions in order, professor."

"They were."

"And you told us what you were after was a bit of glory. Nothing anyone was willing to kill for."

"I told you the truth—I have no idea what they're doing here."

Shaking from the effort, Rachel slowly straightened up and gazed around the cave. Her fear was tied to something nearby. She walked into the circle of statues on weak legs, her knees threatening to buckle at any moment. Some of the figures looked human, but others seemed to have been formed from pure nightmare.

One was a tentacled creature that could contort its limbs to form a humanoid shape. A layer of writhing worms overlaid the misshapen skull, and the worm-like appendages wound into vague arms and legs. Its "fists" were clusters of tentacles that looked like hideously long fingers. Another was a scorpion-looking monster with a dozen legs that ended in serrated blades, a whip-like tail, and two front legs equipped with long pincers. Then there were bloated things, huge wolf-things with dead eyes, and melon-shaped creatures the color of spoiled cream whose bodies were filled with wounds and hungry maws. They couldn't possibly have ever existed. She put her hands out and tried to lock in on the sensation pulling at her. It felt like sandpaper maggots slithered under her skin.

"Rachel?" Professor Fredericks stepped closer to her. His breath came short and his eyes were wide with fear. "What is it?"

She shook her head. She didn't have any words to explain. The sensation of *wrongness* grew stronger, and she followed it unerringly now. She couldn't turn away.

"Beaumont." Doyle continued covering the passageway opening they'd come out of. "Check that tunnel."

From the periphery of her vision, Rachel saw the sec man step into a tunnel she hadn't seen before. He advanced slowly, his weapon pointing into the darkness.

Kneeling, Rachel pursued the grotesque feeling wriggling inside her. An echoing clamor now rose inside her mind; an alien voice, crying for blood and vengeance. Even with the fear surging through her like electricity, she couldn't stop searching for whatever drew her.

Beaumont returned to the cave. "Tunnel goes on for a long way, Doyle."

"Good. Maybe a way out of this." Doyle stared at Fredericks. "Do you know if this tunnel has another end, professor?"

"No." Fredericks watched Rachel as she examined a rough, dirt-encrusted statue almost hidden behind the others. "As I told you before, this cave is uncharted. I don't know anything about what's down here."

"Aztechnology seems to have some idea." Doyle's tone stopped just short of accusatory.

Rachel began wiping dirt away. The earth was loose and easily fell away from the statue. As she worked to expose it, she noticed the figure was some kind of—

"A lizard?" His voice hoarse, Professor Fredericks leaned closer,.

"No." Rachel unburied more of it, pushing the dirt away from the scaled back, the wings, the proud head, and the mighty claws. "A dragon."

"Is that made of—gold?" The professor touched the statue with a trembling finger.

"I don't know." Rachel drew her hands along the savage creature's body. She knew the dragon was longer than she was tall. The metal was dull yellow, and definitely looked like gold. It stood amid a crowd of the monstrous things, head reared back defiantly.

"There's a jewel." Hesitantly, Professor Fredericks took an excavation tool from his shirt pocket and reached for the glittering bauble.

The gem was deep blue with faint scarlet veins threading through it. Mounted in the dragon's snarling mouth, it was almost as large as Rachel's clenched fist.

"Do you feel the cold?" Professor Fredericks held his open palm over the dragon's mouth.

"No." Rachel reached for the gem.

"Allow me." Gently but forcefully, Professor Fredericks pushed her hands aside and reached out to extract the jewel. As soon as he touched the gem, though, something shimmered in the air and knocked him back into one of the statues.

The statue fell and started a chain reaction as it knocked over other statues. The horrifying things fell like tenpins. The *clank* of stone and metal striking hammered Rachel's hearing.

Pale and shaken, Professor Fredericks groaned and tried to

get back to his feet. He failed, and collapsed to the floor,.

Even though she knew she should check on the professor, Rachel was drawn to the jewel. Despite what she'd seen the gem do, she reached for it. The dragon's jaws opened slightly, and she plucked the object from its fanged mouth.

Surprised, but also feeling that everything had happened exactly the way it was supposed to, Rachel examined the jewel. It was egg-shaped. The blue facets gleamed even in the infrared light. She felt the rough texture beneath her fingertips and realized that markings scored the facets.

Then Doyle flew backward into the room, driven by an unseen force.

CHAPTER SIXTEEN

Outrunning the Aztechnology ground troops proved easy. Out-running the GX helo was another thing entirely.

On one level, Flicker admired the skill of whoever was piloting the chopper. But on another, she hated that person. No matter what she did, how deep she risked going into the brush and trees, the helo stayed on top of her.

The heavy machine gun fire and 20mm cannons blazed along her backtrail. The helo's tracking suite was top-of-the-line. She didn't expect anything less. Some of the trees uprooted by the cannon blasts fell into her path. When possible, she screeched around them. Other times she powered over them. The six over-sized tires slid over the trees and spun across the grass.

Activating the recessed six-centimeter spikes within the tires, Flicker felt the ATV grab fresh traction. Bark and white wood pulp erupted in roostertails behind her. Fist-sized chunks of grass and earth spit out as well.

Desperate, knowing the helo was getting her speed and moves down now, Flicker locked the front wheels, shifted power to the rear drivetrain, and risked a rough bootlegger's turn. The ATV came around in a gut-wrenching 180-degree spin as she launched another group of thermographic smoke canisters.

The gray-green smoke filled the jungle, drawing immediate fire from the helo. Trusting the pilot hadn't seen her reversal, Flick-er pinned the accelerator to the floor and rapidly went through the gears. The diversion wouldn't fool him for long, but hopefully it would be long enough.

She shot forward, dividing her attention between the action in the passageway, the geological maps, and the staggered front line of the Azzie troops. As she cleared the smoke cloud, she sent the cave drone deeper into the passageway, mapping the tunnel and racing the dig site sec men in the cave.

"You can get to the underground river." Flicker shifted and juked, sliding across the broken terrain despite the spiked wheels. Shredded countryside lay behind her. "Do you hear me?"

"I'm here." Hawke sounded far away, muffled.

"Grab the package and get out of there. Go to the river." Flicker slewed around a large boulder an instant before an HE round reduced it to rubble. Damn, he was even quicker than she'd hoped. Broken stones rattled against the ATV's ballistic armor. "You're a half-klick away."

"Understood. What's your sitrep?"

"Eyeball deep in drek."

Cannon rounds blew craters in the ground in front of Flicker. She dodged one and hit the NO_x, grabbing enough traction and acceleration from the booster pack to barely hurtle over the second crater. As she landed in an awkward rush, like a three-legged dog trying to make the best of a run across a frozen pond, an HE round hit her directly. The ATV's reactive armor went off in response, minimizing the damage.

The double-blast shivered through the vehicle, and her traction slipped for a moment. Flicker fought for recovery, then got the ATV under control again.

"You got three minutes to get there." Spotting movement ahead of her and recognizing it as Azzie troop movement, Flicker aimed for them.

The GX helo burned ammo as the weapons suite tried to acquire the ATV. Falling debris, smoke, and flames filled her screens. Her exterior audio mics were dampened, but she still felt the crescendo of violence and mayhem opening up around her. The shock absorbers managed to keep the rocking impacts to a minimum.

"If you're not there, I'm leaving without you." Flicker drove through an open space straight toward a new wave of the Azzie sec men. They spotted her and opened fire with small arms that did absolutely null against the ATV's armor.

"We're still underground."

"Get to the river." In the next breath, Flicker plunged into the ground troops.

Before the helo pilot recognized she'd driven among his own people, his weapons chewed through them and slammed them to the ground. One man went down in front of the ATV's reinforced front bumper. Two others bounced up over the vehicle when Flicker hit them. She didn't hesitate, remembering how they'd killed the unarmed laborers.

Realizing what was going on, the GX helo pilot backed off. Anticipating the moment, Flicker pulled another tight 180 and opened up with missiles again, bracketing the helo the moment she got it in her crosshairs.

Two missiles chopped through the GX's security jammers. The helo erupted into a crimson and yellow fireball and turned inside out to vomit black smoke into the sky.

The ATV's alert suite lit up. *"Warning. Vehicle has been targeted by anti-tank missile launcher."*

Evidently the surviving groundpounders hadn't been totally shorn of offensive weapons. Flicker tracked the target acquisition, swiveled her top 7.62mm machine gun toward the danger, and opened fire.

The bullets ripped through the jungle and caught the missile launcher operator as he fired his weapon. The warhead exploded only a meter or two out of the launcher's throat, destroying it.

Before the chunks of the dead man hit the jungle floor, Flicker rocketed forward again, gaining speed as she shot off into the jungle toward Hawke.

CHAPTER SEVENTEEN

Hawke rushed forward, trusting the chameleon suit to buy him a precious few seconds. In the shadows, using only low-light vision, he was just a ghost of blurred movement.

Still, the nearest man reacted at once. His reflexes were smooth and superhumanly quick, letting Hawke know he had wired reflexes as well. Hawke didn't want to kill the man. He and the rest of the sec team weren't like the Azzie troops. These men weren't hired killers—maybe. Hawke was willing to give them the benefit of the doubt.

Never breaking stride—knowing if he did the sec man would easily target him—Hawke ducked below the SMG, grabbed the barrel in his left hand, and ran his right hand under his opponent's left arm. Swiveling and putting his right hip into the other man, Hawke yanked the man off his feet, whirled to the left, and threw him into the sec man standing behind him.

The two went down in a tangle of limbs, their curses filling the cave. As the professor dove for cover, Hawke threaded the maze of statues. The third man's weapon chattered and tore away bits and pieces of the statues around him.

Hawke threw himself to the ground and brought his rifle up, finger squeezing the trigger. A double tri-burst and a shotgun blast slammed into the sec man's chest. Hit at close range, the rounds stopped by his armor but still imparting their kinetic force, the sec man lost his balance and fell on his back.

Hawke rose to his feet and lunged forward. He slammed the rifle's butt against the third man's armored head, pulling the blow just enough to render unconsciousness instead of killing him.

The first man, the one with the wired reflexes, got up almost immediately. Hawke fired two shotgun blasts at point-blank range and knocked the man's feet out from under him, causing him to topple forward. Hawke kicked the man in the head and knocked him out as well.

The surviving sec man reached for his dropped SMG, captured it, and spun to take aim at Hawke. Whirling on one foot, Hawke slammed his combat boot against the side of the man's head and bounced his helmet off the stone wall behind him. Already out, the man crumpled slowly.

The professor and the young woman stood frozen. Blue fire flashed in the woman's cupped hands. Fear etched lines into their faces.

Hawke gestured with the assault rifle. "Let's go."

"No." The professor drew himself up to his full height.

Moving forward, Hawke locked eyes with the man. He spoke in a cold monotone. "Professor Fredericks, either you can leave with me, or I'm going to shoot you in both legs and leave you for the Aztechnology butchers to find."

"Aztechnology? They wouldn't bother us." Worry and uncertainty gleamed in Fredericks's eyes. "I've got permits. You've got to be mistaken."

In his own PAN, Hawke watched Flicker racing cross-country. Time was working against them.

Hawke shook his head. "I don't have time to argue. The Azzies killed your hired help and the sec men."

"Why?"

"I don't know."

"Who are you?"

"The guy who's gonna get you out of here alive. If you want to live." Hawke shifted his focus to the woman. "You're coming with me."

She took a step back from him. "No."

"Either come on your own, or I'm carrying you out of here. Choose now."

Thunder erupted again at the other end of the cave system. Hawke pulled up a link to Flicker's sky drone and saw Aztechnology forces swarming the dig site. Another series of explosions went off, and part of the ground around the dig site collapsed.

Hawke glanced at Fredericks. "They've breached the first cave. You wanna see if they're willing to review your 'permits,' be my guest, but I'm leaving, and she's coming with me, one way or another."

After a heartbeat of hesitation, Fredericks seized Rachel Gordon's wrist. "We're coming."

The young woman looked lost, dazed, but still resisted the professor's tug.

Fredericks pulled again, more forcefully this time. "Come on, Rachel. Staying here isn't an option. We'll get this sorted out soon enough."

"What about the other students?" she asked.

Hawke shook his head. "Hopefully they were smart enough to get to cover topside when the shooting started. Nothing we can do for them down here."

"All right." She swept loose strands of hair from her copper-colored eyes, then shoved the jewel into her backpack.

Fredericks took a final glance at the unconscious sec men, then turned to Hawke. "Which way?"

"This passageway leads to an underground river." Hawke took off at a jog before either of his unwilling companions could ask him what they were going to do next. Truth was, he didn't know what Flicker had planned.

The passageway ran straight and narrow as it plunged through the earth. Hawke kept his speed down. The young woman matched him easily enough, but the professor struggled to keep up. The chameleon suit registered the slight decline, but Hawke was already aware of it. His PAN accessed the GPS marker Flicker had tagged for him.

"I can't . . ." The professor stopped running and braced his hands on his knees as he fought for breath with a wheeze. "Got to stop."

Hawke faced Rachel Gordon. "Let's go."

She shook her head stubbornly. "I'm not leaving him."

"The Azzies are in the tunnels. They'll be on us in seconds."

Her eyes blazed fire. "I'm not convinced going with you will be any better."

"I'm not going to kill you."

"I don't know that."

Hawke put steel in his voice. "If I was going to do that, you'd already be dead."

"Hawke." Flicker sounded as cool and imperturbable as ever.

"Yeah."

"Where are you?"

Hawke took a reading from the GPS marker, then scanned her position as well. She slogged through the jungle, spinning dirt and vegetation in her wake. "Hundred twenty-seven meters out."

"You're running behind."

"I'll be there before you are."

The sky drone blazed a warning, and Hawke picked it up on his connection. Three more GX helos streaked across the treetops as they bore down on Flicker.

"We're cutting this one close." Flicker remained calm, but Hawke knew it was the chems running through her brain, keeping her adjusted and moving. *"The troops in the tunnel're gaining on you."*

Hawke shifted over to the cave drone and watched the perspective dance crazily. The drone's survival suite kicked in as its programming registered targeting acquisition from one of the Aztechnology soldiers. Sleek and quick, the drone avoided two assault rifle bursts that scratched sparks from walls.

Then the video and audio links went black.

Flicker cursed. *"You're blind in there."*

"We'll make it." Hawke grabbed a fistful of the professor's shirt and yanked him into motion. "You just be there when we arrive."

CHAPTER EIGHTEEN

Professor Fredericks stumbled and finally fell as Hawke hauled him through the opening that led to the underground river. Rachel, who'd been supporting the professor as best as she could, went down with him. Flopping onto his back, Fredericks gasped like a beached fish.

"Here?" Rachel glared at Hawke in heated disbelief. "This—*this* is your big rescue?"

Staring out over the wide swath of swiftly flowing river at least a dozen meters below them, Hawke had to admit the escape route didn't look very impressive. Even using telescopic vision, he didn't see a good reason to hope for the best.

The cavern formed a basin, but Hawke didn't know how deep the water was. Both ends were closed, but the river flowed into and out of the area through the limestone, so there had to be tunnels beneath the surface. Even if things went incredibly bad, he could shed his armor and swim for it. If the underground river didn't stay submerged too long. Too long and he'd drown, even with the oxygen-extending filters in his lungs.

Hawke wished he still had eyes on the approaching Aztechnology sec team. At least he'd have known when the drek was going to hit the fan.

"We're here." Hawke peered into Flicker's ATV, then accessed the GPS locators and discovered she was almost on top of him.

"So am I. Grab some cover. I'm going to make a hole."

Ignoring the three GX helos bearing down on her, Flicker loaded four HE rounds in her cannons, selected the target area ahead, and fired. The missiles shot upward, causing the helos to break formation momentarily, then dove back toward the ground.

Explosions ripped across the terrain seventy meters in front of Flicker's ATV. She kept her speed up and aimed for the conflagration as she cut off the automatic warning system. Machine gun bullets and missiles strafed the ground around her and chewed craters into the landscape. The reactive armor blew apart in chunks as the ATV shed its outer skin.

She launched another flying drone and tracked its movement through the twisting flames and smoke clouds. A moment later, the drone marked the gaping twenty-meter chasm in the ground. At first, she thought the combined explosives had failed to break through to the underground basin. Despite the chems lacing her system, allowing her mind to work superfast and unfettered by emotions, a tingle of fear shot through her. Then she clamped down on it and shoved it away.

The drone shot through the opening and relayed images of the basin. The infrared beam peeled away some of the darkness, revealing the spume of rock and earth spilling into the glittering black river below.

She tasked the drone with calibrating the distance from the opening to the river. *37 meters.*

The ATV shivered like an arthritic dog when an HE round impacted its left rear quadrant. One of the tires blew and turned into flaming rubber slag, despite the armor and run-flat composition. Flicker activated a fire suppression system that nulled the fire.

She tapped the brakes, digging the spikes into the terrain, and watched the speed drastically drop. Satisfied, she felt the ATV slew around and topple into the hole. Then she was in free fall.

"Watch out below."

Astonished, Hawke watched the basin ceiling rip apart overhead. Sunlight stabbed into the darkness. Enough of it reached him that the chameleon suit shifted colors to match the surroundings.

For a moment, he thought the whole basin had collapsed. Tons of earth and rock plunged down. Some of the debris struck the stony outcrop where Hawke and the others stood. He turned and shielded the woman. Fist-sized earthen clods and rocks rebounded off his armor. The professor tucked himself against the wall and lay flat, keeping his hands over his head.

Glancing over his shoulder, Hawke saw Flicker's ATV plunge through the opening and fall into the river upside down. The ATV sank immediately as a large waterspout shot up.

"Flicker!" Hawke sprang away from the woman and prepared to leap into the water. He thought he could reach her before the ATV became a watery tomb.

"I'm all right. Wait."

Accessing the sky drone, Hawke watched the three GX helos converge on the pit/entrance Flicker had created. One launched a missile through the hole.

"Down!" Hawke pushed Rachel back into the passageway.

The missile hit the pit's lip and knocked a large section of it loose. The debris splashed into the river just as Hawke used Flicker's latest drone to search the basin. The ATV surfaced upright amid a disturbance in the river only a short distance from the promontory where Hawke had emerged.

"Get down here." The echo of the debris drumming against the ATV sounded strange over the freq. *"You'll have to swim under. There's an airlock."*

Hawke turned to Rachel and Fredericks. "We're going down."

"Down *there*?" The professor looked at Hawke as though he'd gone insane.

"You don't have time to argue with those people." Hawke grabbed the professor and heaved him out into the water. Rachel stood frozen for a moment, then reached for Fredericks too late. Taking advantage of her forward momentum, Hawke planted a hand in her back and shoved her over the edge. Only then did he wonder if either of them could swim.

"The helos are locking onto a target." Flicker spoke calmly. *"I don't know if it's you."*

Holding his assault rifle in both hands, Hawke stepped over the promontory's edge and dropped feet-first into the dark river.

CHAPTER NINETEEN

Cold, black water closed over Hawke's head, chilling him without getting him wet, despite the chameleon suit. Shouldering the rifle, he kicked toward the surface amid more flying debris raining down. He struggled against the weight of the armor, and thought he'd have to lose it. The suit's coloration immediately took on the blackness all around him.

On the surface, Hawke shook his head to get the near-freezing water out of his eyes. He glanced around and spotted Fredericks and Rachel treading water nearby.

"What do you think you're doing?" The professor sputtered and choked on a mouthful of water. "You're going to get us killed!"

Hawke swam toward them. "Swim under the vehicle. There's an airlock. Get inside and let's get out of here."

Waving his arms through the water, Fredericks glared doubtfully at the ATV. Before he could argue, Hawke lunged up and shoved the professor's head under. Bubbles floated up, letting Hawke know he'd caught the man by surprise.

Rachel swung a fist at Hawke and caught him on the side of the head. He caught her arm before she could swing again and shoved her under. Overhead, another missile struck the opening, enlarging it as Rachel fought her way back above the waterline.

"Get down there or we're all dead." Hawke shoved her under again. This time the woman took the message and swam for the underside of the ATV.

"They're almost through." Flicker said. *"If they get down here, we're hosed. I'm almost out of ammo, and the armor's nearly gone. If we get hit again, we could have real problems getting out of here."*

More debris pelted the water, banging off the ATV and splashing all around Hawke. Satisfied that the professor and Rachel were following orders, he dove beneath the water and swam for the bottom of the ATV. Spikes from the tire overhead clawed into his shoulder for a second, then he pulled free and spotted Rachel in front of him.

A cluster of flashing blue lights marked the airlock. The hatch stood open, but Hawke didn't know if Fredericks had survived his dunking. Rachel halted under the opening, then went up, climbing inside the vehicle.

Hawke followed as another missile struck the opening, making the cavern shudder and loosening more earth and rock. Grabbing the sides of the airlock, Hawke pulled himself up into the ATV's passenger cabin. The vehicle rolled on the swift current as Flicker strove to retain control.

"Everybody aboard?" Flicker didn't bother to look over her shoulder. Her onboard cameras relayed everything to her.

"Clear." Hawke hauled his legs up just before the mechanized airlock slammed shut with a smooth *clank.* The interior held six seats in rows of two. He glanced at the professor and Rachel as they hunkered down together. "Sit."

"Who are you?" The professor remained adamant.

Hawke shoved the man back into a seat and the safety belts automatically slid over his body and secured him in place. "I'm the guy saving you from Aztechnology." He glanced meaningfully at Rachel.

Without a word, but definitely not looking happy about her present circumstances, Rachel sat in the seat adjacent to Fredericks. "Where are you taking us?"

"Out of here."

"Why?"

"That's what I was hired to do."

Rachel's eyebrow lifted. "You knew this was going to happen? That we would be attacked? Why?"

Hawke pulled himself into the passenger seat up front and glanced at the console. There was no instrumentation board. There didn't have to be. Flicker was jacked directly into the ATV's OS, which she'd written.

"No." Hawke unzipped the chameleon suit's hood and peeled it down to his neck. "If I'd known we were gonna get this much attention, I'd have stayed clear of this. And you. Now we're stuck with each other." He glanced at Flicker.

The elven rigger sat cocooned in her seat, its datajack connecting her to the vehicle. Her eyes were closed as she used the

ATV's video links.

"Anything I can do?" Hawke leaned back and the belts lashed him in.

"I've got it."

"Gimme a look."

The windshield suddenly pixelated and opened onto the drone view from inside the basin cave. One of the GXs hovered above the enlarged opening, slowly dropping to enter the cave above the river. The rotorwash created waves that slapped the ATV.

Servos whined within the vehicle as it bobbled and settled more deeply into the water.

"What's happening?" the professor asked, a tinge of panic in his voice.

"Relax. We're not sinking, we're taking on ballast." Flicker's voice came from the speakers within the vehicle instead of her meat body.

"Submersible?" Hawke swallowed the small tremor of fear inside him as the ATV sank lower.

"Yeah."

"You didn't mention that."

An image of Flicker's face momentarily showed as an overlay on the drone feed on the windshield. She smiled. *"Surprise."*

Above, the GX swiveled to bring its guns around. Heavy machine gun fire echoed within the trapped space and pinged off the ATV's metal skin and bulletproof transplas.

"We're not as speedy under the water as we are on top of it." The ATV inclined and dove. *"But we're fast enough to get out of here. We're powered by propellers, so we run pretty quiet."*

On the drone view, Hawke watched as they disappeared from view. The acceleration pressed him back into the seat. "You do know where we're going?"

"Downriver. According to the hydrographical maps I've peeked at, there's good chance this channel empties into the Pacific in nine-point-eight klicks."

"This thing can survive ocean depths?"

"Not deep depths, but we can stay down two hundred meters or so. As long as the Azzies don't get a lock on us, we can run for a while."

"To where?"

"Amazonia. The Aztlans and Amazonians still hate each other. I'm counting on that."

"How far are we from Amazonia?"

"Seventeen hundred klicks. Plus or minus a few. I'll know more once we get out into open water."

The thought of open water made Hawke's guts churn. He was no fan of the ocean when he was on top of it. Being underneath it was even more stressful.

"Belt in," Flicker told him.

Without a word, Hawke settled into his seat, pulled on the safety harness, and wished he had more legroom. He worked at telling himself there was plenty of oxygen inside the ATV's cabin too.

The view on the inside of the windshield slid away, replaced by an underwater image of the passageway. In the barely lighted darkness, Hawke spotted the mouth of the river's underwater channel.

"We'll fit?" Involuntarily, his hands gripped the seat arms as they hurtled toward the wall. He couldn't help thinking the ATV would shatter like an eggshell if it hit solid rock.

"Gonna have to. We'll know soon enough if we don't."

Hawke resisted the impulse to close his eyes. Instead, he watched as the ATV scooted adroitly into the passageway with the speed and skill of a porpoise. Cannon rounds exploded in the river behind them and the turbulence threw them from side to side, causing them to carom off the walls for a moment. Then Flicker got back in the groove, and they shot along the underground river.

"It won't take Aztechnology long to figure out the river." Hawke pulled up a map on his PAN and started considering the options. "They'll work out where we've got to re-emerge and try to take us there."

"Null sheen. I've got foolies and a couple other surprises they don't know about. They won't like what they're going to run into." Flicker's image ghosted onto the windshield briefly again. She smiled, then faded. *"Of course, you might not like it either."*

CHAPTER TWENTY

Rachel's senses reeled as she considered her present situation. The big man and his friend—*Flicker*, she remembered—weren't there to save her and Professor Fredericks. Evidently keeping them from getting killed by the Aztechnology gunners was only part of the kidnapping scheme they'd put together. Moving stealthily, she slipped her Fairlight Caliban commlink from a thigh pocket and tried to open an emergency channel.

"You can put your tech away, Miss Gordon." Flicker spoke without turning around. *"You're not going to get a signal through my shielding."*

The big man turned around in his seat and grabbed the commlink from her hand before she could put it away. He closed his fist and the device shattered with a sharp *crack*. When he opened his fist, broken pieces tumbled to the ATV's floor.

"Hey!" Rachel protested, reaching forward.

"Behave," the man said, blocking her hand. "Otherwise I'll trank you, and you'll wake up with a headache that'll last for hours. Doesn't make any difference to me."

Professor Fredericks grabbed her shoulders and eased her back. "Take it easy. We're alive. That's all that matters at the moment."

Forcing herself to calm down, Rachel leaned back in her seat and breathed out in frustration. She shrugged out of the professor's grip. "Who hired you to kidnap us?"

The big man turned his attention back to the view of the river channel. "I've got no idea, and I'm not answering any more questions."

Rachel wanted to fight, but she felt the jewel in her bag radiate calmness. Captured by the mystery the object offered, she removed it from the bag and studied it. The professor's breath feathered against her shoulder as he leaned over and peered into the blue facets. She ran her fingers over the symbols, thinking some of them were starting to look familiar, the same way the scrolls did back in Professor Fredericks's class months ago.

"May I?" Professor Fredericks reached for the jewel.

Despite the reluctance thrumming within her, Rachel held the artifact out for him to touch, but as soon as his fingers got within millimeters of the surface, a shimmer threw out cobalt embers. The hair on the back of Professor Fredericks' hand stood on end and popped with static electricity. He pulled his hand back.

The professor cursed beneath his breath, something Rachel had never before heard him do. He'd always seemed too mild-mannered for such behavior.

He cleared his throat. "Rachel, would you try handing the jewel to me, please?"

Carefully, though the action made her feel wrong inside, and she had to force herself to continue, Rachel attempted to put the artifact into Professor Fredericks's waiting hand. This time, it didn't even get as close before an electrical charge leaped out and lashed his open palm. Professor Fredericks cried out and jerked his hand back. Smoke curled up from his scorched flesh as a four-centimeter circle of blackened skin and blisters appeared immediately. The smell of cooked meat filled the cabin.

"What is that?" His interest captured by the jewel, the big man reached back for it from the front seat.

Stubbornly, Rachel wrapped the artifact in her arms, keeping it back from her kidnapper. He definitely wasn't touching it.

"Hawke!" Flicker warned, her voice blasting from the vehicle's speaker. *"Don't touch that thing."*

The big man halted, then withdrew his hand. His challenging gaze raked Rachel. "What is it?"

"Mine," Rachel said, the word coming out before she knew she was going to speak.

"I don't know," Flicker answered. *"I've scanned it with everything I've got. Whatever it is, it's not tech."*

Hawke glanced at Professor Fredericks, who was blowing on his injured hand. "It throws out energy," the big man pointed out.

"It's not tech," Flicker repeated.

Hawke scowled and drew back warily. "I hate magic."

Magic? The idea whipped through Rachel. All her life, she'd considered herself to be one of the lucky ones. She'd had friends who had studied magic, but when she'd been tested, she'd never had any true aptitude. She was, thankfully, blessedly, normal.

But this artifact *was* magic. And she was the only one who could touch it. She wasn't sure what that meant, but she hung onto all the possibilities it presented.

Whatever else it proved to be, the jewel was *hers*. She was certain of that.

"I just lost my last outside drone." Flicker relayed the information emotionlessly. *"One of the helos shot it down, so I can't see the Azzies anymore."*

"Were they following us?"

"Yeah. Along the surface. Either they've got maps of the area, or they're equipped with ground-penetrating radar. Either one of those is bad, but if they're just using maps, they have to guess at where we are. That gives us a slight edge of unpredictability."

The ATV hurtled down the dark underground passage, running with the swift river current.

Hawke reached under his seat and came up with a med slap-patch that he handed to Professor Fredericks. Then he turned back around and fell silent.

The professor put the slap-patch on his hand, waited for the pain-relieving chems to kick in. All the while, he studied Rachel with a covetous gleam in his eyes.

As Rachel gazed into the murky blue depths of the artifact, she felt the creature's presence on the other side of some unknown barrier. It seemed close enough to touch, but she was afraid to do that because she felt its hunger for vengeance.

Even though Hawke knew Flicker would be keeping an eye on the young woman in the back seat, he watched Rachel's reflection in the transplas window. Her image was captured against the frosted glow of the bright beams carving through the dark river depths ahead of them.

"Breathe slower." Flicker's voice came softly over his commlink.

"I am breathing slow." Her awareness of the tension filling him irritated him. But she was queen of everything inside the ATV. She monitored everyone through the seat sensors. She knew exactly how he was feeling. Even if her tech hadn't ratted him out, she knew him well enough to guess what was going on.

"You're not breathing out enough. If you keep on like you are right now, you're going to hyperventilate."

Hawke didn't bother arguing, or pointing out that his onboard autonomy regulator would adjust his breathing and scrub away the CO_2 building up in his lungs. He nodded, and wished they still had the drone in place so they'd know where the Azzie helos were.

Four objects sped from the ATV, cutting through the water like torpedoes. Trackers automatically showed up on the transplas window, but Hawke knew those were for his benefit. Flicker already knew where they were going.

"Another set of drones," Flicker said. *"Maybe we won't know where the Azzie helos are, but we'll have some idea of what's waiting up ahead of us. The Pacific Ocean's only 732 meters away. Then we're going to be exposed."*

Hawke tested his restraints once more. So far the channel had widened, and their speed had picked up to thirty-seven KPH. Every now and again, the ATV still caught a glancing blow against the limestone walls that rocked the vehicle and echoed within the cabin.

"You know you might not be able to keep this vehicle." Hawke knew Flicker got attached to her rides. To her, they were more than tools. They were her creations.

"I knew that coming into this. That's why I'm going to charge you for the loss of equipment—and for the upgrades I've got in mind for the next one—if I lose this one."

"So, I guess now would be the wrong time to tell you this run's caught me short on cred."

"I can float you a loan, chummer. I just won an Aztlan smuggler's run, remember?"

The cocky attitude in her voice was ersatz, but it made Hawke smile. "I do remember, and I also know you'll be charging me interest. Kind of takes the relief out of the equation."

"I will charge interest, so don't dawdle on the payment." Her voice tightened, became more serious again. *"Hang on. We're hitting ocean in three seconds."*

Hawke braced himself, gritting his teeth and trying not to wonder, if the river let out deeply below sea level, if the ATV would implode. No matter how well built a vehicle was, once it got down far enough, it would crush like a blown eggshell under the increased pressure of the deep.

The water suddenly brightened ahead of them, then they were awash in the ocean currents, jerking ninety degrees to the north to follow the coastal waters. The immediate change in direction shoved Hawke against the vehicle's door. A high-pitched yelp came from the ATV's rear seats. At first Hawke thought it belonged to the young woman, but it was the professor who'd lost his nerve.

"It's okay," Flicker said. *"We're fine. It'll just take a minute to adjust."*

The propeller engines torqued, and shivers ran through the ATV as Flicker made the necessary adjustments. Under her steady control, the vehicle came about smoothly and headed west. All around them, on the other side of the transplas window, fish and sea creatures darted in all directions to get out of their way.

The cavern mouth they'd shot out of quickly faded from view. The sea floor beneath them slanted sharply down, becoming darker till it turned a vivid, impenetrable black. Hawke peered through the windows, looking for the Azzie submersibles he half-expected to be lying in wait. He couldn't see anything, but that didn't mean they weren't closing in.

"I thought we were headed south to Amazonia," he said.

"Not yet. We have to get away from the coast first."

"Are you sonar-equipped?" he asked.

Flicker laughed. *"Do you have six exit strategies for every ambush you walk into?"*

Before he could answer, the forward windshield pulsed again, and an orange sonar schematic appeared. More overlays showed views and intel from the four drones around them. There was so much information, Hawke didn't know how Flicker kept up with it all. He felt a headache coming on.

"Seventeen hundred klicks, huh?" Hawke made it a point to breathe in and out, in and out. "How many hours is that?"

"I can do up to thirty knots in the water. Not as fast as everything topside, but the ATV's pretty nimble."

Hawke worked out the math. "At thirty knots, getting to Amazonia's gonna take a long time."

"Good thing we're not taking the ATV the whole way, then, huh?"

"Then how are we getting there?"

"I'm calling in a favor. Remember when I told you that you weren't going to like this?" Flicker's image formed over the sonar readout and she smiled at him.

Before Hawke could respond, a warning beacon chirped and

the light inside the cabin turned red. "Is that the Azzies?"

"Yeah. They found us quicker than I thought they would."

Streaming lines of air bubbles, small barrels dropped into the water around them. Recognizing them for what they were, Hawke started to yell a warning, but the depth charges all exploded in quick succession, with the resulting turbulence wreaking havoc on the ATV.

CHAPTER TWENTY-ONE

Remaining calm, despite the fact that he was suddenly hanging upside down in the ATV, Hawke blinked, letting the implant enhancements in his eyes quickly correct against the bright detonations of the depth charges.

"Just your luck when it goes bad," Flicker accused. *"You would have a group of Azzie helos equipped for maritime warfare around to come busting down on us."*

Hawke didn't even bother to protest, but he started wondering even more about what made the young woman so valuable. It looked like he was getting shorted on the contract cred from Mr. Johnson, but Aztechnology was pulling out all the stops to get her.

And why had the corp waited 'til now to go in hard after Rachel Gordon? They'd had her practically dossing down with them for the last few weeks. What had changed? The artifact the woman held onto came immediately to mind, and he wished he knew more about it.

Hawke jerked again as Flicker guided them through another series of near misses. The ATV darted and dodged and dived like an agile sea turtle, gaining and losing depth to the point where he started worrying they were going to get the bends from the sudden changes.

"The cabin's pressurized," Flicker told him. They'd worked together closely enough for long enough that she could almost read his mind. *"The atmosphere in here remains constant. Depth changes aren't going to affect us."* She paused. *"As long as we stay inside."*

The depth indicator showed they were 127.3 meters down.

With the oxygen filtration mods done to his lungs, Hawke knew he could make the slow return to the ocean's surface. He figured Flicker would have deep-sea equipment for herself.

But that left the professor and Rachel Gordon as soon-to-be lost cargo. The ocean would take them, and if it didn't and they managed to reach the surface, decompression sickness would kill them or leave them permanently damaged. No cargo delivery, no payout. That potential loss didn't bother him as much as the two dying. He told himself they stood a better chance with Flicker and him than if they'd stayed back at the dig site.

Another trio of depth charges exploded and rolled the ATV sideways again.

"Do you have any surface to air weapons?" Hawke wanted some way to strike back. He hated being helpless.

"I exhausted them keeping you alive back there at the dig. Except for machine guns, I'm empty. And machine guns aren't going to work while we're submerged."

"You could surface, take a few shots." The idea of being up in the open air, above the ocean, was appealing.

"No. Just give me another few minutes. I'm working on something."

"What?"

"You're not the only one I've done runs with, omae. *Now shut up and let me call in a favor from a guy I know is somewhere out here. It's just a question of if he feels like taking on the Azzies to help me out."*

Hawke curbed the instant need to query her about who she was talking about. He knew they each had people the other didn't know about. That was how they worked.

For several long minutes, Flicker ran the underwater gauntlet, somehow avoiding the descending depth charges just enough to keep from taking too much damage. Still, the ATV shook and shivered, twisted and twirled like a leaf in a typhoon from her piloting and from the concussive waves.

"There's a leak!" the professor squawked from the back.

Glancing over his shoulder, Hawke spotted a steady stream of water spraying into the cabin from one of the transplas window seals. Growling a curse, he reached under the seat for the repair kit he'd noticed there when getting the med kit. Grabbing a tube of sealant, he freed his seat restraints and got up.

Strangely calm, like she was somewhere else, and this was just a simsense she could end at any time, Rachel watched her big captor climb out of his seat and start applying the sealant to the high-pressure leak that had opened in the vehicle's roof. The ATV's integrity was rapidly degrading. She felt the truth of that, even though she didn't know how she knew.

She was also suddenly aware of a trio of depth charges angling directly toward them that Flicker wasn't going to be able to avoid. The rigger's sudden fear shattered the icy cool she kept. She changed the direction of the ATV, but there was no way the vehicle was going to make the necessary clearance to escape the explosives.

The blue jewel glowed in Rachel's hands. She felt the heat of it, almost hot enough to burn, and listened to the shrill cry of whatever was contained within it. But some of its power leaked through, filling Rachel up to the point where she thought she might burst.

Needing to get the energy out of her body, Rachel maintained enough presence of mind to direct it at the depth charges. She saw the shimmering blue stream speed through the ocean, then envelop the explosives. In the blink of an eye, the depth charges withered and turned to useless flotsam.

"How—how did you do that?" Flicker asked, communicating through the speaker closest to Rachel.

Staring at the gray detritus that scattered before the ATV and tapped against the transplas windshield, Rachel shook her head. "I . . . I don't know."

"Well, thanks."

The artifact vibrated in Rachel's hands, and somehow, she knew the unleashing of the energy had pleased whatever was inside it. She closed her eyes, held the jewel tightly, and willed it to stay calm.

"Flicker!" Hawke struggled to squeeze more nanobot fixative into the micro-fissure that had opened up in the ATV's armored skin. The gray-green goop spread easily across the surface as the nanites adhered to the metal and ceramic blend, held for just a moment, then got blasted away. The pressure was powerful enough now to lacerate Hawke's flesh. "The sealant's not holding!"

Before he finished speaking, another series of depth charges went off nearby and swirled the ATV around like it was in a blender. Two more micro-fissures spurted into the cabin and he knew the vehicle's integrity was only minutes away from collapsing. The atmosphere pressure had to be getting affected, too.

The ATV dipped and arrowed down, plunging more deeply into the sea. Around them, the water turned bluer and bluer, edging into black.

"Flicker!" Hawke barely controlled the fear of the ocean raging within him. He hated the thought of drowning, of being crushed with no way to fight back. If he was going to die, he wanted an opponent to battle, someone or something he could take on physically.

A fourth micro-fissure blasted open, spraying into Hawke's face and ripping at his cheek. His chem suite worked to sweep away the pain as he jerked his head back, getting out of the jet's path. A pool of salt water was collecting in the bottom of the ATV.

Not understanding why she wasn't responding, Hawke turned to face her. Just as he started to speak, he noticed the outline of the big submersible ahead of them. He guessed the underwater craft was close to a hundred meters long and at least twenty meters wide and fifteen meters deep according to the signature ping.

Hawke also knew Flicker had to see the thing, but she was headed straight for it anyway. With no way to stop it, he braced himself for the collision, knowing the micro-fissures were about to get a lot bigger.

CHAPTER TWENTY-TWO

The luxury of being a rigger was that when jacked into a vehicle, Flicker could see everything. Well, nearly everything. And what she couldn't see with her cams and drones, she could "sense" with her detection software suites.

But she could see Hawke's look of disbelief easily inside the ATV. He was drenched by the incoming seawater, one cheek bleeding from a pressure cut.

"Chill, omae," Flicker told him over their private commlink. *"We'll be safe here."*

"If we don't get fragged when we hit it."

"We're not going to hit it." Flicker feathered the controls, cutting the propellers for a moment and swinging them around to blast forward and slow them. The seat restraints cut into their bodies. Then she switched to the encrypted frequency used by the big submersible.

"Attention, Scorpionfish, *this is* Mantis. *Do you copy?"* She spoke in Spanish more as a courtesy. Every crewman aboard *Scorpionfish* could speak English like a native.

"Hola, Mantis."

Flicker smiled at the cheerful camaraderie in Joaquin's voice. They'd shared some good times over the years. Splitting profits on lucrative runs and dodging heat waves together when Lone Star got serious about enforcing the laws made for deep friendships. Working with him was a nice change of pace every now and again, but they were too much the same to be together long. Too much overlap of skill sets, too much in the way of strong personalities, and Joaquin was too enmeshed in the Ghost Cartel drug biz. To Flicker's way of looking at it, her friend had developed a wageslave mentality to the Camargo Cartel.

"Ah, Flicker, you didn't mention you might be bringing Azzie helos when you visited." His tone was mocking, totally self-confident, another trait that kept a working relationship from any kind of permanence.

She liked meeting with him occasionally, for biz or personal entertainment, just to see what toys he was playing with. The submersible was his pride and joy, though, and he'd developed tunnel vision regarding any other vehicle. Flicker appreciated a broader spectrum.

The exfil through *Scorpionfish* had been set up only as a fallback option. Flicker hadn't mentioned the submersible to Hawke because she knew he didn't like working in deep water.

"I'd planned to be rid of them by now," Flicker replied, *"but you know how these things go."*

"Of course, but this will go beyond the bounds of friendship. Staying in the shadows is our way. This, little one, will put our operation on the map for a time. The Azzies will seek retaliation."

"You have my apologies."

"I'll have your cred to pocket as well. And you'll owe me a favor in the future."

That was the part Flicker dreaded. Cred was cred. That could always be found lying around in one corp's coffers or another. But doing a favor for someone like Joaquin, who was quite capable as a runner—and very well equipped—could get someone slotted up bad.

"We hadn't talked about a favor."

"We're talking about it now."

A trio of depth charges exploded and buffeted the ATV into the submersible.

"And I don't think you have any other offers open, hmmm?" Joaquin *did* enjoy having the upper hand during a negotiation.

"Agreed. A favor to be named later." Flicker knew she'd probably regret the bargain, but hoped she'd at least live through it.

"Thank you."

Flicker tracked *Scorpionfish's* subtle movements as the big boat decloaked and shifted to go into combat mode. Shields pulled back on her bow and topside to flood the firing tubes. For the moment, the Azzie troops didn't know what lurked in the ocean beneath them because the spoofing software rewrote her signature.

"Are you coming aboard?" Joaquin asked. He sounded distracted now and she knew he was running the boat, controlling her every move.

"If you can receive us. I have some repairs I need to make."

"Of course. You know the way."

As Flicker descended into the ocean and maneuvered under the bigger vessel, she tracked the salvo of underwater missiles as they jetted through the ocean for fifty meters, then turned toward the surface.

In the final seconds of their lives, the Azzie helo pilots knew they'd been fired upon. They jettisoned chaff to draw off heat-seekers and tried to cut away, but too late. Locked on, Joaquin's missiles caught the Azzies and exploded, reducing the helos to flaming debris that plummeted into the Pacific.

Hawke stared at the image relayed by one of the drones, gazing at the destruction in wonder.

"Believe it or not, Hawke," Flicker said, *"you're not the only friend I have."* She said that partly out of anger at herself for being forced into the deal with Joaquin. When the drek hit the fan, she knew Hawke would stand with her no matter how deep a problem got. That was something she didn't think Joaquin would do when push came to shove.

She deftly piloted the ATV through the open hatch at the bottom of the submersible and into *Scorpionfish's* flooded cargo section amidships. Bright lights marked the boundaries of the hatch. The ATV squeezed through with millimeters to spare.

The hatch slid closed beneath them, and pumps cycled the water out of the cargo compartment in seconds, leaving them high and dry.

Soaked through, amazed to be alive, and not liking the fact that the larger submersible felt like a giant trap, Hawke undogged the ATV's hatch and pushed himself out of the vehicle. His wired reflexes came online as he peered around, wondering what Flicker had piloted them into.

Bright lights filled the compartment. Other than the twenty heavily armed guards ringing the ATV on catwalks, nothing much was in the cargo area. Hawke resisted the impulse to lift his hands in surrender.

"Hoi," he called out.

None of the sailors responded, and they seemed like an efficient lot.

Flicker started up after him. He reached down and took her hand, easily pulling her up through the hatch.

"You sure you have friends here?" Hawke whispered in her ear.

"Of course." She stepped past him and looked around.

"Flicker, *hola*!" The greeting came from a man on the catwalk who looked to be in his early thirties. Like Flicker, he was heavily cybered for rigging. Implanted tech covered one side of his face. He was handsome and swarthy, wearing a neatly trimmed mustache with fierce sideburns and long hair. A gunmetal gray uniform sheathed his lean body, and a flechette pistol nestled in a shoulder holster. He held out a bottle of wine. "Welcome again to my boat. Rest assured that aboard *Scorpionfish*, you are among friends."

Hawke suspected that last bit was directed at him.

"*Hola*, Joaquin!" Flicker beamed at the man. "Thank you for the assist."

"But of course." Joaquin waved her up with the wine bottle. "Come. Come, and bring your friends, yes? Cook has laid out a light repast from the galley. I thought you might be hungry after your ordeal. And I happen to be in possession of some very fine wine."

"What do you know about our ordeal?" Flicker asked as she stepped down. Hawke got Rachel and the professor from the ATV and herded them after Flicker.

The young woman still managed to glare her displeasure at Hawke, but he noticed she looked worn out, too. "Is this who you were hired by?" A trace of worry gleamed in her eyes. "The person that wanted us kidnapped?"

"No," he said. "Keep moving."

CHAPTER TWENTY-THREE

Every shadowrunner had a history. At least, every shadowrunner still alive had a history. The dead ones got forgotten pretty quickly—unless they'd died spectacular deaths, or were made an example of by the corps. The past events of living shadowrunners didn't often get shared with anyone else. Not even partners.

As a result, Hawke felt uncomfortable meeting Joaquin, because Flicker had never mentioned the man. He felt even more uncomfortable meeting Joaquin over a meal at the captain's table, like they were on a vacation cruise. Especially right after a run that had gone so ragged, and had so many questionable areas and missing information.

Hawke glanced at Rachel Gordon seated to his right, knowing she was one of the biggest questions he had at the moment. That artifact she carried remained in the canvas bag slung over one shoulder, and even out of sight it was still on his mind. He hadn't run across many powerful magical items in his career. In fact, he made it a point to steer clear of such things. To him, magic was an unknowable thing, and people that played with it were pressing their luck. He had friends who swore by it, but he never dealt with it if he didn't have to.

The captain's table occupied a room off Joaquin's personal quarters, and was comfortable without being lavish. The table was real wood, some hardwood from the rainforest, and was bolted to the floor. Vases held cut flowers—the real things, not holos—which indicated the submersible might have a hydroponics lab. If that was so, the flowers—big and bold and filled with bright color—were a showy extravagance.

Around them, trideos broadcast images of ocean bottoms and marine creatures. Many of the images were beautiful seascapes that looked alien compared to the surface world. Other images detailed ancient shipwrecks scattered across the sea floor, and primitive monsters that Hawke wasn't sure truly existed. Soft calypso music underscored it all.

Hawke suspected the meal wasn't so much a dinner as a seduction. The food consisted of Caribbean dishes; fish with coconut-shallot sauce, broiled ginger-lime chicken, rice and beans flavored with chilis, garlic, and cinnamon. Dessert was Bananas Foster.

Their destination was somewhere in Amazonia. Captain Joaquin was being cagey about that. Hawke would have to figure out how they were getting back to the Pueblo Corporate Council. The contract called for the delivery of Rachel Gordon to Mr. Johnson in Santa Fe within a few days.

All during the meal, Flicker talked with Joaquin. They laughed and joked easily, like old friends, but after finishing their excellent meal, the submersible captain asked the steward for a bottle of brandy. Drinks were poured, and they settled down to business.

"It is my understanding that Aztechnology is searching for you with extreme dedication." Joaquin swirled the amber liquid around in his glass.

"They don't know who to search for," Hawke countered before Flicker could reply. He was tired of playing the fly on the wall while the captain trotted out his dog and pony show.

"They do not know to search for *you*, my new friend." Joaquin nodded. "Nor do they know of my good friend Flicker." He gestured with his glass to Rachel and the professor. "But I fear Aztechnology knows very much about these two people. In fact, in the screamsheets they are now outlaws, guilty of absconding with national Aztlan treasures, if one were to believe the tales they tell. Theft of important properties, I fear, is frowned upon greatly in these southern lands. Our history is precious to us, and we have grown tired of people from your country and Europe coming down and taking whatever they want. Such thievery has been practiced for hundreds of years. We are, these days, intolerant of such things."

"We're not thieves," Rachel objected, showing life for the first time since coming aboard. "We were there on a dig sponsored by NeoNET. Whatever we discovered was going to be turned over to the Guatemalan National Archives. We have contracts to that effect."

"Perhaps this is so, and perhaps if things had gone differently, it would have been." Joaquin pointed away from the table. "Or it may be that, according to someone else's plans, you would be dead now. But at the moment, you are certainly being presented as thieves."

The room trideos cleared, pulsed, then returned with images from one of the top newsfeeds owned by Aztechnology. Professor Madison Fredericks and Rachel Gordon were on prominent display. The professor stood speaking in front of a class, and in another video loop, the young woman walked beside her mentor across the college grounds.

Hawke suspected the vids had been tweaked from the originals because both the professor and Rachel looked somewhat nefarious. A pro could have changed body posture and the lighting easily in time to make the media deadlines.

"–learned today of the thefts of Guatemalan artifacts by two foreign thieves," a beautiful reporter announced as she walked among the craters at the dig site. Bloody sheets lay over some of the dead workers strewn over the broken terrain. *"Three of Professor Fredericks' students were taken into custody at the scene, but the search continues for fugitive Professor Madison Fredericks and another student, Rachel Gordon."*

Hawke couldn't tell if the woman was actually on location, or if computer imaging was being used to put her there. News hadn't been exactly true for a long time.

"As we've discovered," the reporter continued, walking through the narrow valley between a dead man's two halves, *"Professor Fredericks has been suspected of other thievery on digs around the world."*

"Lies!" The professor looked apoplectic, his face a deep shade of crimson. He trembled in his seat as he pointed a finger at the reporter. "This story is not true! Why would anyone do this?"

No one voiced an answer for that. The accusations could be true, or they were trumped up charges. Either way, it didn't matter. Whoever was behind the smear campaign was using everything they had to paint the professor as a criminal.

"Most residents in Santa Fe don't know Professor Fredericks very well," the reporter said. *"All they know is that he teaches in the archeology department at the University of Santa Fe, part of the Pueblo Corporate Council, where he had a fairly unremarkable career until the thefts in Guatemala earlier today."*

"'An unremarkable career?' I am considered among the top in my field!" Fredericks looked more pained by that accusation than he did of the one naming him a thief. "They simply haven't talked to the right people!"

On the trideo, the reporter stepped down into a crater. The cam followed her so easily that Hawke knew it was a drone, not carried by an operator.

"At this dig site," she said as she squatted by the large cover Hawke had seen near the hole Rachel and her mentor had gone into, "Professor Fredericks raised an army to kill the laborers working for him, then turned their sights on the Aztechnology protective service units above them. Although we don't know the names of everyone who died, we know that several Aztechnology security guards were killed today."

The camera swept over the bodies that covered the ground.

"*Why* is this being said?" The professor quivered in barely-suppressed rage. "I've never stolen *anything*. There have been objects of questionable provenance that I have taken on occasion, but *never* stolen. I merely held them until the proper owners could be located."

Hawke couldn't help wondering about how "proper" the owners the professor had found had been. Provenance could be changed readily enough. Hawke had been involved in some of that himself over the years.

"*Professor Fredericks is a local resident. He grew up in Santa Fe, but he's traveled the world, no doubt in search of more relics to plunder.*" The camera zoomed in on the reporter, and an image of Rachel appeared beside her face. "*Not so much is known about Rachel Gordon, a master's candidate assigned to Professor Fredericks. According to public records, Ms. Gordon is a student at the University of Santa Fe, studying under the professor. Before that, she was a ward of the state, an orphan, until she aged out of the system. Prior to her academic career, Ms. Gordon was arrested twice. Once for receivership and trafficking in stolen goods, and once for burglary.*"

If Professor Fredericks had appeared discomfited by the charges against him, Rachel Gordon looked absolutely mortified. For a moment, Hawke felt sorry for the young woman. Then he closed that feeling down and put it away. Emotions like that clouded his mind, and didn't belong in the biz at hand.

Who Rachel Gordon was, what she had been, was nothing to him. She was just a contract he planned to cash in. Nothing more. But he also recognized a shower of drek when he saw one.

Evidently Joaquin could, too. The submersible captain waved a hand, and the trideos shut down. "Well," he said with forced congeniality, "that is enough of that."

"I didn't know that deck was stolen," Rachel said in a small voice. "That's what she was talking about. It was a used deck I bought from a friend of a friend. I needed one for school. I thought I was just getting a good price for it. And the burglary charge was bogus. I was just attempting to get some of my things back from a guy I'd been . . . involved with."

"Dear girl," Joaquin said soothingly, "you don't have to explain yourself to anyone at this table. I run contraband into the California Free State, the Salish-Shidhe, and Seattle. Flicker and Hawke stole you away from that dig to ransom you to a contact they know solely as Mr. Johnson. No matter if you did do those things, you're a better person than everyone seated here."

For a moment, Professor Fredericks looked like he was going to object, then decided against it, and slumped in his chair with his arms folded over his chest. He didn't look defeated, but instead had decided not to buy into the fight.

Although he also didn't care for the way Joaquin put it, Hawke knew the captain's words were true. Rachel Gordon was very probably the only innocent one at the table.

The problem was that he didn't know what he was going to do about that yet.

CHAPTER TWENTY-FOUR

According to Joaquin, the voyage to Amazonia would take another seven hours. The captain had directed Rachel and Professor Fredericks to a double berth and placed them under guard. Hawke suspected Joaquin would have liked to put him under guard as well, but had stopped short of that because of his friendship with Flicker.

With nothing to do, he tried to get some sleep, and chose to sack out in the ATV. At least there he had access to an assortment of weapons he could control, and could seal the vehicle off from outsiders if necessary. Not that those things would do any good against the arsenal *Scorpionfish* sported, but attacking the ATV while it sat inside the submersible would raise Joaquin's cost.

Hawke shifted in one of the front seats because the back ones were still wet, trying in vain to find a more comfortable spot. He told himself again how much he hated a long-term op. He preferred to get in and get out, a surgical strike that was over almost as soon as it started.

So far, this mission had been the exact opposite. Boosting Rachel Gordon was already way more complicated than he wanted to deal with. And he was certain it was only going to get worse.

After a few minutes, just when Hawke thought he was on the verge of dozing off, someone knocked on the hatch above. He tapped a control for the topside video and watched Flicker's image sharpen into focus.

"You know the passcode," he growled, partly because he wanted to sleep, and partly because he didn't want to talk about anything until he had his own thoughts on everything properly sorted.

Flicker entered the password and the hatch hissed open. "I do know the passcode, which by the way, allows me more access to this vehicle than the one you have." She pulled herself through and swung down into the pilot's chair, which automatically adjusted for her. "I just didn't want to get shot entering my own vehicle."

Leaning back, she let the neural interface jack into the back of her head. Diagnostics panels lit up on the transplas window, but Hawke knew that was for his benefit. Flicker didn't need them.

"I wouldn't have shot you."

Flicker stared at nothing and everything. "Then take your hand off your pistol."

Unaware that he'd grabbed the Ares Predator until that moment, he released the weapon and folded his arms. The high-pressure wounds he'd received from the micro-fissures stung as he moved, but he ignored the pain. He didn't want to fog his senses with pain management meds.

"You're not happy here." Flicker's voice sounded slightly mechanical, letting him know she was deep into the ATV's diagnostics. "It's easy to see. You're like a tomcat in the territory of another tomcat. You don't say much about it, but it shows in the way you move."

Hawke laced his fingers behind his head and stared through the images on the transplas to the two guards on the railing above. "I guess Joaquin isn't too happy about me being here either."

"No, he's not. The two of you are a lot alike."

"Is this going to be a problem?"

"You and Joaquin? No. He's a professional. Like you. Anyway, he's not doing this for you. He's doing it for me."

Hawke intended to let that go and not comment, but found he couldn't.

"I didn't figure I'd see you again tonight." He didn't mean to say that, or to sound accusatory, but he did and the words were.

"Joaquin and I are friends. We like a lot of the same tech and we think a lot alike, but we don't have a physical relationship."

"That's none of my biz." It wasn't, and he felt slightly guilty for bringing the matter up. Still, he was on a submersible in the Pacific Ocean with a tempo runner he didn't know. If things got tangled, he wanted to know which side of the line Flicker would come down on.

"No, it's not, but I want you to know because I don't want your wondering about it cluttering up your mind."

Hawke didn't say anything for a moment. "You might have mentioned him earlier."

"That we're friends?"

"That you knew he'd be out here waiting, and he'd be willing to give us a lift if we needed it."

"I was counting on not needing it. I figured you'd have everything on the op wired." Flicker paused, and while she was silent, several servos within the ATV whined and rumbled to life. Lights chased each other in indecipherable patterns on the transplas. "We got surprised, and we're lucky to still be alive."

No, Hawke told himself, *we're* skilled *enough to be alive.* There was a difference.

"Besides," Flicker opened a new diagnostic routine on the transplas and problem areas lit up in red, "there was a fifty-fifty chance he would have been gone by the time we needed him. He's got his own biz, and he takes care of it."

"Running cargo for the Ghost Cartels." Hawke couldn't help putting his dissatisfaction with that choice of work in his words. He hadn't wanted to mention that either, but it was bothering him. He didn't like the idea that Flicker would traffic in tempo. Pharmaceuticals were worse than BTL chips. At least a chiphead didn't end up with serious physical problems from his narcotic of choice. "The cartels run tempo."

Tempo was a Bioengineered Awakened Drug that had spread around the globe in short order. Rumor had it users could perceive astrally, even if they had no magical abilities. It was instantly addictive, and even the beetle-heads gave up their chips to try it. Frequent usage built up a tolerance, though, and more of the drug had to be used to trip the effect, which compounded the physical damage.

"I don't like tempo or the other cascade of BAD brands either, but I don't get to decide what hits the streets. Neither do you." Flicker's tone sharpened a bit. "I also don't get to tell Joaquin how to make his cred. *Scorpionfish* is his masterpiece, and the overhead on this beast is voracious. He takes the work he can get."

"Point taken."

"And whether I told you about him before we came out here is not the problem eating your guts now."

"I'm fine."

"No, you're not. I saw you watching Rachel Gordon over dinner tonight. You're wondering what you're supposed to do with her."

Hawke made his voice flat, the way he did when he was talking biz. "I'm taking her to Mr. Johnson in Santa Fe just like I agreed."

Flicker hesitated. "Maybe you should reconsider that."

"I don't back out on deals. You know that. My word is what keeps me in biz."

"You were lied to about this run. *We* were lied to about this run. Mr. Johnson didn't mention there would be any interference from Aztechnology, and we nearly got hosed because we weren't informed of that. If we'd known, you would have turned him down flat or increased the crew. At the least we need a bump on the payout."

"Agreed." Hawke didn't like getting lied to. It was just one of the downsides of the biz, however. There was also the possibility that Mr. Johnson really hadn't known Aztechnology would be so interested in the dig or what was found there. Secrets always got so complicated and twisted there was no way to know who really knew what.

Then he wrapped his brain around something else. "Mr. Johnson didn't contract for the artifact. He contracted for Rachel Gordon. Seems to me like Mr. Johnson would have wanted the professor because he would know more. He's the one calling on the shots on the dig. I don't know why Rachel's so important."

"That jewel, whatever it is, seems almost—possessive of her."

"You talk like it's alive." That thought had slid through Hawke's mind too, and he hadn't liked it, either. Magic on its own was bad enough—this, whatever it was, though, made him uneasier by the minute.

"Maybe it is alive. You and I have both run the shadows long enough to see even more unlikely things. You should have brought a mage."

"Maybe Joaquin has someone onboard we could use."

Flicker's image appeared on the transplas, cocking a disparaging eyebrow at him. "Do you really want to pull Joaquin into our biz so deeply, *omae*?"

"No."

"Me neither. And I'm going to chalk that suggestion up to fatigue and *not* assume you were testing me."

"I wasn't." But Hawke knew some part of him had chosen that possibility as a loyalty check, and he felt guilty about it.

"What do you know about NeoNET?"

The query caught Hawke off guard. "It's located in Boston, in the UCAS." He didn't do much biz in the United Canadian and

American States, preferring to stay west of the Mississippi River or in Asia and Europe. "It formed after the Matrix Crash in 2064." He frowned. "You think they're interested in Rachel? Doesn't scan to me. They're hardcore tech-based. Besides that, they already had her. They could have picked her up at the university."

"Then she's only part of the target."

"Mr. Johnson didn't mention that."

"It could have come up later."

"Why would NeoNET fund the dig? I didn't see anything at the site that screamed tech at me."

"I'm still digging into that. The TransAsia branch has a lot of big players behind the scenes, but I've scanned one of them: Ayuni Sukenobu."

"I don't recognize the name."

"I'd be surprised if you did. She's one of the chief software designers. Her grandfather helped found the corp, so she's got a lot of blue-chip stock. She also has a serious jones for archeology. According to the intel I got from the blackboards, she owns four dinosaur skeletons worth millions of nuyen, and those are just the big items in her collection."

"She buys bones?"

"That's what skeletons are, Hawke." Flicker could sound incredibly snarky when she wanted.

"There weren't any dinosaur bones at the dig."

"There were lots of statues. I captured footage of them from the drones and from when I broke through to the river. Maybe there's something there she likes."

"Doesn't scan. I got the contract on Rachel before she found her artifact."

"That young woman and the weird glowie could be tied in somehow."

"There's no mention of magic in her background."

"No, but how else are you going to explain the relationship she and that thing have? Because those sparks and the way it won't let anyone but her touch it tells me they do have a relationship."

"I don't know." Hawke's head hurt from chasing all the angles of the run. He didn't know enough to put everything properly into context.

"You don't know what's at stake in this run, and you don't know what you're going to do with Rachel Gordon," Flicker said. "My suggestion is to go talk to her. Get to know her a little better.

Then skull it out. You do people better than I do."

Hawke silently disagreed with that; Flicker was social engi-neering him right now, and both of them knew he was letting her. "I'll talk to her in the morning. I got the impression she's not in the mood for conversation now, and I'm running on vapor."

"*Early* morning. We'll be hitting Amazonia shortly after noon. We need to have a game plan in place by then."

"Agreed." Hawke might have said more, but he wasn't sure. With Flicker there watching over the ATV, knowing he was locked securely away in what might be hostile territory, not knowing what he'd claimed a piece of, sleep took him.

CHAPTER TWENTY-FIVE

Rachel woke, surprised she'd been able to sleep. She lay on the bed in the prison ship—there was no other way to think of the submersible, even after the fancy dinner last night—still dressed in her mud-spattered clothing.

A twinge of guilt over not being a proper guest ached within her when she noticed the bedding she'd tracked mud over, but the feeling quickly passed when she recalled the circumstances under which she'd been housed there. She also needed a shower. It was one thing to be a woolly beast on a dig site, but being in the company of people who bathed regularly promoted attention to cleanliness. Last night she'd crashed after dinner, and maybe she'd thought about a shower and clean clothes for a few seconds before that.

Since there were no windows in the room, it was full dark except for the light from Professor Fredericks's deck. The holo projector was broadcasting a shimmering blue screen with Mayan pictographs moving across it.

She had no idea where she was within the vessel. She knew the room probably had another name than simply "room," but she didn't have enough experience with submarines to know for sure.

She also didn't like the thought that dozens, perhaps hundreds of meters of water separated her from the surface. Being in the submersible was somehow worse than being trapped underground yesterday, or running the river channel. Drowning had always been a big fear of hers.

Yesterday. It was hard to believe her life had changed so much in one day. And it was even harder to acknowledge that she might not be able to go back to that life again.

She still had no idea what her captors intended for her, or who they were working for. Who wanted her so badly that they were willing to have her practically kidnapped? Why would she be valuable to anyone? She'd been an orphan all of her life, unclaimed by anyone.

Breathing out, she pushed away the tension and anger coursing through her. She couldn't dwell on the past. She had to be on the lookout for an opportunity to escape.

But to where? Thinking about that made her want to scream. She couldn't go to the authorities, and disappearing into the underground in some third- or fourth-world country didn't appeal to her. But she knew she could do it. All she had was herself. And she had skills and knowledge she could barter into something.

She glanced over at Professor Fredericks, who was still sleeping. At the dig, they'd had separate tents. The present accommodations felt invasive, but he hadn't shown any signs of it bothering him. Even though their "host" hadn't granted them access to the Matrix, and they were cut off from the outside world, the professor had been working on his rebuttal to the media stories. She'd heard him reading his words aloud until she'd gone to sleep. Rachel didn't know what he could possibly have to say, and she didn't know if he would ever get the chance to say it.

Still, this morning—if it was morning—she felt surprisingly rejuvenated. She wondered what time it was and peeked at the professor's deck, where the glowing time/date stamp read 0702 hours. She'd slept longer than she'd anticipated, but not as long as she'd thought.

The deck's screen page showed a bas-relief cut of a Mayan artifact that had been discovered in 2012. On the stone, a Mayan warrior in a feathered headpiece, thick necklace, wide belt, and loincloth sat on the ground. More decorative pieces made irregular columns around him.

Rachel remembered the piece. As an archeology student, Professor Fredericks had been on the dig that had discovered it. It had been, until now, the highlight of his career.

At least, as far as she knew. Despite her determination not to give into suspicion, she couldn't help wondering if the stories about his thievery were true. A number of archaeologists, when they found something important—or valuable—succumbed to greed, or covetousness at the least.

During her time with the professor, she hadn't exactly put him up on a pedestal. After all, he had insisted on keeping her "feelings" about the artifacts secret. His reasoning had been logical: if they'd gone to an outside source, they wouldn't have had control over the dig. So he'd fabricated some research and presented a proposal to potential endowment prospects. She still didn't know why NeoNET had agreed to fund the dig.

Just like she didn't know why Aztechnology had shown up at the site and started shooting. All of that had taken place right after the discovery of the artifact. She couldn't discount that the unearthing of the jewel was possibly the catalyst for all of the death and destruction. That was the only thing that had happened since the beginning of the excavation.

Guilt cut into her when she wondered if simply surrendering the jewel would have stopped the bloodshed. She hadn't considered that at the time. She'd just taken the artifact and run. She couldn't imagine giving it up now, however. At least not until after she'd divined its secrets.

Not even to Professor Fredericks.

Thinking of the jewel, she glanced at the other side of the bed and spotted it *floating* in the air a full meter above the floor, slowly revolving on an invisible axis. It's soft, blue glow illuminated that side of the small room

Surprised, Rachel stared at the artifact. Then, she sensed the mysterious presence come alive inside it. Slowly, she approached the jewel. She reached out her hand and the artifact floated to her, coming to her like a pet.

The awareness of the creature inside transmitted through the jewel directly into her mind. It knew she was there. She was certain of that. At the same time she stared at the artifact in fascinated wonder, fear trickled through her too, eating away at the foundation of curiosity that pushed her to open up to its wants.

Someone knocked at the door.

For a moment, the artifact glowed more brightly. Embers orbited only centimeters away from the multi-faceted surface. Then the glow extinguished and the artifact settled heavily into her hand.

The knock repeated. "Rachel. We need to talk."

She recognized Hawke's voice. Her first instinct was to ignore him or refuse him, but doing either wouldn't help her figure out what was going to happen to her. She wanted to know. Besides, she couldn't lock the door anyway. The man could just walk in if he wanted.

"Give me a minute." She retreated to her backpack and put the jewel inside the cargo compartment, then checked for a compact mirror, knowing she probably had a bad case of bedhead. Then, realizing she wanted to make certain her appearance was good for her kidnapper, she settled for running her hands through her hair and letting it fall. Unwilling to leave the artifact behind, she shouldered the backpack and walked to the door.

Opening it a crack, she looked at Hawke's stained and ripped clothing, and took satisfaction in knowing the big man didn't look any better than she did.

"We need to figure out what we're going to do," he said.

"About what?"

"You."

That caught her off guard, but her anger had been waiting just under the surface. "I thought you already had that figured out. I'm some kind of prize you get to trade in for a reward."

"That wasn't how it was supposed to be. I didn't get the chance to discuss things with you before Aztechnology started shooting. Everything I knew changed when the corp brought out the big guns. I'm looking at options." Hawke paused. "For *all* of us."

Even though she was afraid, Rachel didn't want to let it show. She also didn't want to believe him, but his words sounded true. She told herself that a professional abductor was probably also a skilled liar. "Why? So you can demand more cred for kidnapping me?"

The big man didn't blink. "That's one of the options, sure, but that's not the deal I'm offering."

"*Now* I get a deal? *After* you kidnap me?" Rachel couldn't reel in the anger coursing through her. From the corner of her eye, she caught a glimpse of the jewel glowing strong enough to be seen through her backpack. She calmed down with an effort, knowing it was responding to her on some emotional level.

Hawke frowned. "Kidnapping you wasn't part of the arrangement. I agreed to meet with you, talk with you, and get you safely out of Aztlan. But only if you agreed to leave. I don't kidnap innocent people."

"Really? Who do you kidnap?"

His answer came immediately. "People who've stolen things—cred or tech—that doesn't belong to them. Those people are criminals, and I don't have a problem taking them."

"But you're not a criminal?"

"I provide a service—what some consider an illegal service—but I don't just work for anyone, and the jobs aren't just about the cred."

Rachel considered what she knew about shadowrunners, how they targeted corps and wealthy people. "You and your . . . what do you call the guy that hires you?"

"Mr. Johnson, typically."

"Mr. Johnson, right . . . so, you and he are on a first name basis?"

Hawke took in a deep breath and let it out. "Do you want a vote in what's done with you or not? This is your only chance."

Unable to think of a casual dismissal for the question, Rachel nodded. "I do. Should I wake Professor Fredericks?"

"No. He's not part of the package."

Immediately feeling traitorous, Rachel shook her head. "No. You're not just going to throw him overboard—"

Hawke winced in displeasure. "We're *under* water. We're not throwing anyone overboard."

"—or *jettison* him, or fire him through a torpedo tube or anything. I want to know he'll be okay."

"All right, but let's you and I talk first."

"Flicker's not going to be part of this conversation either?" Rachel didn't care for that. She felt like she'd get more sympathy from the female rigger. The woman was probably the only reason Hawke was there now.

"Flicker goes where I go on this run. I make the decisions. That's the only way we operate when everything's in play."

"All right." Rachel stepped through the door and closed it behind her. She followed Hawke as he strode through the narrow passageway, nearly filling the entire space with those wide shoulders.

CHAPTER TWENTY-SIX

"What do you know about NeoNET?" Hawke sat at a small table in the *Scorpionfish's* top-of-the-line galley and studied Rachel Gordon sitting on the other side. Between them, a Renraku white noise generator provided privacy from the sailors eating, drinking, and talking at other tables.

"Not too much." Rachel shook her head and sipped her cup of coffee; not soykaf, but the real drink, made from real coffee beans. The scent was delightful to Hawke. "I'm aware of the corp, of course. Their ads are all through the media. I've got some of their entertainment devices. They help fund some of the programs at the university. Other than that, I don't know much other than what you see in their advertising."

"But you knew they funded Professor Fredericks' dig."

"I did."

"Fredericks didn't talk to you about that funding?"

Rachel smiled, and it was easy to believe she was telling the truth. Hawke's onboard deception reading software suite and his own personal experience agreed with his impression.

"Professor Fredericks talked to me about NeoNET just long enough to tell me the funding had come through. That's all. After that, there were brief mentions of packing, travel arrangements, and passports. Most of his communication with me was about the dig and what he hoped to find."

"What did he hope to find in Guatemala?"

A quick smile and a shrug covered her slight hesitation. Even without the deception reading software, Hawke knew he wasn't about to get the whole truth. She was holding something back. That was natural.

"He hoped to find what we found," she answered. "Artifacts."

That was mostly the truth. Hawke chose to stay with it, see if he could ferret out what she was holding onto.

"He wasn't looking for anything special?"

"No."

"Did NeoNET know what artifacts you people were supposed to find?"

"*Hoped* to find," she corrected. "You never know for sure you're going to find anything. You go to a dig in the hopes of finding *something*. I helped write Professor Fredericks's grant proposal. He laid out his research into the area, the faint mentions of a small village that might have been there thousands of years ago. There wasn't anything substantial. We were just hoping to find some record of those people."

"Where did he find out about the possible location of the village?"

"In Mayan records we were able to translate." Rachel took a breath. "If you want to know more, I'd have to get my deck and show you."

"That's all right." Hawke didn't want to look at images of Mayan symbology with Rachel Gordon any more than he wanted to discuss circuit boards with Flicker. Those were just details. He needed to figure out the big picture. The fact that Rachel wasn't giving him the whole truth was a big piece of that. "Tell me about the blue jewel you found."

Rachel shrugged again, almost pulling off nonchalant. "It's blue. It sparks sometimes. There's a lot of what I think is Mayan inscriptions on it."

"You *think* it's Mayan?"

"Exactly. What's there is like nothing we've ever seen before." That was the truth. Curiosity shone in her eyes.

"Is that unusual?"

"There are a lot of dead languages in the world. Some of them didn't get rediscovered until after UGE hit the population. Then some of the things that we've known about for centuries suddenly became clear. Mostly things in the elven tongues. We still aren't sure why that is."

Hawke knew the answer to that one. He'd liberated a tablet in the past that had been covered in a dead elvish script. "Some people think the elves have been in the world before, that they died out, then came back when the virus started mutating people. Others say that the elves have always been with us, just in hiding."

She studied him. "Which do you think is true?"

Hawke grinned, enjoying her attempt at deflection. She was a fast learner, even if she was only a college student. "I'm no expert, and I don't care. The elves I know, and I know only a few, aren't saying. Either they enjoy their mysteriousness, or they don't know either."

"It's my opinion that both of those things are true."

"Tell me why you can touch the blue jewel, but Fredericks can't."

"I don't know."

There was just the slightest hesitation before she answered, just enough to register to Hawke and ping the deception suite. Maybe she didn't know, but she had her suspicions.

"Is it magic?"

"It doesn't appear to be technology-based. Your rigger friend seems to agree with that."

Hawke sipped his coffee, hating that he enjoyed it mostly because Joaquin provided it. "Tell me about Ayumi Sukenobu."

Rachel's brows knitted in confusion. "I don't know that person."

That sounded like the truth to Hawke, and he let it go. "All right, let's talk about you. Tell me about yourself."

The questioning turned awkward for Rachel, especially given she was trying to hide her knowledge of the artifact as well. Even with her backpack sitting under the table between her feet, she could still sense the presence of the being contained within it. Hawke gave no indication he was aware of anything unusual.

Rachel never liked talking about herself, because it always reminded her of how little she knew. But at least they weren't talking about the artifact, and Hawke didn't seem as scary now that he was sitting across from her with a cup of coffee in his hand instead of a weapon.

She shrugged. "There's not much to tell. I'm an orphan. No family to speak of. I was dropped off at a shelter only a few days after I was born. I guess whoever had me couldn't wait to get rid of me." Although she tried to mask it, she was sure some of the old bitterness echoed in her words. If Hawke noticed, he gave no indication. "After I aged out of the system, I started college, graduated with my bachelor's, and immediately started on my

master's." She heard the emotionless way she said that, so practiced after all these years.

"No records of your birth parents anywhere?"

"None. When I was older, after I'd met a few people who liked
to break into things on the Matrix, I had a friend hack into the orphanage's records. She found nothing in the files that linked me to
anyone. I just . . . appeared." Even now, it was still hard to imagine
how that could have happened.

"Did you try DNA files?"

"I did." Rachel couldn't help wondering why Hawke was so
interested in her. Then she realized he didn't know why his "Mr.
Johnson" wanted her either. That orphan kid part of her that never
truly went away was curious and apprehensive, thinking maybe
the big man knew something about her past that she didn't. But
she remained afraid to get her hopes up, because that old hurt
never stopped aching. "I didn't find any matches."

Hawke's eyes narrowed.

She knew that not finding anything through a DNA link was
interesting. Most people around the world were tagged with DNA
these days. Drug testing was mandatory for a lot of corps, and
other agencies—like Lone Star—kept a prodigious amount of records on everyone they came in contact with.

She was also looking for *two* parents. The odds of both of
them not being in a database somewhere were astounding.

"It's possible my birth parents were killed in an accident shortly after I was born," Rachel said, rewinding all the old arguments
she'd had with herself over the years. "Maybe their DNA was never registered."

"If they were accident victims, their DNA would have been on
file. The same goes for crime victims."

And criminals. Rachel knew Hawke was thinking that, and she
was surprised he didn't mention that possibility. He didn't seem
like the kind of guy that would go easy on someone.

With all the possibilities that were open to DNA recording,
Rachel had ended up with only two logical conclusions: either her
parents had taken care not to end up in a DNA database somewhere, or someone, possibly someone other than her parents,
had expunged those DNA records.

As a child, and sometimes even as an adult, Rachel had felt
certain that a choice had been made to deliberately cut all ties with
her. Even after all these years, it was hard not to feel that way. Oth-

er acquaintances she'd made had always found something about themselves; a trail leading back to a deceased or incarcerated parent, or someone who had left because they were too young and unable to raise a child. Sometimes there were good endings.

She had found nothing. That had made her feel even more lonely.

Looking Hawke in the eye, she lifted her chin and refused to let those old hurts demean or define her. "Whoever my parents were, they chose not to acknowledge me. That's not a problem for me."

Hawke nodded and, thankfully, moved on in his interrogation. "Why the interest in archeology?"

"I like old things, the idea of culture and other times." That was the easy answer and she knew it. The truth was she liked the idea of history, of evidence that things had happened *before* the here and now. Mostly because that field was so different from her own life. Her life as she knew it had begun twenty-three years ago. No depth. No history. Just a date recorded in the data files of a nondescript orphanage in a small town outside Philadelphia.

Hawke's gaze flicked from her to the doorway, and Rachel turned to see what had captured the big man's attention.

Professor Fredericks, bleary-eyed and looking slightly frantic, stumbled into the galley. When his gaze fell on Rachel, he sighed and relaxed slightly. "Ah. There you are. I've been looking for you."

"Sorry. I should have left a note." Rachel felt only a little guilty about that. During the dig, she'd looked after the professor more than he had looked after her. She couldn't help feeling he was more interested in the artifact.

"This is a submersible," Hawke said as he pushed back from the table and stood. "There aren't many places to go. I'll leave you two to breakfast. We'll be making port in another three hours." He looked at Rachel. "Flicker has arranged for new clothing to be dropped off in your berth."

Rachel hated the way he could just get up and leave, and the way he could still plan his life while hers had been brought to a complete standstill. Even if she was able to escape Hawke and get off the submersible, the charges presented by Aztechnology still waited out there.

"Are you ashamed of the way I look?" she demanded, thinking she might throw him off-balance. "Maybe you want to tidy up your captured prize?"

He regarded her frankly. "No. I just thought you might like to wash up and get into a fresh change of clothes. If you want to stay looking like that, it's fine with me." He turned without another word and walked away.

Rachel watched him go, somehow feeling a little more vulnerable without him there.

She hated that, too.

CHAPTER TWENTY-SEVEN

When Hawke returned to the cargo compartment with two break-fasts from the galley, he found Flicker lying on a mechanic's creeper under the ATV. A welder's torch flared in her hand, illuminating the scarred underside of the vehicle and throwing off sparks. Several other tools hung from the ceiling on electrical cords, and robot arms under her control repaired dents and dings and reapplied ab-lative armor. She hadn't told him how much the repairs were going to be, but he knew it'd be costly just from watching all the activity.

"Did you learn anything?" Flicker rolled out from under the ATV, but the suite of robot mechanics kept working, controlled by her neural interface. She switched the welding torch off and the blue flame disappeared with a soft *pop*, like a bubble bursting.

"Did I learn why Mr. Johnson is so interested in Rachel?" Hawke shook his head, not at all happy with his answer. He hand-ed her the breakfast box and a bulb of orange juice. "No, and I don't think she knows either."

"There can only be two reasons." Flicker ticked them off on her oil-stained fingers. "Either Mr. Johnson wants the girl, or he wants the artifact."

Hawke sat on the floor across from her, his legs crossed to support the breakfast container as he opened it to reveal eggs, sausages, wheat cakes, and heavily-spiced shredded potatoes. "The artifact hadn't even been found at the time we accepted the run."

Flicker took out the disposable fork and dug into her food. He'd guessed right that she'd skipped breakfast.

"That doesn't mean Mr. Johnson didn't know it was going to be found." She was great at playing devil's advocate. "Look at it that way, *omae*. We're always the *last* people to see all the cards face up on the table. The Johnson might not be the only person withholding intel. Or flat out scheming on us."

"That doesn't scan either. Given the way Aztechnology came gunning, they would have nabbed the artifact earlier if they'd known it was there in the first place."

"*If* they'd known." Flicker chewed and thought. "Aztechnology had someone inside the dig team. It might help if we knew who it was."

"There were a lot of locals on the op. Aztechnology could have had any number of informants."

"I know." She stabbed a sausage and popped it into her mouth. "Why doesn't Mr. Johnson want the professor? Seems like he'd know more than a grad student."

"Because the professor can't touch the artifact."

Flicker nodded as she chewed, then swallowed. "That's how I had it figured, too. So someone, somewhere knew that the girl would be able to connect with the artifact, then sent Mr. Johnson to hire you."

"Yeah." There was no other way to look at the series of events.

"The girl has a connection, whatever it is, to the artifact. But what connects you to her? Why did Mr. Johnson reach out to you? Or whoever's behind him?" The note of suspicion in Flicker's words held a sharp edge.

Hawke looked at her. "I don't know." He didn't promise her the truth. He didn't have to. As deeply as they'd gone into the shadows together, often the truth was all they had between them.

She sighed irritably. "For once, I think I might be happier if you were holding something back."

"That's not how I work."

"I know. But I don't like how we've been zeroed out on this."

"Neither do I." Hawke ate a few more bites and let the silence between them stretch. He wasn't certain which one would be the first to break it.

Finally, her breakfast gone, Flicker put the box aside and wiped her mouth with the back of her hand. "The smartest thing we could do is lose the girl, the professor, and the artifact somewhere in the ocean between here and Amazonia."

Hawke didn't bother replying.

"But I know you're not going to do that." Flicker wrapped her arms around her bent knees while the mechanical arms continued working on the ATV behind her.

"No."

"It's not just the payday, is it?"

Hawke shrugged and nodded at the ATV. "Those look like some expensive repairs."

"Those *are* expensive repairs."

"I can't pay for them with what I've got put away right now. We need a score."

"*A* score, yeah. But we don't have to have this one. Joaquin will allow me to owe him for a while."

"Still have to pay the loan off."

Flicker frowned and her aquamarine eyes narrowed. "It's the girl, isn't it?"

With Flicker looking at him like that, Hawke knew he had to give up that rough spot that was bothering him. "She's an orphan."

Flicker shrugged. "She's had a hard life. So did a lot of other people. Like you and me. We grew up in the system, too."

Hawke nodded. "That means we both know she has no one looking out for her."

"She's got her professor."

"Does he look like the kind of guy who'll stand up when the drek hits the fan?"

"Not our problem."

"No, but if we get her to the Johnson, we get a pile of cred and she gets a way out of the mess she's in."

"You hope." Flicker lifted a sarcastic eyebrow. "So, me and you? Against Aztechnology?"

"We're lucky it's just me and you. We're easier to hide."

"Gotta hide the girl, too."

"Yeah. Think she'll go along with this?"

"If she doesn't, she's on her own, and we find another way to pay for the repairs."

"But that's—that's *insane*!"

Professor Fredericks stood in front of Hawke and gestured wildly for a moment. Then his mouth locked into track with his brain again. "You want us to *aid* you in our own kidnapping so we can be turned over to someone whose identity *you* don't even know?"

Arms folded, face blank, back to the door inside the little room the two had been assigned, Hawke nodded. "Yeah."

"You expect us to just . . . just *agree* to this?" The professor was on the edge of spluttering.

"The deal isn't for you," Hawke stated bluntly. The other man's histrionics were getting on his nerves. "I'm willing to try to get you out of this mess for free. It would be a lot easier to just park a bullet between your eyes."

Instantly he knew he'd gone too far, because Rachel's face hardened at that. She folded her own arms, closing herself off.

"And that would be more kind than letting you fall into the hands of an Aztechnology black ops interrogation," Hawke went on. "I'm offering you your only chance out of this."

Fredericks paled a little at that. When he breathed out, he looked a little deflated. "All right. Just tell us what you need us to do."

Hawke shifted his gaze to Rachel. "Does that go for you, too?"

Lips pressed together in a tight line of defiance, she nodded.

Even without his deception software, Hawke knew she was lying.

CHAPTER TWENTY-EIGHT

Shortly before 1100 hours, the *Scorpionfish* docked without incident at an underwater base several kilometers off the Amazonian coast.

With the submersible at a dead stop, rocking slightly in the ocean currents, and the vibration of her idling engines sending a tiny quiver through her body, Rachel tried not to think dark thoughts. She wanted to live, to survive this . . . whatever it was that had happened to her, and get back to her life.

Things aboard the vessel had changed. Two guards stood at attention outside the door. They had requested, politely but firmly, that Rachel and Professor Fredericks remain in their room until someone came for them.

Freshly showered and dressed in the casual women's clothing Flicker had arranged for her—probably from the few female sailors aboard—Rachel felt a little more confident and a lot cleaner. She almost felt rested, and couldn't help thinking the artifact was probably part of the reason for that. Some of the bumps and bruises she'd acquired during her "rescue" were healing fast, a fact that had caught her attention.

She worked on her deck—still without a connection to the Matrix—while they waited, sorting through her notes about the excavation. Some were private, things she kept encrypted, even from Professor Fredericks. She wasn't sure how to deal with the presence she kept sensing from the jewel, and she didn't know exactly why she wanted to keep that secret from the professor. She just knew it had to be done—in the same way she'd known where to find the jewel.

Finally, the door opened, and Hawke stood there in clean street clothes; slacks and a shirt under a lightweight, loose-fitting jacket. Casual attire a tourist might wear, except he looked like anything but a tourist. Her glimpse of a matte-black pistol butt underneath one arm destroyed the already weak illusion. Wraparound sunglasses masked his eyes. Somehow they looked more normal than his eyes did, like this semi-masked version of himself was who he truly was.

"Let's go," he said.

Rachel shut down her deck, tucked it into her backpack, and joined him at the door.

Moving a little more slowly, a little more uncertainly, Professor Fredericks looked at Hawke. "You're sure we'll be safe?"

"Yeah." The big man's features remained bland. Light gleamed off his freshly-shaved head.

Rachel almost wanted to ask Hawke if he would lie just to get them moving, but didn't. She already knew the answer was yes, and she only wanted the professor to know he couldn't trust these people. From Professor Fredericks' wariness, that was something he'd already grasped.

In the hallway, Hawke took the lead, easily stepping through circular doors between compartments. Also dressed in new clothes and with a messenger bag slung over one shoulder, Flicker brought up the rear. The vessel was better lit now, or maybe Rachel just hadn't noticed how things had looked when she'd been brought aboard.

A few minutes later, they entered a small room with an airlock, presumably for divers to depart and enter. Captain Joaquin stood there with his hands clasped behind his back. He was neatly groomed, and wore a big smile.

Two guards stood beside him, on either side and just a step back.

"Ah, Flicker," Joaquin said, looking at the dark elven woman. "It's a pity we couldn't spend more time together."

She smiled at him. "Perhaps our paths will cross again soon."

"I shall hold you to that." The smuggler took her hand and pressed the back of it to his lips.

Rachel noticed the brief grimace that tweaked Hawke's lips, then quickly vanished.

"Make sure you take care of my ATV."

Joaquin nodded gallantly. "Of course. I'll drop it off in San Diego on my return trip in a week or so. We have a mutual friend there who can store it until you're able to get it."

"That will be fine."

"I trust you can get it home from there?"

"I can."

"Then I wish you good luck in your endeavors." Joaquin nodded to one of his men, who operated the airlock with a keypad. Hydraulic systems hissed, and the door opened to reveal an area big enough to fit a dozen people.

Looking all around, Hawke stepped inside the chamber. Rachel knew the big man didn't like the enclosed space, and she couldn't help thinking about how easy it would be to trap them in there and simply flood the room with ocean water. She swallowed hard as she joined him, followed by the professor and Flicker.

A bright film of perspiration covered Hawke's forehead as he stood, quiet and still, while the airlock closed.

"It's okay," Flicker said. "The airlock's connected to a pressured delivery tube. Nothing's going to happen."

A moment later, the hatch behind them opened into what looked like a small elevator shaft. Flicker led them all inside. The airlock closed, then the platform they were standing on rose with a humming vibration.

"How far under are we?" Hawke asked.

Flicker shook her head. "Doesn't matter."

"It does if decompression is a problem."

"It's not. Everything's kept at surface pressure. We'll be fine. Null sheen, *omae*."

Before she knew it, Rachel was sipping her breath, certain her lungs were getting heavier. She'd never been more than forty meters down while scuba diving. Panic rose with each second they ascended.

"We have to start worrying once we hit the coast." Flicker took some small drones half the length of Rachel's forefinger from inside her jacket and held them in her hand for a moment. They took flight and hovered overhead noiselessly. "Amazonia's friction with Aztlan heats up there, so if anybody's looking for us in the area—and they could be—there could be fallout."

Getting prepared for the dig in Guatemala had deepened Rachel's knowledge of the two countries' fight over Bogota. Hualpa, the feathered dragon who was Amazonia's head of state, had declared the nation to be eco-friendly, and the industrialization and consumption of natural resources would be stopped. Aztlan and Aztechnology were unwilling to relinquish their hold on the area. As a result, guerrilla wars broke out constantly along the malleable border.

The platform slowed, then stopped, and the hatch irised open onto a new room that looked like an ill-lit basement. An old man stood on the other side with a smile. He wore khaki shorts, a Hawaiian shirt, and a sombrero tied beneath his leathery chin.

"*Hola, amigos, amigas*! I am Julio. I will be your boat captain to the mainland today." He waved a wrinkled hand toward a set of wooden stairs barely visible in the gloom. "Please, step this way."

CHAPTER TWENTY-NINE

Seated in the stern of the old man's fishing boat while waiting to get underway, Hawke hated the fact they were out in the open in the small harbor. He didn't have control of the op at this point, and there was nowhere for them to run. Even the Ares Predators slung in shoulder leather and the expanding katars sheathed under his jacket didn't give him any real degree of comfort.

Flicker finished speaking with the old man, arranging the cred transfer for the ride to the mainland, and joined Hawke on the thinly-padded seat. "You need to chill, *omae*. It's just a boat ride. Zero threat."

Hawke just shot her a doubtful look as she released her drones up into the air and down into the sea, then resumed his scan of the area. There were no boats in sight, nothing that could threaten them.

Unless they were hit with some kind of missile, or some other submersible rose from the depths. He told himself Aztechnology wanted Rachel Gordon and the jewel in one piece, then held onto that thought as best as he could.

The old man lived on a rocky atoll thirty-six kilometers from the mainland, putting him out in international waters. The island was something less than five kilometers in area, stretching mostly east to west, and housed Julio's Marine Salvage, an expanse of fence-enclosed junk that took up most of the flat land in front of the shark's fin outcropping of bare rock that stabbed into the blue sky.

Several wrecks lay across the salvage area, mostly decrepit hulks that looked like they'd fallen apart at sea and been towed to the island for stripping. Julio and his sons worked a metal recla-mation operation on one end of the salvage yard, melting down scrap that couldn't be sold as parts. Black smoke wafted steadily into the blue sky. The other side of the salvage area had a well-tended garden and flowerbeds.

The stink of the antique diesel engines gave Hawke a headache. Even the boat's heavy fish aroma couldn't blunt the hot, oily stench. Bundled nets to the sides and behind the boat banged against masts and support poles.

"I'm not picking up any noise around us." Flicker sat with her deck open on her thighs. Blue holo screens showed images relayed by her airborne drones flying high above them. Four more patrolled the area underwater.

"What about Joaquin?" Hawke couldn't let go of his suspicions about the tempo trafficker.

"Already gone. He's got deliveries to make."

"Do you know anything about our captain and his crew?"

"Julio's a small-time fixer I've met once before. Some branch of family to Joaquin. He looks out for the old man, and the old man keeps gossip from the coast flowing to Joaquin, intel about traffic in international waters. Don't let the decrepit salvage yard fool you. Julio is well connected. His crew are his sons, and it's all family biz."

Atop the tower, Julio waved his yachting cap. He'd traded the sombrero for it. "*Hola, amigos, amigas!* We go. Prepare yourselves."

The thready engine noise suddenly leveled out as the twin diesels powered up with more thrust than Hawke expected. Within seconds they were cutting across the ocean, heading for one of the small, nameless towns dotting the western coastline of Amazonia, near the Aztlan border.

Despite all the open space around them, Hawke was grimly aware they would be even more vulnerable in the town than they were on the ocean, but at least an urban area was more familiar than the endless azure water.

As they neared the small harbor twenty-three minutes later, Hawke studied the low limestone seawall that kept back the ocean during storm season, and knew it would never be enough during a full-blown hurricane. Small stone houses with red clay tiles that didn't always match dotted the broken coastline and marched up into the sharply rising hills beyond the harbor. Broken tree stumps and the ruins of collapsed buildings lay farther south, showing past tropical violence, and the fact that the general population had diminished.

Hawke's PAN tagged the Matrix, logged in under a fake ID, and identified the town as Playa del Iguana Verde. The coordinates were off, however, so maybe this was only part of the town, and it had been truncated in some way. More probably lay on the other side of the hills, at the end of the dusty roads zigzagging up into the thick forests.

A fistful of pleasure craft dotted the small natural harbor, most advertising for tourists in a half-dozen languages. Docks built of quarried limestone blocks extended into the ocean, but some were completely underwater, showing only strips of slight, gleaming white. At least two of the docks were broken apart, with wide gaps between the pieces. Some of the locals still tied up small fishing boats to mooring areas, and along the empty spaces between them fishermen sat in folding chairs whose legs were wet only up to the first few centimeters.

Julio pulled the fishing boat in to one of the intact docks. Old rubber tires on the hull thumped gently against the limestone as his two sons vaulted from the vessel with lines they quickly made fast to the iron mooring cleats.

"See, *amigos* and *amigas*? You are delivered safe and sound." Julio grinned brightly from the open pilot cabin. "Go, and may luck be with you."

Hawke stepped onto the boat's coaming and dropped to the wet limestone. Curious glances and idle speculation from crews aboard nearby boats drifted his way, but he ignored them. Anyone from Aztechnology would be much more stealthy.

Rachel and the professor followed and joined him on the dock.

"Just remember," Hawke told them, "right now you're safer with us than without us. None of us wants any kind of law enforcement looking at us too closely. Amazonia's extradition treaty with Aztlan might be sketchy, but the UCAS authorities might not be so generous. Either way, everyone will be interested in the artifact you have."

Hostility shone in Rachel's copper-colored eyes, and Hawke realized he'd never seen that color before. "Wouldn't it make more sense just to threaten to kill us if we try to escape?"

He didn't reply, didn't try to explain that he didn't work that way. If things hadn't gotten so slotted at the dig site, they could have met under different circumstances, and maybe had a different relationship. Now he didn't need her understanding. He just needed to regain control of the situation.

He nodded the pair forward as Flicker joined them on the dock. "Move."

Rachel's hesitation showed that she had more to say, or maybe she was considering calling to the onlookers for help, but the professor took her by the wrist and spoke in a low voice that Hawke's enhanced hearing picked up.

"We don't have a choice. Just do as he says for now."

For now? Hawke didn't know what the professor had up his sleeve—or *thought* he had up his sleeve—but it wasn't going to happen. He followed Fredericks and Rachel as they headed off the dock.

They walked through a cargo area where stevedores and 'bots moved freight, shifting crates, barrels, and sacks between lighters and small warehouses. Once they were past that and the row of bars, restaurants, and supply stores that catered to whatever crew was in port, they walked up a wide set of cracked stone steps into the town proper.

The main area of Playa del Iguana Verde surrounded a low, wide fountain, where an artesian well blasted a line of sparkling water straight up like a whale's spout. In the center of the fountain, a large stone iguana stood with its massive head raised. The creature didn't look friendly, and Hawke wondered why it had been chosen and what story might lie behind it. Faded and worn hotels, shops, and cantinas advertised goods and services in LED lights, and in voice-overs between canned *carnivale* music blaring from PA systems.

"So, where do we find this fixer you know?" Hawke asked Flicker. In the southern hemisphere, she had all the connections. That was one of the reasons Hawke had called her when he'd learned Rachel Gordon was in Aztlan.

She pointed her chin ahead of them. "Ferreira has an electronics market a few blocks ahead."

The fixer was supposed to have a vehicle and supplies they could use to get to Distrito Caracas. The city lay beyond the Muralha Verde, the "Green Wall," and though the sprawl was technically within Amazonian borders, Distrito Caracas operated as a free city-state for all intents and purposes. Once there, Flicker knew someone else that could get them back to Pueblo Corporate Council lands so Hawke could make his meet with Mr. Johnson.

The plan was ragged, a patchwork thing, but doable.

Then Flicker dodged to the right and yelled, "Sniper at three o'clock on the roof!"

Just starting to move, already raking the rooftops with his enhanced vision, Hawke felt a high-velocity bullet graze his temple hard enough to jolt his head sideways. His reinforced skullcap kept the round from penetrating, but the glancing blow jarred his brain, causing his vision to double and vertigo to dance through him.

Drawing a Predator, he fought to stay on his feet and find cover, but a second bullet thudded into the subdermal armor right over his heart just as the loud *crack!* of the first shot reached his ears.

CHAPTER THIRTY

If the heavy-caliber bullet had only struck flesh and bone, it would have passed through Hawke's chest and staggered him at best, leaving a fist-sized hole he might not have recovered from. But since all the velocity expended against his subdermal armor, the round knocked him backward. His wired reflexes came online automatically as his adrenal pump flooded his system.

The world slowed down as he managed to keep from falling by spreading his feet and shifting his center of gravity. He spotted the third bullet streaking toward him, and threw himself to the left. The round slapped the ground behind him, creating a long scar before bouncing up and speeding off toward the harbor.

Hawke ducked and rolled as the fourth bullet blasted through the air only centimeters behind him as the sniper tried to follow his movements. When he reached the cover of a nearby building, one of the Predators came up and he opened fire, throwing a salvo of slugs in the rifleman's direction.

A hundred and forty-three meters distant, the building was a three-story stone hotel, a monolith from the town's better times. The Amazonian flag flew out front, while LED panels scrolled the room rates and availability. Although the distance was too far for accurate shooting with the Predator, the slug-thrower still peppered the building with rounds that shattered one of the LED panels in a shower of sparks.

"Hawke!" Flicker called over the comm. On the other side of the narrow, dusty stone street, she opened her messenger bag and unleashed a swarm of drones.

"I'm fine." Hawke glanced down at himself to make sure. Pain flooded through his chest, and a trickle of blood soaked into his shirt, but the onboard med suite was already taking away the hurt and coagulating the wound, as well as the one on his head. He cursed and glanced around the corner at the sniper's position.

Rachel Gordon and the professor had reacted slower than Hawke and Flicker had, but they'd reached the fountain wall and now lay on the ground, hands wrapped over their heads.

A few blocks down the main thoroughfare, a large GMC Bulldog step-van shot out of a cross street and roared toward the fountain. The two axles in the rear had four tires each to support the vehicle's tonnage, and the stiff suspension showed in the way it rocked as it raced along. Painted a nondescript gray and green, the van featured no windows except the bullet resistant front windshield.

A hatch popped open on top, allowing a gun turret to lock into place. Heavy-caliber machine gun rounds sprayed along the building where Hawke had taken cover. He ducked back as the bullets chewed chunks out of the corner and threw stone splinters everywhere.

His back to the wall, Hawke took a breath, and was glad the effort didn't hurt as much as he thought it would. The chems had cleared most of the foggy dizziness from his mind and vision.

"Read me in, Flicker."

"Datastream coming to you now."

Hawke braced himself. Even though he'd been given access to her drones through his cybered vision before, the translucent overlay of images was a staggering amount of visual data to take in.

An image of the downtown area overlaid Hawke's normal vision. Through the drone-view, he watched the van skid to a stop beside the professor and Rachel. The screech of tortured rubber grated on his hearing as a dust cloud roiled around the vehicle. A side door popped open, and two armored men jumped out and ran toward Rachel and Fredericks. The men wore featureless black combat armor, and moved like they'd trained together.

The professor was already getting to his feet. He had both hands wrapped around Rachel's forearm, and was dragging her toward the two approaching gunmen. It was possible the gunmen had ordered the professor to do that, but Hawke didn't think that was the case.

"Flicker."

"I see them."

Suddenly, Hawke's view of one of the sec men zoomed in fast, and he knew the rigger had coaxed the drone to greater velocity. The image held him as the little machine closed on one of the gunmen. The man's forehead suddenly filled the view, and the datastream went dark.

Instantly, another view opened up. This one showed the gunman's profile as the back of his head erupted in a spray of blood and bone when the drone blasted through and dropped in pieces to the ground.

Fredericks shied away from the dead man as blood spattered the side of his face and shoulder. He kept pulling Rachel toward the van. The surviving gunman caught the woman's other arm and helped drag her along.

Several of Flicker's finger-length drones smashed into the van's windshield, but didn't penetrate the barrier, ending up shattered or embedded in the transplas. Others trailed after the professor and the other gunman, closing in for the kill.

Just before the drones overtook their two targets, another of the armored men stepped from the van's door with a metal bar trailing a power cord. He held it straight out and the video and audio feeds from the drones suddenly went dead.

Flicker cursed.

"I'm dark," Hawke said over the commlink.

"They hit my swarm with a degausser," she said. *"Knocked out their magnetic fields. They're toast. New feed coming online now."*

Almost instantly, a new translucent image shaded Hawke's vision. He watched as Rachel and the professor were pulled aboard the van. "Can you take out the sniper and the turret gun?"

"I can."

"Keep me in the loop with a visual on the van."

"I will. What are you going to do?"

"I'm gonna recover our cargo." Hawke edged to the bullet-riddled corner of the building, held his position, and watched the big GMC van wheel around in a tight turn, sunlight reflecting from its cracked windshield.

The sniper atop the building suddenly went slack as one of Flicker's remaining drones zipped through his eye and into his skull. The moment he dropped his sniper rifle, Hawke raced around the corner and leaned into the speed the wired reflexes gave him. He ran for the fountain, to the body of the man lying there, and snatched up the Ares Alpha assault rifle/grenade launcher combo as he pursued the van.

CHAPTER THIRTY-ONE

Accessing his PAN, Hawke pulled up a map of Playa del Iguana Verde and tracked the Bulldog's progress. The vehicle was headed out of town, but the road curved around a steep incline that slowed its progress. The all-terrain tires slipped on the dirt road as it slewed around the bend, spitting dust as they fought for traction.

The turret gun spun atop the van and opened fire again, struggling to lock on Hawke as he broke from the straight course he was on and headed through a nearby cluster of buildings. Bullets crashed into the buildings around him, leaving smoking craters. An instant later, a swarm of Flicker's dart drones slammed into the turret. Although it tried to turn, the gun couldn't sweep around, and the whine of its overstressed motor was almost lost in the main engine's roar.

Slinging the Alpha assault rifle over his chest, Hawke ran, feeling the adrenal pumps supply his body with fuel as the reinforced muscle tissue bunched and propelled him forward, pumping his arms and legs like pistons.

"Hawke!" Flicker sounded out of breath.

He knew she was trying to keep up, and he knew she'd never be able to match his speed. He didn't know how many drones, if any, she had left other than the one still trailing the Bulldog. "Watch yourself. I'm going for the van."

As he closed on the first building, Hawke leaped onto a battered truck parked in the alley, then jumped and caught the low edge of the roof. Hauling himself up, he threw his body onto the top and rolled to his feet. Then he was sprinting again, propelling himself forward like a human bullet. When he reached the end of the roof, he leaped across the narrow alley and caught the roof there, slightly higher than the last one.

By the time he reached the third building, trees and brush covered most of the surrounding area except for switchback trails that led from dwelling to dwelling. The rooftops were islands of mostly level ground that allowed him clear passage and stair steps up into the nearby hills and jungle.

The ghostly image of the Bulldog grinding up the incline remained printed across his vision. He ran and leaped and ran again, gaining a small lead that allowed him to reach the dirt road across the crest of the hill before the van barreled around the curving road below, barely visible through the thick jungle canopy separating him from it.

On level ground now, the Bulldog accelerated, trailing a cloud of dust as it hurtled along. As the brush and tree limbs slapped his face, Hawke knew he was scant centimeters from being too late for the intercept.

If he missed, Rachel Gordon and the jewel would be in the wind.

"What are you doing?" Rachel fought against the armored man who held her pinned face-down against the van's floor in the cargo area. She kicked at his legs, hoping to topple him. The armored suit proved too strong for her, though, and she couldn't move him. She rolled again, trying to get her hands free while the man struggled to secure her hands behind her back.

"Stop!" the man ordered, the suit's PA system making his voice thunder inside the vehicle.

She kicked him in the face, putting as much of her weight into it as she could manage, and only numbed her foot when it impacted his helmet.

"I don't have to be gentle," the man warned. A transparent strand oozed out of one of his armored arms and he looped it around her left wrist. *"Keep it up, and I'll break something."*

The presence in the jewel grew more agitated in Rachel's mind. She didn't know how the others couldn't feel it. Bracing herself as more of the strand played out, she fought to keep her remaining wrist free.

"Rachel!" Professor Fredericks stood against one side of the van, holding on to cargo netting covering the wall. "Rachel, calm down!"

Calm down? Rachel couldn't believe what she was hearing. Her arm still throbbed from where the professor had yanked her toward the van. He wasn't putting up a fight at all. In fact, he seemed almost happy to be there.

"They're here to help," Professor Fredericks told her.

"Lies!" The voice was a cold, razored rebuttal sliding through Rachel's mind. *"Betrayer!"*

The armored man captured her other hand and bound them together. Her mind spun as she tried to hold onto her shifting realities. The Aztechnology soldiers had almost killed her. Hawke and Flicker had taken her captive. And now Professor Fredericks—the one person she thought she could trust on the dig—didn't seem to be who he was supposed to be either.

"What did you do?" she demanded, turning to face him with an accusing stare.

Guilt pulled at the professor's haggard face. He winced in pain and ran a hand across his forehead. "What I had to do, Rachel. Just go along with them. They're not going to hurt you. Everything's going to be all right. I swear."

"Liar!"

The armored man yanked Rachel to her feet, almost popping her arms out of their sockets, and pressed her back to the cargo netting beside Professor Fredericks. She lunged at the professor and tried to kick him, so furious she couldn't control herself. If she couldn't hurt the guy in armor, she would hurt her betrayer.

The sec man knocked her foot away before it reached Professor Fredericks, numbing her leg from the knee down. She slumped against the cargo net and the man started to ooze more strands, tying her to the netting like a spider trapped prey.

"She's not listening to you." The sec man nodded to Professor Fredericks. "Make yourself scarce."

Nodding, his face ashen, the professor sidled away, heading toward two other armored men in the cargo area. The van's speed increased steadily, the growl of the engine growing louder.

The man holding Rachel popped his faceplate, revealing round features with burn scars that marred his right cheek and tightened his right eye. "I'm gonna trank you. Keep you docile for the trip back."

A hypodermic needle slid out the end of his forefinger and dripped two drops of clear liquid.

"I need her backpack," Professor Fredericks said.

"Sure," the sec man replied as he stabbed the needle into Rachel's throat under her right ear.

Pain bit into Rachel's neck, and fire flooded her veins. In the next heartbeat, her senses started to fade. Her vision dimmed as the voice from the jewel rose to a furious shout. Someone pulled at her backpack, and it started to slide away.

Then something heavy thudded against the van's roof.

CHAPTER THIRTY-TWO

Landing on the Bulldog, Hawke struggled for find purchase as his momentum carried him across the vehicle in an uncontrolled skid. For a split-second he thought he wasn't going to secure a hold, then he managed to grab the frozen gun turret.

The barrel turned blistering hot as the gun unleashed a salvo that missed him and caromed from the Bulldog's roof in ear-splitting whines. Between bursts as the weapon reloaded, one of Flicker's drones zipped into the barrel, and when the gun fired again, a heavy-caliber round met the drone blocking the muzzle. With a muffled detonation and harsh clang, the turret gun vibrated and the barrel shredded, leaving curled metal strips peeled back.

"The gun's offline," Flicker informed Hawke over the commlink.

"No drek." Hawke figured he'd been only a couple centimeters away from needing a hand replacement. As it was, his arm ached all the way to his shoulder before the med suite shut the pain down.

"I've commandeered a vehicle and I'm coming to you."

Still accessing one of the next wave of Flicker's drones that had just arrived, Hawke spotted a sec man about to climb onto the roof. He drew a Predator with his left hand and waited till the guy stuck his head up.

Mercilessly, Hawke shot him, but the curved bullet-resistant face shield kept the rounds from penetrating. Still, it was hard to not react to getting shot in the face, especially when the impacts rocked his head back. Hawke knew for a fact it was harder still to imagine *not* taking some kind of massive injury.

The sec man recovered from the frontal assault and leaned back outside again to search for his target. This time Hawke braced himself on the gun turret and whipped his body around to plant both feet in the guy's face. Knocked from his perch, the sec man sailed off the Bulldog and smacked into a tree on the side of the road before rolling into the brush.

"Be careful on your approach," Hawke called. "You've got one off in the weeds, and I don't think he's down."

"I saw." The roar of an engine underscored Flicker's response over the commlink.

Holstering the Predator, Hawke reached for the Alpha, slipped the sling off the rifle, and let the weapon slide off the van, hating to see it go. He looped the sling around the turret, let out the slack as far as it would go, and tested its strength. Using the sling to secure himself, he curled over the vehicle's side until he was hanging next to the open cargo door.

The driver must have spotted him, because the door slid closed. He drove along the edge of the road, trying to brush Hawke off into the trees. Several branches slapped or dug into him, splintering against the armor, but battering him against the vehicle.

Bouncing against the Bulldog's armored hide, he pulled a thermite grenade from his vest and slapped it onto the door's locking mechanism. He primed the detonator through his PAN, then scrabbled back along his tether to put distance between himself and the explosive.

When he judged he was far enough away, Hawke detonated the grenade. A wave of heat blasted over him as his sound dampers muted most of the explosion. The door hung awkwardly now, leaving a gap where it joined the vehicle's frame.

"I need a peek," Hawke said over the commlink.

"Coming up."

The drone's view changed as it dropped altitude and matched the Bulldog's speed, pacing the partially open cargo door. Inside, Professor Fredericks cowered against the far side while protected by a sec man. A second sec man held Rachel Gordon hostage in front of him, pressing a pistol to her head. She looked dazed, her copper eyes glassy and faded.

"I can give you one distraction," Flicker said, *"but that's all. Which target?"*

"The guy by the professor." The other man was occupied holding Rachel hostage.

"On your go."

Hawke shifted his weight, clinging to the rifle sling as he gauged momentum, and set himself. "Go!"

The drone's view veered as it darted inside the van. It closed on the sec man, but he had his pistol up and was aiming. Hawke grabbed the broken door, set his feet, and heaved, wrenching it from its mooring as the driver headed toward the bole of a large tree. As Hawke tried to get inside the GMC, only meters away from being smashed into the tree, the sec man's bullet smashed into the drone, and his view of the interior went black.

Unable to dodge the trees the driver steered the Bulldog against, Hawke flattened against the vehicle and hung on. Branches tore at his armor, one of them shredding his shoulder rig, tearing it loose. Both Predators fell and disappeared under the churning wheels. He reached for one of his katars and fisted the punching dagger without telescoping the blade.

Up front, the driver gestured frantically, and Hawke thought the man might have seen the pistols get stripped away. He was out of time. He whipped around the cargo doorway and threw himself inside.

Landing on his feet, ducking beneath the sec man's line of fire, Hawke felt the heat of two bullets burn past him, then he was pushing up, launching off his toes with all his strength and speed, following the katar as he telescoped the blade. His body trailed the weapon in a straight line as the nano-edged point slid into the sec man's face shield and the skull beyond.

Gripping the dead man as he fell, Hawke spun the body around to use as a shield. He pulled the katar behind his impromptu cover as he faced the surviving sec man. The cargo area was large enough for both them to stand with a couple meters between them, but that was about it.

"If you don't want her to die," the man threatened as he angled his weapon under Rachel's jaw, *"you'll exit now. Otherwise, I blow her head off, and you and I take our chances with how this shakes out."*

Fredericks shrank away even further, as if trying to pull himself into the cargo netting and van wall behind him.

"Flicker . . ." Hawke subvocalized over the commlink.

"Almost there."

Almost wasn't going to help. Hawke faced the sec man and considered his options. If he leaped from the van, all bets were off, because they no longer had anything worth holding onto in whatever game Mr. Johnson had brought them into. He and Flicker would have to run, drop so deep into the shadows no one could find them. If they did, they'd have to keep running because they didn't know all the players, and probably wouldn't find out until one showed up to frag them.

No, giving up wasn't an option because they couldn't escape from or buy their way out of all the drek they were in.

But there was no way he could take out the sec man before he killed Rachel. For an instant, Hawke wondered if her death might get Flicker and him out of whatever this was. If Rachel died, maybe nobody won. And there was no percentage in revenge. Players only continued the game while a win was still possible. With her gone, would everything reset to zero?

Hawke pushed those thoughts aside. Whatever else she was, he felt certain Rachel Gordon was an innocent, and those people got handled differently when he was in the game. He set himself, waiting for an opening, determined to make the best of it.

"Time's up," the sec man said. "Move or watch her—"

Before he could finish his threat, before Hawke could launch any kind of attack, a bright blue nimbus enveloped him, and the stench of burning flesh filled the cargo van. His armor turned cherry-red at his head, chest, and groin as he released Rachel and staggered back with a rising scream.

The woman dropped to the van floor and struggled to rise.

With an anti-climactic *bamf!*, the sec man dropped to his knees. His armor fell to pieces off his body, and charred meat that used to be a man spilled out, twitching on the floor.

Hawke cursed, feeling the after-effects of the magic that had been unleashed. He stepped back, not knowing what had happened, unsure if it was finished.

Professor Fredericks bent down toward Rachel, but ignored the woman, reaching instead for her backpack. Before his fingers touched the material, a black fog drifted up from it, forming into a hideous mouth filled with long, serrated fangs. It snapped at the professor, driving him back against the van wall.

"Back!" a voice from nowhere said.

The professor turned his head, hiding his face as he begged for mercy.

The thing—and it wasn't just a mouth now, Hawke saw glowing red eyes as well—turned toward him. For a moment, he thought it was going to attack him, and he didn't know what he was going to do about that—or even what he *could* do.

Then it vanished.

"Hawke!"

Realizing only then that Flicker had been repeatedly calling for him, Hawke said, "I'm okay." He couldn't help wondering if he was telling himself that more than he was telling her. The back of his neck still prickled in fear. He hated magic.

Cautiously, Hawke approached Rachel. He put the katar away, then hesitantly reached out to her, waiting for the fog to manifest again. He was surprised when his fingertips rested against her carotid, then concerned because her pulse was weak.

So who killed the guy threatening her? And what was that—thing?

He glanced up at Fredericks. "What'd he give her?"

The other man just shook his head, like he was going to deny everything, but knew he'd come too far to do that and couldn't answer.

Hawke pointed a katar at Fredericks. "I'm not gonna ask again."

"A—a sedative. That's all, I swear." His eyes were wide and frightened behind his dust-covered glasses. "Just something to knock her out so she could be handled more easily. She wasn't going to be hurt."

Hawke didn't bother to point out that Rachel had only been a finger twitch away from having her brains scattered across the van. He grabbed the professor's shirt with his free hand and yanked the man off his feet, throwing him to the floor.

"You and me are going to talk soon. For the moment, stay there and you won't get hurt."

Fredericks rolled up into a fetal position next to the sec man Hawke had killed and nodded, wide-eyed and terrified.

Looking up at the video feed on the ceiling that allowed the driver to view the cargo area, Hawke said, "It's just you now. Don't make me come after you."

After a moment, a man's voice asked over the speaker, *"What do you want?"*

"Pull over."

"How do I know you won't kill me?"

"If I have to stop this vehicle myself, I will kill you."

The van slowed immediately and pulled to the side of the road.

CHAPTER THIRTY-THREE

Once the van had stopped and the driver had fled into the jungle, Hawke stooped and picked Rachel Gordon up from the floor. He strode to the cargo door, kicking burned pieces of armor and sec man out of his way. He paused at the door and looked back at Fredericks, who gazed up at him fearfully.

"Get up and follow me," Hawke ordered. "If you try anything, I'll kill you."

Fredericks had to try twice to get to his feet, then followed shakily. "They're going to kill me anyway."

Hawke ignored that for the moment. This wasn't the time or place to talk about those things, but it would be soon. He stepped down from the Bulldog as Flicker drove up in her commandeered four-wheel-drive king cab pickup. Dents, holes, cancerous rust, and mismatched paint scarred the vehicle's exterior. The engine coughed and wheezed, and exhaust trailed in a writhing gray line behind it.

"You call that a pursuit vehicle?" Hawke asked.

Behind the cracked windshield, both hands wrapped around the steering wheel, Flicker shrugged. "Beggars can't be choosers, *omae*. It was the best I could get on short notice."

"Is there going to be any pursuit from town?"

"None from the locals. They don't want to buy into anything this heavy."

"What about local law?"

"There isn't any. One of the reasons I picked that destination."

Hawke opened the passenger door, flipped the seat forward, and slid Rachel Gordon onto the back seats. He made her as comfortable as possible, but didn't touch the backpack. Whatever that jewel had unleashed, he could still feel it buzzing in the air.

Flicker turned to look over the seat at the young woman. "She okay?"

"They gave her a sedative. I want to get her checked out, but I think she's gonna be all right." Hawke didn't want to get into the black fog-thing, especially since he had no idea what it was. He looked at Fredericks. "Get in the back."

The professor gazed at the truck bed, then back at Hawke. "It looks like they've been hauling pigs."

From the overwhelming smell of dung in the truck bed, Hawke agreed. "Get in or I put you in."

Fredericks clambered into the truck's rear and hunkered down against the cab.

Hawke set the timer on an incendiary grenade for one minute, then pitched it into the Bulldog's cargo area. He slid into the pickup's passenger seat, moved it back as far as it would go, and still wasn't comfortable.

Flicker engaged the transmission, making the pickup jerk forward, then let out the clutch and they got underway. "This beast's old school," she said, shifting gears. "Nothing cyber about it."

"Good—makes it harder for anyone to trail us. Let's find a hole to crawl into."

Behind them, the incendiary went off and flames climbed out of the van, engulfing the entire vehicle in seconds.

Hours later, after the sun had dropped into the Pacific and full dark filled the jungle, signaling nocturnal predators to come out to hunt, Hawke stared at the bombed-out remains of a tempo drug lab that had almost been reclaimed by verdant growth.

Somewhere in the distance, a jaguar screamed.

Now that the adrenaline had drained from his system, his body was demanding payback for the earlier use and abuse. He curbed the immediate need with a cocktail from his med suite, but knew he couldn't keep the coming lethargy at bay for long. He needed some rack time, or at least a period of quiet.

When the site had been an enterprising business, it had consisted of four buildings: the lab where the drugs were manufactured, a warehouse for the chemicals and finished product, a barracks for the workers and guards, and a main house for the ops boss and close crew. All of the buildings were constructed out of cheap plascrete blocks. A nearby runway, too limited for anything other than STOL aircraft, ran east and west. Brush and young saplings choked the fast-vanishing airstrip.

Since he'd found no one on his recon, Hawke stood near the main house and gave Flicker the all clear over the commlink.

Minutes later, lights doused and trailing exhaust that looked ghost white in the darkness, Flicker parked the pickup in the warehouse. Getting inside was easy because someone had blown the building's front and left side out. The four-wheel-drive strained a little to get over the debris, but eventually lurched into the waiting darkness. After Flicker switched the ignition off, the engine rattled noisily for a moment before spluttering to a halt. It sounded like it was on its last legs.

Hawke slung the Remington 950 sniper rifle over his shoulder and strode toward the pickup. The rifle was part of the gear Flicker had gotten from another fixer. After everything that had gone down in Playa del Iguana Verde, they hadn't wanted to use the contact there, just to be on the safe side. Even if the man didn't have anything to do with the ambush, any follow up investigation might root him out.

The second fixer had charged them triple for the supplies and narrow drop window, but Hawke had made her earn part of the fee by requiring a drone delivery. After a check to make sure the weapons, food, and water weren't carrying tracking devices, Hawke had called Flicker in and they'd picked up the cargo. After making certain there were no other trackers on the shipment, they'd quickly departed the site.

Rachel Gordon was still unconscious in the pickup's rear seat. Seeing her lying there, pallid and boneless, worried Hawke as he gathered her in his arms, but thoughts of the dark entity and the hard way the sec man had died also kept him wary. Stomach tense with anticipation, he carried her to the sleeping bag Flicker had prepared on the ground.

"There might be some salvageable hammocks in the barracks," the elven rigger said with a frown as she looked around with a chem-powered camp light. "We need to get up off the ground if we can. You'd be surprised what tries to crawl into bed with you around here."

Hawke nodded at the professor, who sat on the edge of the pickup bed. "You okay with him while I go see what's lying around?"

"If he tries anything, I'll shoot him."

"Fine, but don't kill him. I still wanna talk to him."

"The way he set us up back in town, he's got it coming."

"Maybe, but that's one of the things I wanna talk to him about." Hawke left the Remington with Flicker and picked up one of the two assault rifles they'd had delivered. He went off to raid the bombed-out barracks, knowing he'd be surprised if anything was left, because whoever had destroyed the drug operation had been pretty thorough.

CHAPTER THIRTY-FOUR

A short time later, Rachel slept on one of the cots Hawke had rescued from the mangled barracks. Judging from the number of skeletons he'd found—both assembled and blown apart—the attack had caught a lot of people off guard. He guessed the other two buildings were probably in the same condition. Luckily, there weren't any dead in the warehouse.

"Look," Professor Fredericks said when he returned, "can I just explain—"

"Shut up," Flicker said, "or I'll shoot you in the foot. You won't be dead, but you'll wish you were."

Sitting on an empty crate nearby, the professor closed his mouth, drew his feet closer to him, and sat meekly, even though Hawke knew the man wanted to try to weasel out of his predicament. Letting him stew and wonder about his future would soften him up.

In the glow of the camp lantern, Flicker ran a portable med scanner over Rachel's body. "There aren't any physical injuries that would account for her prolonged unconsciousness."

"Could this be a result of the sedative?" Hawke asked.

"I ran the bloodwork. She was given a variation of Bliss, but the amount shouldn't keep her under for this long."

Bliss was a street drug derived from poppy opiates. Normally, narcosoldiers and various military field operatives used it as pain management. Hawke's onboard med suite used a variant of it.

He sipped a water bulb that had been in their supplies. The night's heat drew moisture from him, soaking his shirt. "Maybe she had a reaction to the drug."

"I'd think that would show." Flicker took in a breath and let it out. "I *think*. I'm not a med tech, Hawke. I just interface with machines. Everything I'm seeing tells me she's gonna be fine. She just . . . isn't."

"Let's hope she stays healthy."

"Then there's this other thing." Flicker put the device away and slowly reached for the backpack that remained strapped to Rachel.

When she got within a half meter of it, something blurred the visual spectrum around the unconscious woman. Static electricity crackled up Flicker's arm, making her short-cropped hair lift a little.

With a displeased hiss, she pulled her hand back, and the static charges disappeared. "I can touch her. I can check her over with the scanner. But any time I make a definite move on that backpack, that's what happens. It *knows*, Hawke, and that freaks me out."

"Then we don't touch it."

"I don't like not knowing what it is."

"Curiosity kills, Flicker."

"I know, but knowing things keeps you from getting killed." She turned away from her sleeping patient. "Whatever's in that backpack, I don't like it. And I get the impression it isn't too chill about us either."

Hawke shifted his attention to Fredericks. "I'm gonna talk to the professor."

"Give me a minute." Flicker picked up a med kit from a nearby worktable she'd found in the lab building and took out a sterilized cloth and cleaning solution. "Let me take care of your wounds."

"I'm fine." Hawke started to walk away, but she grabbed him and held him in place.

"You're fine when I tell you you're fine. In this heat and this jungle, wounds can get infected fast. You do that, you're slotted because we don't have much in the way of antibiotics, and even your med suite might not cover every weird bug variant out here." Flicker applied the disinfectant liberally, the astringent smell tickling Hawke's nose as it stung the side of his head. Her wipe came away bloodstained.

Even though he felt certain his med suite would take care of him, Hawke let her work. Flicker thought best when her hands were busy. She calmed down when she had things to do. After a few minutes, she was satisfied and stepped back.

"While you're talking to the professor, I'm going to work on the pickup. We've got a lot of ground to cover in the morning to get out of Amazonia. You can fix dinner. I don't want to eat out of a can if we don't have to."

"Roger that."

"I don't know what we found." Professor Fredericks mopped the back of his neck with a sterilized wipe. It might have helped him relax and maybe even cooled him off somewhat, but it didn't remove any of the pig dung odor clinging to him. "Whatever's in Rachel's backpack is as much a mystery to me now as it was when we found it."

Hawke's deception suite told him the professor was telling the truth. At least about that. There were a lot of other things that didn't add up, and his explanations triggered the appropriate responses from the detection software.

"What were you looking for there?" Hawke knelt by the fire he'd built inside a loose ring of plascrete blocks and placed bacon slices on a skillet perched on a makeshift grill he'd created out of security mesh. Flicker's food inventory had been wide-ranging. Even more surprising, the requests had all been met.

Fredericks shrugged. "Just about anything. We went to Guatemala based on some translations from other artifacts I'd been working on."

Some or all of that was a lie. Hawke turned the sizzling bacon over with a combat knife. He couldn't control the fire's heat, so cooking the bacon slow wasn't an option. He had to settle for turning it often.

Now he raised it and poked the grease-stained blade at Fredericks's throat, causing the man to rear back and fall onto his haunches. "You're lying."

"We *didn't* know!"

"Then you're lying about the translations." Hawke fixed the older man with a hard stare. "We're out in the middle of nowhere. You nearly got my partner and me killed. No one will hear you scream, the jungle will bury you, and unless you can tell me something I don't know, right now you're just extra baggage."

"You told Rachel you'd get me out of this."

"That was before you signaled your playmates. Now you and I have a new deal. You talk, or I drop your body in one of the other buildings with all those dead people. And I don't care which way you go. But one way means my partner and I have more to eat tonight."

The professor's sweating face paled in the flickering firelight.

"Now try again," Hawke suggested as he went back to tending the bacon.

CHAPTER THIRTY-FIVE

A few meters away from the campfire, Flicker worked under the pickup's hood. She'd found a small toolkit in the vehicle, and gathered a few other tools from the small, mostly-stripped motor pool. They didn't have any replacement parts, but she was cleaning the ones she could get to, and tuning them up as best as she was able. Fuel was the biggest problem. The pickup's tank was almost depleted, but she'd told Hawke she had a workaround for that.

"We weren't there because of any specific research," Fredericks stated. When the deception suite pinged, Hawke glanced at the man again, even though the professor's dispirited tone made him inclined to accept that statement as the truth.

The professor leaned back. "We *had* to do research in the end to provide a basis for the funding request we sent to NeoNET. That was just blue smoke and mirrors. The real reason we were there was because of Rachel." He pursed his lips and grimaced. "She's got this . . . gift. I don't know what else to call it."

"What gift?"

"There are these artifacts my department's had for years. They're thousands of years old. Maybe something that goes back to the Second Age, an era of this world we've barely been able to guess at. One is some kind of bell, as near as we've been able to figure, and we have no clue about the other things. I don't have images, or I'd show you. They're covered with a language we've never seen before. It's not Mayan or Incan, or anything we've ever discovered. Though some of the characters look like elvish."

Hawke took the bacon out of the pan and poured reconstituted eggs into the grease. The smells woke up his hunger, but his attention was focused on Fredericks and the feeds from Flicker's three surviving drones patrolling a perimeter around the building.

"I was writing a paper on another artifact. Rachel was helping me with the annotations. She saw the bell and the other things, and she just started translating some of the language inscribed on them." Fredericks shook his head. "Just started translating out of the blue, even though she had no background in whatever language it was. *Nobody* has ever had a background like that."

"What'd the translation say?"

"We're not sure. Rachel was only able to provide glimpses, not a full translation. It talks about something called the 'Becoming,' or the 'Anointing,' words to that effect."

"But you have no idea of what's supposed to 'become' or be 'anointed?'"

"Not a clue."

"No mention of the jewel?"

"None."

Hawke used his knife to ease the scrambled eggs from the grease and put them on three disposable plates. "Then how did you find the artifact?"

"Rachel found it. After she started reading the language on the artifacts, she also started dreaming about a jungle. Eventually, we narrowed it down to somewhere in Guatemala. We didn't know exactly what location the dreams were showing her at first. Discovering that took months of searching through landmarks and topographical maps and satellite searches she remembered from the dreams. *Months.*" Fredericks squeezed his hands into fists, which shook with the effort. "It was so hard being so patient. We got fragments spaced out over many weeks—it was intolerable! Sometimes I felt like Rachel knew, but she just wasn't telling me."

"Is that what was happening? She was holding something back from you?" From the corner of his eye, Hawke caught Flicker pausing her work to listen.

"No. At least, I'm convinced that wasn't what was happening. Rachel is a giving person. She's guileless. And she trusted me. At least, until today." Fredericks sighed, looking distraught and guilty, and Hawke couldn't help wondering if the professor had only then realized how he'd taken advantage of the mentor-student relationship. Or maybe he was just feeling sorry that he'd been caught. "She just didn't know." He sipped his water bulb. "Eventually, though, we figured it out."

"That's when you put your dig request through, and got the funding grant."

"Yes." Fredericks placed the water bulb on the ground at his feet. "Faculty puts those requests out and hopes someone will bite. I knew if we revealed everything—Rachel's ability to translate some of the documents, her dreams—we'd have a better chance at getting someone to fund us. But we couldn't. We would have lost too much control. So we did the best we could, and I—*punched up* the data when Rachel had finished."

"Why NeoNET?"

"Because they agreed to fund us. There's no other reason."

"You don't have a relationship with anyone there?"

Fredericks shook his head. "If I'd had someone like that, I would have called them. We had to wait almost three months for the request to get answered."

"Who brokered the deal?"

"The cred came straight from NeoNET. It was just deposited in an account I could draw on."

"You didn't try to find out who put up the funding?"

Fredericks shook his head. "You've never been involved in academia. You don't care where the funding comes from because you're so glad to get it. I never asked. I was just grateful."

Frustrated, Hawke activated a tin of freeze-dried, self-heating biscuits. "How did Rachel find the jewel?"

"We'd been onsite for a few days. We moved around because she felt like we were getting close to something. She'd have these *visions*. There was nothing else we could call them. But while we were in Guatemala, the visions grew stronger and more frequent."

"Did she have any idea what it was you were getting close to?"

"No. Just . . . something."

"And it was tied into those artifacts?"

"She believed it was. I hope it is. But I don't honestly know. And right now it really doesn't matter because whatever that artifact is, it's *something*." Fredericks met Hawke's gaze. "You saw what happened in that van with that guard who was threatening Rachel."

"I did." Hawke knew it would be a long time before he didn't think about that.

Fredericks shivered at the memory, grimacing and looking sick. "She did that. Or that jewel did that. I'm not sure which. I'm not even certain you can separate one from the other at this point.

She's different, and that jewel is like nothing I've ever seen."

Hawke let that pass without comment, though he felt the same way. "Who were the men in the Bulldog?"

Fredericks ran a hand over his face and hesitated.

"I saw you drop the broken commlink after you got into the pickup," Hawke said. "Don't try to lie about it. Where'd you get it?"

"From one of the men aboard the *Scorpionfish*. I took it without him knowing while they were marching us out."

Hawke's estimation of the professor jumped a couple notches. Fredericks had taken the commlink without Hawke or Flicker noticing, either. The man definitely bore closer watching.

"They were mercenaries," Fredericks said. "I contacted Neo-NET, and told them Rachel and I had been abducted."

"NeoNET sent that team?"

Fredericks stared at Hawke. "I thought so."

"Did you ask them?"

"There wasn't time, but they seemed to know what was going on."

Hawke guessed the sec men were mercenaries in the area who picked up a contract. NeoNET couldn't have mobilized a team into Amazonia so quickly. His thoughts chased themselves. For every question the professor answered, the problems they faced just became more complicated.

He took the biscuits from the tin and placed them on the plates. Then he called Flicker over to eat.

CHAPTER THIRTY-SIX

"Careful with that," Flicker advised as Hawke hoisted the 100-liter barrel into the pickup truck's bed. "That stuff's explosive."

"Thanks." Hawke set the barrel down and ran a finger under the word *FLAMMABLE* stenciled in white in both English and Spanish on the black barrel. "I got that."

"Sorry. Just making sure." Flicker looked exhausted. She'd been up most of the night working on the pickup, either preparing it for the trip or because she couldn't sleep. Hawke wasn't certain which was the cause, but she wasn't in a good mood this morning. "Now get out of the way and let me work."

Hawke stepped away from the pickup truck as Flicker vaulted over the side with her makeshift toolkit, a rubber hose, a drill gun, and two metal restraints she'd fashioned from salvage. The pickup idled much better than it had the previous day, purring like another vehicle. The electric drill had been altered to run off the pickup's battery.

A short distance away, Professor Fredericks sat on a plascrete block under a tree that blocked the early morning sun slanting through the canopy. The jungle was so green the sunlight looked like it was tinted emerald.

"It took a little doing," Flicker said over the spinning drill, "but I adjusted the pickup's carburetor to run off the methanol in that barrel instead of gasoline. Methanol's wood alcohol and acidic, so using it for fuel is going to produce a lot of wear and tear, but those two barrels I found should get us to Distrito Caracas before the engine gets totally fragged. From there we can make the jump back to the Pueblo Corporate Council. Then we check in with your Mr. Johnson and see what's what."

"Sounds good."

She glanced at Hawke. "That's still the plan, right? We deliver the woman as originally agreed?"

Hawke nodded. "That's still the plan." He wasn't exactly keen on the idea, especially given the present conditions, but he thought it would at least get Flicker and him out of the hot seat.

"Good." Flicker pulled a screwdriver from her pocket and attached a clamp to the rubber hose. "I asked because the way you've been checking up on her, I was starting to think you were taking her on to raise."

"No." The comment left Hawke feeling a little irritated and embarrassed. But Rachel Gordon still hadn't come back from wherever she was. As long as she was in a vegetative state, he couldn't do anything to help her. She'd be better off in the hands of someone who could look out for her. "I'm just looking for the payday."

"Uh huh." Flicker put another screw in the drill and sunk it into the pickup bed. "You have to remember, she was already in a pile of drek when you found her."

"I remember." But now Hawke also knew that Rachel Gordon hadn't put herself there.

"All you've been doing—all *we've* been doing—ever since is hauling her out of all the hurt trying to fall down on her. Whatever she's got going on, whatever that jewel is, it's none of our biz."

"I know. She's got warning labels on her even plainer than the ones on that barrel." Not wanting to deal with the direction the conversation was taking, or acknowledge his own nascent reluctance about their parts in Rachel Gordon's future, Hawke went to get the second barrel of methanol.

They made Distrito Caracas just after sundown, and the sprawl was alive with festive neon lights that washed across the pickup's cracked windshield. Sins came with fees in Distrito Caracas, and several establishments offered flashing trideo lists to catalogue them.

Flicker drove, almost as much a part of the pickup now after hours spent speeding through the jungle as she was in a cyber-equipped rig. She shifted gears instinctively, listening to the engine and just knowing what needed to be done and when. She was proud of the way the vehicle had held together, proud of the way she'd made it better than it was.

And part of her already felt a twinge of guilt about leaving it in some alley. It had done everything she'd asked and more, and she didn't like the idea of just abandoning it once it ceased to be useful. That was how she was about things she worked on, though, and she knew it. They weren't use-and-lose things. For a time, they were a part of her—even this mundane, rusty bucket of bolts.

That insight into her own mindset was what gave her a view into Hawke and how he was functioning while on this run. She'd known him for years, and she knew how he operated and what he thought about most situations.

His mind was unsettled now, and it was all because of the sleeping woman in the back seat. Flicker wanted to reach into his skull and fix his thinking. He just needed an adjustment, and his hesitation would go away. People needed to be more like machines, she'd decided a long time ago.

As she rolled down the final hill into the waiting sprawl, she looked at Hawke and knew she needed to ease some of the pressure he was feeling. She was partly responsible for his present mood, after all. "Look, I spoke too soon this morning. I was wound up and, haven't had any real sleep in two days."

Hawke looked at her. He'd sat quietly in the passenger seat for most of the day with the assault rifle in his lap. During lunch, he'd been polite while passing out sandwiches and bottled water, but he'd stayed quiet and kept his attention on the landscape, scanning for hostiles.

Flicker nodded over her shoulder at Rachel. "You should meet with Mr. Johnson in Santa Fe and see if you can figure out what's going on. Don't just hand her over without knowing more. It wouldn't be right."

"'Right?'" A smile twitched his lips. "We're not in the business of right and wrong, remember? We provide services."

"We're in the business of right and wrong for *us*. That's what I forgot this morning. That's what I'm telling you now." Flicker watched the streets as she cruised through them. The vehicle didn't have an electronic signature to speak of. She and Hawke kept their PANs dark. The address for the guy she needed to speak to was in her head. "To the best of our knowledge, Rachel's hands are clean in this. I don't care about the professor. He betrayed a sacred trust, took advantage of a student, and he needs to be held accountable for that. Or at the very least not profit from it."

Relaxing a little in the passenger seat, Hawke watched the pedestrians drifting to and from the various venues along the winding streets. Security helos and drones tracked the airspace, but Flicker knew none of them would get involved in a simple street crime. They were there for the people who paid expensive security premiums.

"If I'd known we'd be in this deep," he said, "I wouldn't have taken this run. I don't go looking for trouble."

"I know, but we're here now. Let's deal with it. Okay?"

He nodded. "Okay."

Flicker watched as her companion's body language relaxed. They weren't out of the drek right now, not by a long shot, but at least they were in sync again. As usual, she'd take what she could get at the moment.

CHAPTER THIRTY-SEVEN

"This is the place," Flicker announced as she doused the pickup's lights and let the night close in around them.

During that last moment of light, Hawke caught a glimpse of a small, white plascrete warehouse on the outer fringes of the downtown business sector. A faded sign that read *MILHAZES' IMPORTS AND EXPORTS* hung on a thick pole over the double entrance doors. Low-key sec lighting illuminated the area in a haphazard fashion, but state-of-the-art cams watched from barely noticeable black transplas observation blisters Hawke located when he looked for them.

Three man-sized shadows waited in front of the double doors. Cloaks and long coats covered them from their necks to their ankles. The outerwear was too hot for the weather, but it was great for concealing weapons and other nasty surprises.

This section of the sprawl had gotten old, and was in need of an overhaul and a few coats of paint. It was also the perfect place for the man they were there to see. Two longer warehouses sheathed in battered, corrugated plasteel lined the narrow, dead-end street leading to the warehouse.

"Nice killbox," Hawke commented, recognizing the terrain for what it was. "The warehouses on either side keep people blocked in so they can't get out after they enter." He glanced over his shoulder and watched as a large truck rumbled out of an alley and rolled up behind them, blocking any quick exit. "And they close up afterward."

"Dorival's careful." Flicker checked the mirrors, but Hawke knew she was also in contact with her three drones running recon. "That's why we came to him. The guy is totally wiz when it comes to getting people and things out of Caracas on the DL."

"You said you two know each other," Hawke said as he eased

his assault rifle into a better position.

"For years." Flicker pulled the pickup to a stop twenty meters from the warehouse and killed the engine. Slowly, she removed the keys from the ignition and laid them on the dashboard, in plain sight of the sec cams.

"And you've always been friends?"

"More like we did some good biz together. The way I figure it, Dorival still owes me a favor, but he might not see it that way, because it was a close call. He makes it a point to keep his books balanced. Either way, I'd rather talk to him over anyone else I know in Amazonia. Especially this close to Aztlan."

"Works for me." Hawke pushed away his doubts. Whatever happened, Flicker had the best chance of arranging passage back to Santa Fe in a short time. The longer they took, the more time the opposition—still largely unknown—would have to organize and close off their potential escape routes.

"Then put the rifle on the dashboard," Flicker suggested. "Show some good faith."

Reluctantly, watching the three men through the bug-splattered windshield, Hawke did as he was told. "I don't suppose they're going to show good faith."

"Sure they are. They're not going to kill you 'til they have a good reason. You can keep your personal weapons, but if they put in an appearance, those men will shoot to kill."

"If I have to make them appear, I'll be shooting to kill."

Flicker grinned, but the effort wasn't totally humorous. It, like leaving the keys and the rifle on the dash, was for show. Her eyes were bright and her fingers trembled for a second before she regained control. "Okay, let's get out. Slowly. With your hands up."

Although he didn't want to go along with the directions because surrender was alien to him and usually only delayed getting dead, Hawke opened the door, then raised his hands above his shoulders and slipped out of the pickup. When nobody opened fire, his next breath was a little more relaxed.

In the back of the pickup, Professor Fredericks didn't move. He'd slept most of the day, courtesy of the drug Flicker had given him to keep him unconscious. Neither of them wanted the professor to give into any temptation to call out for help while they were in Caracas. For the moment, the plan was to keep Fredericks alive and with them.

A male elf wearing black clothing and ruby-lensed wraparound sunglasses, despite the night, stepped forward. His pale blond hair was pulled back in a ponytail that hung past his narrow shoulders. He smiled.

"Hello, Flicker." His voice was soft and held what Hawke thought was a Brazilian accent, from somewhere in South America, but not from Caracas. He pulled at the black gloves he wore, thin enough to be another layer of skin.

"Good evening, Artur," Flicker replied.

"It's been a while."

"I've kept myself busy."

"I saw your run up in Aztlan on the trideo broadcast." Artur smiled a little more broadly. "Racked up a few nuyen on the bets I laid out. The people I was with don't know you like I know you. Reminded me of old times."

"I don't know what old times you're talking about," Flicker said, but she was smiling.

Artur chuckled. "You always did know when to keep your mouth shut. That's one of the things Dorival likes about you." His eyes cut to the pickup. "Looks like you've fallen on some hard times, *chica*." His gaze turned to Hawke. "And maybe fallen in with some bad men."

"He's my friend."

Artur's pale blond eyebrows rose behind the ruby lenses. "You don't claim many of those."

"I don't, so remember that when it comes to him. Now, I'd like to see Dorival, please."

"Sure, sure. Put your hands down. You two look like scarecrows or something." Artur waved at them to follow him as he strode toward the warehouse.

Gears whined somewhere inside, and the warehouse doors jerked into motion. Tracked grooves ran across the ground. Hawke looked at the massive, heavy gates and realized it would take some serious ordnance to get through them. Despite its battered appearance, the warehouse was a fortress.

"I've got two people in the pickup," Flicker declared. "Both unconscious."

"They'll be fine. If they wake up, my crew will keep them company. No one will get hurt."

Hawke didn't like leaving Rachel Gordon there because she and her magic were wild cards, but she had the thing in the backpack to protect her. Flicker would have been on her own if he hadn't accompanied her, less protected than Rachel, and he liked that even less. He followed the two elves into the building.

"I can get you to the Pueblo Corporate Council. That's not a problem, though the transfer is not without its difficulties. You say time is a factor. The best I can do is three days. As you know, moving goods and people through these areas is always risky. Some times are just less risky than others. Moving people with as high a profile as the two people you're traveling with is even more perilous."

Dorival sat behind a small, elegant desk that was more of a showpiece than functional. Hawke didn't know much about furniture, but he'd traveled in Europe, and thought maybe the piece would have fit someplace that specialized in Old World antiques. The desk set off the rest of the room, holding down one end of a Persian rug while the two wingback chairs Flicker and Hawke occupied anchored the other side. To their host's right, trideo images showed international markets, mediacasts, and front pages of screamsheets.

Artur and three of his men sat quietly in chairs at the far end of the room.

The smuggler baron, as Flicker had called him, was also an elf. He seemed older than Artur just because of the way he acted, the timber of his voice, and the way he dressed in a modest-looking, summer weight tan suit that Hawke was willing to bet cost a lot more than appearances led him to believe.

Dorival's dark brown hair was parted in the middle and cropped at his jawline on both sides. His pointed ears poked through his locks and the top of the left one was pierced with a gold hoop earring that must have held personal attachment because it was nothing special-looking. His goatee was long enough to have a definite fork shape to it.

"Time is a factor for us," Flicker said. "If it's a matter of nuyen—"

Dorival held up manicured hands. "Please, Flicker, after everything you and I have done together, I wouldn't try to squeeze extra out of you for transportation. This is a safety issue. I can get you where you want to go without anyone being the wiser in three days. I'm not going to endanger my record *or* you by trying to best that when I know it's not comfortably possible to do so."

Flicker thought for a moment, but didn't confer with Hawke

because she didn't want to appear to defer to him in front of the smuggler. "If we take the three-day deal, how do you plan on getting us there?"

"Easy enough." Dorival shrugged. "I own some shipping stock on a freight line that does a lot of business in the Caribbean. An ocean voyage will get you into Havana, and I've got air transport from there to Denver."

Hawke liked the sound of that. Denver was the Free Range Zone, technically a sovereign state with United Canadian and American States, the Confederation of American States, and the Native American Nations involvement. The sprawl had been a smugglers' paradise for years, due to its association with the other regions.

"Denver's good," Flicker said.

"Denver is better than good right now." Dorival grinned. "Aztlan has been weak there ever since Ghostwalker kicked them out in 2062. That's as good a buffer zone as you can get from Aztechnology right now."

"All right," Flicker said. "Let's do that. How soon do we leave?"

Dorival spread his hands. "The ship sets sail at six in the morning. I've taken the liberty of making arrangements for you ahead of time. All you have to do is accept."

"We can do that." Flicker started to get to her feet, but Dorival held up a hand to stay her departure.

"Tell me about the young woman you have with you. Rachel Gordon."

Hawke didn't move, but mentally prepared himself for a firefight, thinking he needed to take out Artur first because the elf was the most dangerous man in the room. As if guessing what Hawke was thinking, Artur stared back at him, grinning broadly.

Flicker shook her head. "She's a package I'm holding for someone."

"Maybe I can pay you more for her, and offer you a way to disappear for a while," Dorival said.

"The same way you'd sell off cargo you were holding for a client to another client to get a better deal?" Flicker's voice was flat and her face was impassive.

Dorival's face flashed annoyance. "I would never do that."

"No, because a client has already bought your services, and those services and your word of honor are the only things you can put up for sale. I remember you telling someone that a few years ago. He didn't listen, and ended up dead."

Frowning, Dorival leaned back in his chair. "A contract should be binding."

"It is, and we're already locked in. We have a code, too."

"I understand. Pity. We could have both increased our profit margins."

"What do you know about her?"

Dorival gave Flicker a sad smile. "I'm sorry, but that information is directly from another client, and I am not at liberty to discuss it."

As he listened, Hawke wondered if they'd be better off making other arrangements to get back to Santa Fe.

"You have a client who knows we have the woman?" Flicker asked.

"No." Dorival shook his head. "If that were the case, I would be working at cross purposes. I simply have a client who asked me to keep a look out for one Rachel Gordon, in the event she came this way. I don't have a direct contract with anyone to provide information as to who is looking for her. That client will never know she—or you—were here."

He rose and offered his hand and Flicker rose and took it. "Good luck on your trip."

"Thank you." She headed out of the room, with Hawke following.

CHAPTER THIRTY-EIGHT

When Hawke found Rachel Gordon still asleep in the back seat of the pickup, his stomach muscles untightened a little. He knew he wouldn't relax any more until he was back in Santa Fe.

Professor Fredericks was still unconscious as well, though that was expected. He was going to stay more or less comatose for the next three days so he wouldn't be more of a threat than he already was.

Four sec men stood near the truck. A lean guy covered in tattooed sigils peered through the window at Rachel. His hard, vulpine face revealed hunger and a trace of fear. Neon tats swam across his scarred features. He held his right hand palm flat against the transplas. A shimmer spread out across the window, but didn't penetrate the barrier.

As Hawke neared the truck, he felt an uncomfortable and oppressive uneasiness that he recognized as magic usage. Nothing else ever caused the writhing, whiplike tremors that raced through his heart that he was currently experiencing. His hand dropped to the butt of the Predator on his hip.

"What are you doing?" he demanded.

The man ignored the question, concentrating on the sleeping woman. In the next instant, a multi-segmented creature as large as a German shepherd, sheathed in shiny, black armor, with at least ten legs and four leathery wings appeared, floating centimeters above Rachel. As soon as it manifested, a thin, long tail whipped around from behind it and exploded through the window, sending shards of transplas everywhere.

Yowling in fear, the man stepped back and grabbed his right hand with his left. The black creature crouched protectively above Rachel. Hesitating a moment, Hawke forced himself to keep walking to the truck.

The mage fell to his knees as blood dripped between his quivering fingers. Flesh dangled from his palm, and two of his fingers hung loosely. He spoke in a harsh language Hawke didn't recognize, and shimmering light spun and danced across his wounds. The blood flow slowed, and some of the mutilated tissue slowly pulled together.

Glancing up, tears running from his pain-filled eyes, the mage fixed Hawke with his desperate gaze. "What is that slotting thing?"

"Dangerous," Hawke answered. The hair on the back of his neck lifted as he stood less than a meter from the door.

The creature continued floating over Rachel, its feet resting on her now. Its clawed appendages didn't leave a mark on her skin. Ducking its wedge-shaped head under one wing, the thing cocked its gaze to watch Hawke with a dead-white pupilless eye.

Tentatively, Hawke reached for the door, gripped the handle, and tried to think good thoughts. With his hand on the handle, he paused for just a moment, then pulled the release and opened the door.

The thing opened a cruelly curved beak to reveal a barbed tongue that extended at least fifty centimeters before slipping back into its mouth.

"Easy," Hawke said in a soothing voice, not even sure if the thing understood him on any level. "We're all friends here. It's all null sheen."

Slowly, he slid into the passenger seat, and tried not to wonder if that barbed tongue could penetrate his reinforced skull. He carefully watched Flicker as she scooted behind the wheel because she had no such protection. Glancing over her shoulder, moving slowly, she released a tense breath and closed her eyes for a second. Then she opened them and remained still. "If it hasn't attacked by now, it's not going to."

Hawke hoped that was true. If it did come after them, he *might* be able to distract it enough for Flicker to escape, but he had no idea if he'd be able to follow.

The creature shifted, turning so it could keep both of them in view, as Flicker started the pickup. Wired reflexes online, Hawke kept watch over the thing in the reflection from the windshield. If it tried to attack either of them, he intended to try to stop it. If he couldn't, then he would try to destroy the artifact.

The truck blocking their retreat slid back into the alley, opening the street again. Flicker used the rear-view mirrors to back them into the opposite alley, then turned the truck around and accelerated.

A block from the smuggler's offices, the creature evaporated, leaving nothing behind. Only then did Hawke realize he was covered in sweat. He took a deep breath and released it.

"Hungry, *omae*?" Flicker's voice sounded only a little strained.

"Yeah." The last of their food had disappeared hours ago.

"I know a place near the harbor where we can get some authentic Brazilian food. I also know another place where we can get Matrix access so you can leave a message for the Johnson about the new timetable without getting us compromised."

"Sounds good. Let's contact Mr. Johnson first. That way we can enjoy the meal."

Games by Cabrice was a small shop on the other side of the sprawl from the import/export biz. The neighborhood was low-rent, filled with street skels, hard guys, and joyboys and -girls hanging out on the corners. The street was a twisting, potholed strand between single-story and two-story buildings that operated behind blackout transplas under neon ads.

Flicker parked two blocks down from the shop and set up watch with her remaining drones while she assembled others out of supplies she'd gotten from Dorival.

Hawke walked the two blocks with his hands in his coat pockets, which were cut out to allow instant access to the Predators. The street people noticed him, but they read the warning signs that said he was a man on a mission and wouldn't be screwed with and kept their distance. A couple joytoys of both sexes tried hitting him, but sidled away quickly enough after getting a good look at the expression on his face.

Although on full alert, Hawke couldn't help thinking about Rachel Gordon and the creature that had manifested to protect her. He didn't know enough about magic to know if a mage could track them through whatever it was. That thought was only slightly less unsettling than knowing the thing could apparently pop out of wherever it hung out when it wasn't on this plane any time it wanted to.

The fact that Rachel Gordon was still unconscious bothered him a lot, too. He didn't know if she would survive three more days in the shape she was in. For all he knew, the artifact was living off her life energy, and he'd be delivering a corpse by the time he got back to Santa Fe.

Of course, whoever was controlling Mr. Johnson might already know that.

He entered the shop, and a small silver bell over the door dinged once, a thin note that carried throughout the building. Gamer gear—cyberdecks, sim modules stacked with VR experiences and games, AR gloves that allowed the wearer to interact with the Matrix on a more "physical" level, and simrigs all mixed with tech Hawke didn't recognize—filled shelves and hung from boards on all four sides of the room. Dubstep club music slammed the walls.

"*Hoi,* chummer." The ork clerk was young and relatively svelte for her kind. Make-up blunted the protruding brow and brought out her sea-green eyes, which must have been cybered, because the color was unnatural. She wore her blonde hair in cornrows that made her pointed ears stand out even more. Her shorts and crop top revealed curves and muscle in equal measure.

Hawke approached the counter, noting the observation blisters on the wall behind her. From the way her right hand dropped behind the counter, he knew she was armed, too. He stopped just out of her reach.

"You know what you're looking for?" she asked. The light glinted from her fangs. "Or maybe you want a suggestion? *Crystal Phage III* just got released this week. So did *Milky Way Warlord.* That one's a multi-player RPG that allows you to build a galactic empire. Very wiz, in my opinion. Or if you want some simsense encounters, I've got a full range of history sensies. If you're looking for something more *playful,* I've got bootlegs of *A Night With Angelina McAdams.*" She smiled. "Lots of replay value in that one, I promise."

"I was told I could get private access here."

The carefree manner dropped from the clerk's face. "I don't know you."

"I don't know you either." Hawke placed an open credstick on the counter. "I was told you provided special services to people who had the right price."

She made no move to pick up the credstick. "The price isn't all that's required."

"The password's 'kestrel.'"

For a moment, the clerk held his gaze, then she nodded and reached for the payment. "I can hook you up."

CHAPTER THIRTY-NINE

Hawke used the simsense rig the clerk provided to make contact with Mr. Johnson. Although his body was riddled with cyberware, the idea of leaving his flesh while he took a joyride through the Matrix left him cold. The simsense rig didn't provide the complete immersive kind of experience with the settings he used, so he could still see/hear/feel everything going on around him.

He opened the commlink to the SIN Mr. Johnson had provided, knowing the System Identification Number was a false one. Chances were, they'd have to burn it after this use, and time spent on the connection wouldn't last long before it turned up as a fake.

The commlink buzzed for attention, and it went without being answered long enough that Hawke thought the SIN had already been burned and almost hung up. Finally, though, the connection went through.

"Hello?" The person at the other end was using voice-masking software.

Hawke's own voice-masking software was built-in. He gave the password they'd agreed on after leaving Tang's, then received the countersign. It still didn't mean he was talking to the Mr. Johnson he'd met. The man could have been replaced by design, or been intercepted. The shadows shifted constantly, so no one ever truly knew what was going on.

"Events have gotten sufficiently fragged on the recruitment drive that I'm gonna be a day late delivering."

"I've seen the stories." Even with the masking software, the speaker didn't sound happy. *"What happened?"*

"I'd ask you the same thing, but we don't have time for that." Hawke kept up with the passing seconds on his PAN. "I'll be arriving in three days. Do you still feel comfortable with the prearranged meeting place?"

"Yes. I think so. But I was given specific directions about the time frame."

"If three days doesn't work for you, just let me know, and the deal's off. There's plenty of other buyers for this package. I've already gotten a local offer."

The reply came immediately. *"No. Three days will work. I'll make it work."*

"Good. I'll see you then." Hawke broke the connection.

Clothed in darkness, Hawke sat in the small room Flicker had arranged in Caracas. He'd known getting her for the run was a good idea, but since things had gone sideways, she'd been even more solid than he'd thought she would be.

Or than she would have to be. That thought curdled inside his mind as he scanned the street through the west-facing window. A few pedestrians were out, mostly the sprawl's poor walking home after a late shift or partying.

On a threadbare couch, Fredericks slept, his mind blotted by the slap patches they kept administering to him. Rachel slept on one of the room's two beds. Like the professor, she hadn't stirred. Hawke had been worried when he and Flicker had been forced to carry her inside the room, but her otherworldly guardian hadn't made another appearance yet. IV bags attached to her arm kept her pumped with fluids and calories. Even then, he'd expected to see some negative impact on her physical health. But her vitals had remained solid. He felt fairly certain that was due to the thing that had latched onto her.

It was still there, hiding wherever it hid. Hawke felt its vibrations rattling inside his chest like the angry growls of a muzzled beast. He couldn't believe how sensitive he'd become to it.

A few minutes later, the pickup pulled into the alley beside the building where Hawke waited. He watched the cyberdeck stream images from the rigger's drones. Flicker was alone and carried food cartons. His stomach rumbled in anticipation.

The rigger had locked down the room using gear she'd salvaged from the drug lab site. The cybersec wouldn't stop anyone from getting in, but it would slow their entry and give plenty of warning.

The maglocks on the door clicked almost silently as they released, allowing Flicker to enter. She crossed the room and set the cartons on the small, square table marred by knife scars.

Flicker glanced at Rachel. "Still not awake?"

"No." Hawke stood, leathered the Predator he'd had sitting in his lap, and joined her at the table. The cooked meat smells and spices tickled his nose, and his hunger spiked. "She can make it three more days, but we need to keep her hydrated."

"Null sheen. I'll arrange for some more IV rigs to feed her meds and glucose. We'll keep her as healthy as we can." Flicker handed Hawke a plate and locked eyes with him. "We don't know what that artifact is. There's the possibility that she won't come back from wherever she's gone."

"I know." Admitting that bothered Hawke. He wasn't much older than Rachel Gordon, but he was certain he'd seen more of the world than she had. Now it was possible she wouldn't ever see anything else.

Unless she was somewhere in the astral realm. That thought concerned him, too. He wondered if Rachel was even now standing next to him, yelling at him in frustration to help her. Or maybe she was prey for astral beasts and predators. He'd heard about that, though he'd never experienced it.

"Mr. Johnson and his people probably have a way to deal with this." Flicker doled out the meal, filling Hawke's plate with *acarajé, bolinhos de arroz, empadinhas de palmito,* and *coxinha.* She passed him a bulb of beer and they sat to eat, keeping watch on their surroundings through the drone array.

Hawke popped an *acarajé* ball into his mouth, savoring the fresh shrimp, black-eyed pea, and onion concoction. The beer was weak, but it was cold and that was fine.

Flicker used a spork to cut into the *empadinhas de palmito.* The honey-yellow mini-pie split easily, revealing hearts of palm, sautéed onions, and black olives. "Something crossed my mind while I was out."

Lifting an inquisitive eyebrow, Hawke forked up a chunk of *coxinha* and ate the deep fried morsel. The chicken filling was made with catupiry cheese, not cream cheese, which was used in other places. It gave the savory snack a subtle but definitely different flavor. "What?"

"Why the Johnson wanted you to pick up Rachel Gordon at the dig in Guatemala, not at a hotel or in a sprawl."

Hawke shook his head. "Maybe no one knew about her 'til then."

"Or maybe Mr. Johnson wanted a package deal. Rachel and the artifact." Flicker picked up a *bolinhos de arroz* with her fingers and bit it in half. Parsley and onions showed in the rice fritter.

"There was no guarantee we'd get both."

Flicker regarded the sleeping girl. "Wasn't there? She and that thing have been inseparable since we recovered them. And we were told where to pick up the woman." She dove back into her food. "It's something to think about, *omae*. I'd hate to find out somebody's been jerking our strings from the start when its too late to do anything about it."

CHAPTER FORTY

Three days later, just as Dorival had promised, Hawke and Flicker landed in Denver. Also as promised, no one was waiting for them. Their arrival remained clandestine.

Before clearing the airport, Hawke arranged medical support for Rachel Gordon through an ex-CrashCart caregiver who'd gotten sideways with a superior who had then sabotaged his career. Hawke had received medical attention from the man during his CrashCart days, and helped set him up in the shadows after his dismissal. Other runners used him these days as well, and he operated private facilities in a half-dozen sprawls, always working through off-grid channels.

Fredericks was returned to consciousness and immediately demanded to be released or to see Rachel, who still remained in a coma. Ignoring his demands, and later his threats and pleading, Hawke parked the man under lockdown with a street samurai he knew.

"I don't like the idea of you going to this meet on your own." Flicker stood outside the door to the small hospital room where Rachel lay unconscious, monitored by several med devices—as well as some of the rigger's drones. "Especially not with me in Denver and you in Santa Fe."

"Mr. Johnson came looking for me," Hawke said. "The guy knows me. Maybe he doesn't know you. If that's the case, I wanna keep it that way." He gazed back inside the room where Rachel slept. "Besides, somebody's gotta keep an eye on the goods."

"I know." Flicker leaned against the white wall and crossed her arms. Despite the relative quiet of the last three days, she looked worn. "What do you think Mr. Johnson's going to do if she's still like this when we hand her over?"

"Pay us. A deal's a deal, and I'm not settling for less than I was promised." Hawke nodded at Flicker. "See you soon."

Flicker wrapped her arms around herself. "Take care of yourself."

"I always do."

At 2318 hours, two minutes early to the meet in Santa Fe, Hawke braked his Yamaha Growler dirt bike to a halt in an alley across the street from the Hellstorm Club and lowered the kickstand. He removed the helmet and hung it just behind the motorcycle's large gas tank.

The desert outside the sprawl was filled with abandoned mines that hollowed out large sections of the Sangre de Cristo Mountains and cut through the Pecos Wilderness. When the mining had played out, smugglers set up underground supply runs. The go-gangers protected their retreat routes with anti-aircraft fire and booby-traps in the tunnels. Hawke knew the area well.

Wearing temporary tattoos, and dressed in road armor he'd bought from a fixer when he first hit the sprawl, Hawke knew he blended in with the locals. Go-gangers frequented the Hellstorm Club, and most citizens knew to stay out of the area.

Deep-throated roars of designer machines and heavy rolling stock blasted between the two- and three-story buildings on either side of Zelazny Avenue. All of the structures sported the flat, pueblo-style roofs. That architecture, Spanish Pueblo Revival, had been enforced in the sprawl since 1912, and reinforced with a later zoning ruling in 1957. The NAN, particularly the Hopi and Zuni tribes, had added their own unique artistry to the area with bright colors and designs woven into storefronts and neon signs.

As he crossed the street, Hawke automatically shifted into the go-ganger swagger that would help him blend into the environment. His jacket bore the colors of the Eye-Fivers out of Seattle. If challenged by any local talent, Hawke would claim his visit was to duck heat from Knight Errant while catching up with some local friends and looking for side work to cover his food and housing. The story would hold up for the next hour or two, but he planned on being long gone before then.

By then, if the meet worked out, Rachel Gordon and her black phantasm would be someone else's problem, and Hawke and

Flicker would split a fat recovery fee.

He looked forward to that, and tried not to wonder what would happen to the young woman. She wasn't his responsibility. Flicker was right about that: Rachel Gordon had her own problems, and Hawke wasn't about to take them on. Surviving in the shadows meant staying away from anything more than temporary responsibilities, and having only quick, infrequent partnerships as the need arose. His life was about moving fast, lethal when he had to, and staying small in the shadows. He didn't take on permanent relationships.

And no matter where Rachel went, it had to be an improvement over letting her fall into Azzie hands. He'd brought Flicker into this fragmire, and owed her an escape route and a payoff, if that could be arranged.

As if sensing he was thinking about her, Flicker spoke in his ear. *"I've got drones covering the street to keep an eye on you, but I'm getting a lot of interference from black ice covering the local hubs and the high usage in the area. My coverage is spotty at best. If I was there, it might be better."*

"Understood. We'll work with what we have."

"I'll try to get inside the club's security, but if I can't, I'll watch through the windows and walls whenever I'm able."

"Just keep an exfil route on deck for me." Hawke wasn't expecting trouble, but too many players were after Rachel Gordon to think everything would go smoothly here.

"Null sheen, omae. I've got your back." One of the small drones buzzed Hawke, reminding him she was there, then it flew high and disappeared against the light haze.

Industrial metal blared through the club's batwing doors. Pushing through them, Hawke filtered his audio pickups as he slotted an open credstick for the troll bouncer minding the entrance.

"Enjoy, chummer," the big street sam growled. He flew the deep purple and black of the Ravens, one of the NAN biker gangs. "Careful with the Cactus Water."

The local brand of alcohol had a small but dedicated following, and was carefully policed by the go-gangs. If bad batches of hooch got out, blindness, nerve damage, and birth defects trailed afterward. And the stricken were usually dead before sobering up, either killed in a fight or just flatlining. Since most of those victims tended to be bikers, the go-gangers watched the suppliers.

Inside, the bar occupied the wall to the left, and a balcony ran the length of the back of the room, overlooking everything. A raised stage along the right wall featured a six-piece band with synth instruments. The lead singer was a delicate-looking female elf with a flared raspberry Mohawk tipped in white and showing a lot of skin. Her baritone vocal cords had to be cybered, or maybe it was magic, because her voice was huge. She sang in German and sounded menacing and depressing. The crowd of bikers and hangers-on threw themselves at each other in a frenzy on the dance floor.

Above the writhing mob, a holo of a mechanical buffalo herd ridden by go-gangers charged across a mesa and leaped into the air. A scarlet haze of novacoke vapor streamed up from many of the dancers, adding its pall to the holo.

Hawke circled the room, staying away from the dancers and deftly avoiding the servers. When he reached the other side, he went up the stairs and discovered Mr. Johnson sitting at a small table against the back wall in the shadows. He had to have paid a small fortune for the spot, which was a noob move, because people would remember him.

The man wore casual clothes, but still couldn't fit in with the crowd. Two go-gangers had already posted up on him, in case he turned out to be a fed trying to infiltrate. Instead of being dismayed by the presence of the enforcers, Hawke felt buoyed by their proximity. That meant no one else had set up on the Johnson. The man hadn't attracted rival corp attention.

Yet.

Hawke slid into a chair on the other side of the table. Mr. Johnson frowned at him, started to object, then looked again, seeing Hawke for who he was at that point.

"You made it." The relief in his voice seemed heartfelt.

"I did. This is gonna be quick."

Nearby, three sec men in street clothes shifted in the loose triangle they used to keep Mr. Johnson under observation. Mr. Johnson tilted his head and subvocalized a few words. The sec men remained at a distance, but still on overwatch.

Mr. Johnson looked around in confusion. "Where's—" He stopped.

"Not here." Taking care to not be seen, Hawke drew one of his Predators and sat with the weapon in his lap. Even with the go-gangers and sec men keeping watch, he wasn't taking any chances.

Mr. Johnson shook his head. "I don't understand. You can't just show up here empty-handed. We had a deal."

"We still do. I've got your package, but I want to set up a drop to make the exchange."

"This *is* the drop. I've got a helo waiting nearby." Mr. Johnson's face reddened, and his voice turned coarse.

"She's in a coma."

Mr. Johnson's face turned white. "You hurt her?"

"Not me. That artifact she's saddled with is responsible for that." Hawke had no other culprits in mind for Rachel's continued lack of presence. Whatever the stone was, he was convinced it was keeping the woman out of the loop for the moment.

"The—*artifact*."

Although Mr. Johnson tried to sound casual, Hawke knew the man was in the dark about what was truly going on. His deception suite agreed with his assessment. Mr. Johnson had *not* known about the artifact. That was disappointing, because it told Hawke there were a number of other things the man wouldn't know.

Mr. Johnson put his hands on the table and interlaced his fingers. He leaned forward and tried to sit taller, but there was no way he could match Hawke in a size competition. "People are not going to be happy with the way you just hijacked this operation. You were told that time was of the essence, and you come here, tonight, a day late."

"I'm still alive, and I've got your package. The way I scan it, that's a bonus."

"The people I represent are *not* going to be happy."

"What *people*?" Hawke pinned the man with his gaze.

Cowering a little in spite of himself, Mr. Johnson drew back slightly. "Don't worry about other people. You're dealing with me."

"Fine. We also need to talk about my fee."

"Your fee has already been established."

"You led me to believe this was a simple recruitment effort." Hawke tapped the table top with his forefinger, underscoring his words. "It wasn't. I drew fire from Aztechnology and a mercenary group put into the field by NeoNET." He name-dropped to see if he could get a reaction out of the man.

The corp names didn't seem to faze Mr. Johnson. "Once you go south, you know you risk dealing with Aztechnology."

"Your package was in Guatemala—smack in the middle of Aztlan. What's more, the Azzies were already watching the dig site, and they had a large team sitting there, ready to capture the package when the word came down. That tells me the job's worth more than you're paying me. Add the NeoNET presence as well—especially since they funded your package on the dig—and I got promoted to the big leagues without being told." Hawke glared at the man, remembering all the near-misses he and Flicker had survived over the last few days. "Now I want big league pay."

"I don't know anything about that." Mr. Johnson ran a hand through his hair, brushing it back from his forehead. "I'll have to talk to my people to get you an answer."

Hawke nodded. "That's fine, but tell those people that mercs are out hunting for their goods while they choose to haggle over a few more credits."

"It's not going to be a few more, though, is it?"

Hawke smiled, but there was no mirth in his expression. "No, it's not, but I get the feeling they can afford me. Whatever that artifact is, it has to be worth a lot. And there's a reason—maybe more than one—your boss or bosses didn't go after the package themselves, and chose to send someone like me. Whoever it is will pay."

"When should we—?"

A hole suddenly appeared in the back of Mr. Johnson's hand as he brushed at his forehead again. His eyes went wide, the black pupils expanding to drown the irises like tide pools pulling in flotsam. Sitting there, he quivered, then scarlet leaked from behind his damaged hand and ran down the left side of his nose to drip onto his chin. Already dead, he went slack and toppled forward.

CHAPTER FORTY-ONE

Spinning into motion, his wired reflexes coming online, and the world slowing down around him, Hawke threw himself to the floor, Predator clenched in his fist, before Mr. Johnson's corpse hit the thin carpet. Adrenaline fired through him as his gaze swept the club.

Two of the sec men scanned the room while the third crouched low and headed for Mr. Johnson.

The surrounding club patrons had no clue what was going on, and just eased away from Hawke 'til a young ork in metal-studded leather froze in his tracks and dropped to the floor. The guy gasped and choked on blood gushing from his mangled throat where a large caliber bullet had plowed through flesh and bone. Like the first shot, Hawke hadn't heard the second over the pounding beat.

Now realizing a threat was among them, the crowd ducked for cover like herd animals fleeing a predator. Several pulled heavy caliber pistols, looking for the shooter. Hoarse screams and curses filled the air. The raucous music played on, rocking the building's interior.

Hawke took solace in the presence of Mr. Johnson's sec men. He wouldn't be the only one looking for the shooter, and they'd both provide cover and confusion. The downside was they'd be watching over him as well.

The sec man beside Mr. Johnson laid a hand on the side of the dead man's throat. Mr. Johnson stared up at the ceiling. A small, neat hole wept a slow trickle of blood.

"You!" the sec man roared. He was human, a combination of steroid and cyber, a meat shield and heavy bruiser who got paid for fighting other people's fights. Plastic surgery had turned his

features into average, brown on brown. He was a component that could be placed anywhere and fade into the background till he took action. He pointed a silencer-equipped Hammerli 620 pistol at Hawke. "Drop your—"

Hawke shifted his hands slightly, keeping the sec man's attention there, rolled to his side, then kicked him in the temple. Immediately unconscious, the sec man slumped beside Mr. Johnson.

"Hawke?" Flicker called over the commlink.

"I'm busy."

Scrambling back, Hawke reached Mr. Johnson's side and ran his free hand through the corpse's clothing, hoping for a commlink or anything he could use to get more information.

A short distance away, one of the remaining sec men took three bullets to the chest, but remained on his feet. Either his subdermal armor hadn't been compromised, or chems slamming through his body kept him up and moving. He extended a Colt Cobra TZ-120 and snapped the folding stock out, then fired at figures taking cover beside support pillars on the other side of the room. Hawke didn't know if those figures were assassins or club security or paranoid bikers, but they were trading shots with the sec men.

Finding nothing on the dead man, Hawke rose into a half-crouch and looked for an escape route. He rapped a fist against the window behind him and discovered that it was reinforced transplas, bullet-resistant and bombproof. He'd need major explosives or an anti-tank missile to get through it.

That left the entrance and exits on the first floor, all of which would be heavily guarded and would form chokepoints that would work in favor of any hostiles surrounding the building. Hawke had no way of knowing how deep the opposing numbers ran, but with corps involved, he guessed the effort would be more than a skeletal team.

If the target had been Mr. Johnson, the hitters weren't giving up. Either Hawke had been on the list with him, or the assassins were looking to add collateral damage to make a statement.

"Hawke–" Flicker tried again.

"I need that exfil *now.*" Hawke stood and grabbed the sec man closest to him, yanking him off balance. The guy had been shedding bullets like raindrops. Synthskin ripped away from the bodyguard's face, exposing the steel beneath. He looked more machine than human.

Distracted, the sec man swept his free hand back while his other continued firing the Cobra. Hawke ducked the blow and hustled the sec man toward the steps. The big man's body vibrated when struck by the incoming heavy caliber bullets, but none appeared to do any significant damage.

"Let go, you fragging drekker!" The sec man swung another punch, then started to come around with the pistol.

Hawke chopped the man's wrist with the barrel of his Predator. The impact didn't knock the other man's weapon away, but it did block the blow. A bullet smashed into the sec man's forehead just over his right eye, and rocked his head back on his thick neck. By then Hawke had him to the stairs.

The man's foot moved out from the first step, found nothing, and he toppled over. Hawke raced down beside the falling man tumbling down the steps, knowing he was in the open now and speed was the best defense he had. More bullets caromed off the stairs, rails, and the dead man's armor.

"*Stand by for exfil.*" Flicker's voice was tight but controlled. "*Ready for overlay feed.*"

"Bring it online." Hawke experienced a split-second disruption in his vision, then the drone feed came through. The angle told him Flicker's drone had entered the club and was angling for the high ground to give him a complete view of the area.

Two guys in biker leathers took aim from the second floor. Hawke didn't know if they were part of the hit team, but they were definitely gunning for him. Bullets cut the air around him. He put two rounds into the first man's bearded face and watched him stagger back, either mortally wounded or momentarily sidelined.

Reaching the bottom of the stairs, Hawke pushed and shoved through the crowd, feeling bad when bystanders took bullets meant for him, but knowing he'd gotten caught in crossfires himself on occasion. Someone who went to places like the Hellstorm had to expect to get blown up at some point. That was just how the odds played out.

"*Exfil through the back of the building,*" Flicker said. "*The club owners have a private exit there.*"

"And they'll have security to protect it." Hawke angled for the bar. He used his forearms like battering rams, colliding with people and knocking them out of his path when they didn't clear quickly enough. Bruised flesh and broken bones gave way before him. Pained yelps and curses trailed him.

A pair of heavy caliber rounds thudded against his back, but flattened on his bulletproof armor. Hawke kept running toward the bar. One of the bartenders swung around to face him, bringing a stubby Enfield AS-7 combat shotgun to bear.

CHAPTER FORTY-TWO

Wrapping his free hand around the short barrel, Hawke pushed the shotgun aside just as the bartender fired. The barrel heated immediately, but Hawke stubbornly held on. Riding out the recoil, he pulled the weapon forward, but was unable to wrench it from the bartender's grip. Instead, he stopped his momentum and shoved the shotgun back into the man's face.

Nose broken and streaming blood, half-dazed by the impact, the bartender stumbled back into his partner, who was turning toward him. Hawke spun, chambered his right leg, and fired it into the first bartender's chest, driving him into the second. Both went down in a tangle of flailing limbs.

Through the drone's view, Hawke spotted three men heading toward him. Their paths were direct and simple, and they shot anyone who got in their way. One of them went down in a hail of bullets fired by one of the club's enforcers, but the other two killed the shooter with combined machine pistol fire.

Then the lead gunman, a human dreadnought much like Mr. Johnson's sec man, turned his attention back to their intended prey. He fired two short bursts and the bullets peppered the wall of liquor bottles behind Hawke, sending broken glass and alcohol tumbling to the floor.

Hawke leathered his Predator and double-fisted the Enfield. The 8-gauge combat shotgun had a 24-capacity drum slung under its barrel. He aimed at the lead gunner and fired twice. Instead of double-ought buckshot, the shotgun was loaded with ceramic slugs designed to render impact damage without penetration. Against bulletproof clothing or subdermal armor, the slugs delivered sledgehammer blows.

Struck in the chest and face, the assassin broke his stride and dropped to a crouch. The second man veered from his direct approach and triggered a new volley of rounds that left long scars in the bartop.

Hawke dropped below the bar, still able to watch his opponents through the drone interface, and crouch-walked to the far end. Near the corner, the PRIVATE door sat partially ajar. Without pause, he slammed a shoulder into the door and drove back the guard taking cover there. Hinges shrieked as they tore free of the jamb.

Whirling as he entered the room, which turned out to be a small kitchen outfitted in plasteel, Hawke leveled his captured shotgun at the man sprawled on the ground. Burly and bearded, the go-ganger reached for the pistol he'd dropped during the collision.

Hawke blasted the pistol. The ceramic slug shattered on impact, but the weapon spun across the floor out of the man's reach.

"Don't," he warned.

The go-ganger held up his hands in surrender and broke eye contact, becoming immediately submissive. "Just doing my bit, chummer. Working for the cred. No personal investment. I'm done."

The three cooks here had already hit the floor. All of them wore casual jeans and tee shirts bearing the Hellstorm Club logo. They were wageslaves, no fighters among them.

"Through the kitchen," Flicker directed.

"If this comes out into an alley, they'll have people there." In spite of his own concerns, Hawke headed for the kitchen's back door.

"You're not going into an alley." Tension tightened Flicker's words. *"And the alley wouldn't be a concern anyway. Someone's got a private helo hovering over the club. I'm trying to identify it now."*

"That's the Johnson's ride."Hawke cursed as he burst through the next door and discovered two go-gangers standing watch over a door to the right. Both men immediately pointed their weapons at Hawke.

Ducking and bringing up the Enfield at the same time, Hawke pumped a rapid salvo of shots into the men's center mass, not wanting to kill them because they were—relatively—innocent bystanders here. The ceramic slugs knocked both men back into the wall behind them as the detonations blasted through the room.

"There's a rooftop access panel to your left on the ceiling," Flicker said.

Hawke looked and spotted the panel. Three metal rungs stood out on the wall. "I see it."

"Go up."

Crossing to the rungs, Hawke dropped the Enfield and climbed fast. The ceiling panel was locked, but it broke open the second time he slammed a fist into it. He scrambled up, hearing the coughing men recovering behind him as he heaved himself up into the darkness, throwing the panel closed behind him. The access tunnel ran straight through the second floor, where another panel barred his exit. Bracing himself, he drove his fist into the locking mechanism again and again.

Through the drone's vision, he kept an eye on the two gunmen headed in his direction. Three other men, probably a back-up team, followed them. Pausing briefly at the door he'd broken through behind the bar, they rushed into the kitchen, which was now empty, then into the next room.

The two recovering go-gangers barely had their weapons in hand before the new arrivals opened fire and cut them down. Hawke redoubled his efforts to break open the sturdier roof hatch. Finally the lock shattered and rained broken pieces down into the room below.

Drawn by the falling debris, the gunmen crowded under the ceiling access. Hawke barely shoved himself through the opening before bullets ricocheted off the access tunnel's sides. He hit the pebbled rooftop and rolled, then pushed himself to his feet and drew one of the Predators as he swept the area for opponents.

The loud *whop-whop-whop* of helicopter rotor blades closed in on him. Flicker transferred the video feed from the drone inside the club to one she had flying nearby in the night. Hawke picked up the helo in the dark sky just before an infrared searchlight fell over him. His vision suite alerted him to the increased light spectrum.

"Move!" Flicker yelled. *"To the west side of the roof!"*

Hawke sprinted and heavy caliber bullets pounded the pebbled roof in his wake, dogging his heels. As big as the Hellstorm Club was, he ran out of space quickly. "Flicker—"

"Jump. There's a delivery truck parked in the space below you."

Trusting his partner, Hawke reached the building's edge and leaped, picking up the solid top of the truck five meters out. He waved his arms and legs to keep his balance, couldn't, and hit the truck's roof on his side. His breath rushed from his lungs, which felt like they were on fire, and his senses spun, but he managed to get control of his wild skid across the metal just before he dropped off the side.

He landed in a crouch on the ground. Bullets from the helo's machine gun ripped through the truck like it was made of paper.

"North," Flicker said. *"Along the street. I'm running the Growler over to you now."*

As she spoke, Hawke spotted his motorcycle rounding the corner at a sharp angle, the rear wheel drifting almost even with the front tire as it powered through traffic.

Pushing out from the truck just far enough to spot the helo adjusting its position overhead, Hawke raised the Predator and fired four quick shots at the transplas bubble where the pilot sat. The bullets wouldn't penetrate, but getting shot at was still a distraction, and the helo jerked in reply.

Then the helicopter instantly turned into a roiling orange and black fireball. Hawke registered the looping contrail of a surface-to-air missile launcher fired from somewhere on the other side of the Hellstorm Club. Either one of the go-gangs had struck back at the interloper, or there were two groups of heavy hitters on-scene.

Pieces of the destroyed helicopter rained down in flaming bits around Hawke and the street as the Growler skidded in his direction. He holstered his weapon and caught the motorcycle's handlebars, pulling himself atop the machine while it was still moving.

"I've got it," Hawke said, transitioning control from Flicker between heartbeats. He leaned over the handlebars and twisted the throttle. The motorcycle shot down the street, weaving easily between the confused traffic trying to get out of the area. He accelerated again, heading for the safety of the smuggler routes. A brief glance at the rear-view mirrors showed no evidence of pursuit.

But it would be coming. Hawke was certain of that. He just wasn't certain what he was going to do about it.

CHAPTER FORTY-THREE

In the dream that wasn't quite a dream, Rachel knew she was in terrible danger. Even though she was aware that she was sleeping, or something close to that, on some primitive level she was certain that if she died here, she would be dead everywhere.

Just . . . gone. That scared her more than anything she'd ever known.

She hid under a rocky overhang that reminded her of the broken land in Guatemala, but the terrain spread out a few hundred feet below her wasn't anywhere in Aztlan. At least, it wasn't in the Aztlan she knew. Maybe at some later date, after a drastic climate change or genetically modified organism got loose, the entire world would look like this. Doomsayers had been forecasting an apocalypse along those lines for decades.

Instead of the normal rain forest fanning out below her across the tall hills and deep valleys, a vast, towering jungle unlike anything she had ever seen—*except maybe in my dreams*—covered the broken terrain. The land lay in cracks and sharply angled pieces. There was nothing soft about it. From the destruction that wasn't covered by jungle and brush, it looked as though something huge and monstrous had run rampant through the whole area.

Or perhaps monstrous *things* had warred here at some time and left this ancient battleground behind to be claimed by the encroaching jungle that was slowly filling the scars.

The thought made Rachel shiver, even though the temperature was hot and humid. Her clothing, khakis and a fitted pullover she remembered from her early college days, stuck to her skin. She wore a ball cap. When she took it off, she discovered it was from Tufts University, where she'd gotten her undergrad degree. She pulled it back on and scoured the countryside again.

Creatures roved the jungle. Only *creatures* wasn't quite the word she was looking for. These things that crawled and scampered and ran weren't like anything she'd ever seen. They looked like—prototypes of later animals. Scales covered most of them, but a few furred things leaped from branch to branch in the trees.

"Part of you knows this land. Some piece of you remembers this."

The voice came from inside Rachel's head, "loud" enough that it hurt. Startled, she shifted on the ledge, sending a handful of scree pouring down the steep incline. Even though the voice mixed with her thoughts, something told her it was close to her.

She spun, rising from her hunkered position to stand. She wished she had a weapon, the staff she sometimes used in the brush, or even a camp knife. Anything would have been better than standing empty-handed before the thing that stood behind her in the cave mouth.

Covered in iridescent scales that looked green at first glance, then blue at another, the creature stood more than three meters tall. Its massive head, shaped like an ax blade, bobbed low between its pointy shoulders to avoid contact with the rough, white limestone ceiling. Virulent red eyes sat on either side of its narrow face. Its arms and legs were too short for the long body, but the limbs were thick with muscle. Faded gray scars stood out against the beautiful scales.

"You recognize this place on some level, don't you?" The thing cocked its head at her, fixing her with one crimson eye.

Rachel didn't try to answer. She couldn't. *This is a dream. Just a dream. Wake up!*

"A dream?" The thing laughed, the growling, gurgling noise sounding like rocks banging together. *"This is no dream, Rachel Gordon. This is a warning."*

"A warning about what?" she asked.

"That change is coming. That your life will no longer be the same. That you must accept the loss of your old life, and embrace what is yet to be if you are going to survive."

"Who—who are you?" Rachel had to struggle to keep her voice from cracking. "Where am I?"

"Where you are now is not important. It is what you do here that matters. I am a messenger. You have nothing to fear from me." Raising an arm, it gestured at the world beyond the cave's mouth. What looked like a cloak hung down from its shoulder and disappeared in the shadows of the cave. *"What you have to fear lies out there."*

"What do I have to fear?"

"Those things that would kill you."

"Why can't I wake up?"

"Because sleep is necessary at this point. You must rest in order to be renewed."

"Are you talking about Aztechnology? Are they who I'm supposed to be afraid of?" If that was the case, Rachel already feared the corp. Actually, she didn't think she could be more fearful of it. Memory of the firefight in the Guatemalan caves had haunted her for however long she'd been asleep. Occasionally, she'd heard bits and pieces of conversations between Hawke and Flicker, and sometimes from Professor Fredericks as well. But none of that made any sense.

She wanted to turn back time, to when things were clear and simple. She wanted her life back, wanted to read musty tomes and sort through gigs of edata on pottery and botany and ancient peoples. She wanted history to be times that were long gone, that couldn't hurt her.

She didn't want whatever *this* was.

The thing turned its head and fixed her with its other eye. *"No. Humans are a threat, but there are greater menaces you must be aware of."*

"Are you talking about the artifact?" Although the jewel intrigued her, Rachel would have gladly given it up. Well, maybe not gladly, but she would have traded it for control over her life.

"Cling to the artifact as it clings to you. It will give birth to you, Daughter. Only then will you be strong enough to take care of yourself. You will have powerful enemies awaiting you after the dreams. You will need to become powerful, too."

"What are you talking about? What do you mean?"

"Now that you are revealed, you cannot hide." Dark light glinted in the thing's eyes. *"You cannot hide here, and you cannot hide in that other world."*

"Where am I?"

"In the womb. Growing stronger."

"How do I get back?"

"When you are strong enough, then you will go back. Until then— you must survive." The thing unfurled curved wings and leaped for the mouth of the cave.

"Wait!" Rachel trailed after the creature. Her boots wobbled over broken pieces of rock and almost went out from under her. She regained her balance by placing a hand against the rough rock.

The creature leaned out into the sky and took flight centimeters beyond her reach. A dark shadow fell across it almost immediately, alerting her to the predator in the sky above.

A nightmarish cloud of pale corpse flesh floated right above the cave mouth. Putrid and bloated, it had dozens of arms and tentacles hanging from its lower half. Above that, a massive, bulbous blob held a horrific face that looked like it had been beaten into the fleshy physique. The features were childlike and the maw moved constantly, opening to expose jagged, broken teeth that poorly fit the huge mouth.

Awed, filled with razor-edged shards of fear, Rachel pulled back into the cave. She forgot about the winged messenger as the bloated form turned toward her. The face looked childlike, though stripped of innocence, but its two huge, staring eyes held dark malignance.

Waving its arms and tentacles, the bloated thing wheeled much more quickly than Rachel would have guessed. It swung on its axis and dove, keening like a horribly wounded thing as it closed on her.

In full flight now, Rachel hurried backwards, tripped, and hit the ground. She lifted her hands and feet to fend the thing off, but knew that would only delay the inevitable. It was going to devour her. Tears streamed from her eyes as she shivered in shock and terror.

Then, incredibly, the bloated thing filled the cave mouth and could go no farther. Realizing it was stuck, the creature screamed again, the horrible noise echoing throughout the cavern. Glistening hands and tentacles reached for Rachel, and she regained her senses just in time to scramble back to avoid capture.

Gathering her feet under her, not knowing where to go, she turned and fled into the darkness at the back of the cave.

CHAPTER FORTY-FOUR

On the bed, Rachel Gordon suddenly arched her back and screamed through the oxygen mask covering her nose and mouth. The machines connected to her flatlined and went dark as she fought her restraints.

Seeing her distress, thinking the young woman was in her death throes, Hawke started forward. He didn't know what he could do, but he had to do something.

Without getting out of her chair, Flicker put a hand against his chest with enough strength to get his attention. "Easy, *omae*. There's nothing you can do."

"She's dying!" Hawke protested, but didn't fight past Flicker's barrier.

"No, she's not." Flicker removed her hand. "She's done this before. A few times. If you touch her, that thing comes out to defend her. Trust me, you won't enjoy the experience." She touched the bruised swelling on the side of her face and turned her head to reveal scratches along her neck that looked like they'd been made by talons.

Abruptly, Rachel went limp and dropped back onto the bed. The machinery came back on with a chorus of chirps, and the readouts resumed functioning. As it did that, a team of nurses and a doctor filled the room, but they didn't try to touch their patient either. Evidently they had learned things the hard way too, because a few of them also showed bumps, abrasions, and bruises. They waited for a little while, checked the machinery, and took their leave.

Hawke took a breath and tried to relax. Even a few hours later, he was still adrenaline-maxed from the debacle at the Hellstorm Club. "This happened before?"

"A few times."

"What's causing it?"

Flicker shook her head. "It's nothing physiological. Whatever's triggering this is coming from inside Rachel."

On the bed, the young woman looked worn and pale. Her blood pressure had dropped.

"Whatever was holding her steady is losing its grip," Flicker said. "Maybe it can't keep up with the demands Rachel needs to fight whatever she's battling." She looked at Hawke. "We need some outside help. The doc here has some astral people. They've been able to monitor some of the activity going on in Rachel's mind and body, but not all of it. None of them have seen anything quite like this." She paused. "It's almost like she's possessed or something."

Hawke rubbed at his chin tiredly. He'd been thinking the same thing. "Do they have any recommendations?"

"No."

"I might know a guy." Even as he thought that, Hawke recoiled from the idea. He'd dragged Flicker into this situation. He didn't want to pull anyone else in.

"I think you should get him."

"I don't want to get anyone else involved."

"Then you should get the doc to give her a lethal dose and end this."

Hawke turned to stare at Flicker. She returned his gaze full measure. "I'm serious. For you. For me. And for her. One way or another, this needs to end."

Hawke didn't say anything.

"But you're not going to do that, are you? Because killing innocents isn't part of who you are." Flicker's small smile held no humor, only sadness.

"No, it isn't."

"Then you can leave her somewhere. Contact NeoNET or Az-technology, and let them know where to find her. If you want, you could let them both know and let them fight over her."

"No."

Flicker nodded. "Because even if either of those corps know how to fix what's wrong with her, she might as well be dead. They'll take what they want and jettison the rest as soon as they have it."

Hawke knew that was the truth.

"You won't kill her, and you won't give her up. And every

minute we just sit here without working toward resolving this situation is another minute we get closer to being in some corp's crosshairs—and she gets closer to dying."

Hawke knew she was definitely speaking the truth.

Flicker took his hand in hers. "We need help. That's what it comes down to."

Trying to think, Hawke searched her aquamarine gaze. "You know I've always worked with one or two runners at a time. Only for short times. That's a rule I've had since I started in this biz."

"I know. Stay small and hard to find. I remember. I've done that too, Hawke."

"It's what's worked for us."

She looked up at him and squeezed his hand. "It's not working anymore. This . . . whatever it is . . . is too *big.* If we're going to deal with it, we've got to get bigger. For starters, we need someone who can get inside Rachel's head, in spite of that artifact. Or just help us *understand* that fraggin' thing better."

Hawke wanted to just turn away and leave, get some alone time and get his thoughts together. Better than that, he wanted to take Flicker and start running.

"If we run," the rigger said, as if reading his mind, "we'll never stop. However this works out with Rachel and the corps looking for her, they'll still want to bury us because we know more than they want us to. Or they'll think we do. So we've got to deal with them from a position of power. The only leverage we have is helping Rachel."

Hawke looked at the young woman in the bed, saw the pain on her face, but maintained his silence. His thoughts spun and collided, returning again and again to the idea that he'd filled out their death certificates, and the corps were closing in to sign off on them.

"We know Aztechnology is involved," Flicker went on. "Neo-NET. And there's a third party, someone the Johnson was working for. He's dead, and whoever he was working for is still out there, expecting us to come through with Rachel. But even if we could find out who hired us, I don't think we can trust them."

"Neither do I." Hawke breathed out. "Like I said, I know a guy. He's wiz with astral stuff, and he lives for problems that don't have simple answers."

Flicker nodded and smiled. "Yeah, but we're going to need more. We need a decker, somebody who can get into the Matrix and see what's there that none of these people want us looking at."

"I know someone like that, too." Hawke took another breath and tried to relax as his personal paradigm shifted. He couldn't go back to what he was. He'd changed the minute he'd accepted this run. He just hadn't known it at the time. "We'll need more muscle, too. Some cyber and some mage stuff, because this is gonna get really nasty before it's over. And there's another woman, someone who might be good with the cultural history that's probably attached to this artifact." He paused. "I can get us a team, but nothing's ever gonna be the same."

"I knew that before you did." Flicker released his hand. "Get whoever you need. Bring them here and let's deal with this. It's the only way we're getting out of this alive."

On the other side of the room, Rachel Gordon arched up again, this time floating completely off the bed, and nearly pulling the heavy unit from the floor. The med machinery around her winked out.

Hawke resisted the urge to go to the young woman's assistance. Black lightning flashed in her hair as it billowed out from her face.

"I've got this," Flicker said in a tight voice. "I don't know how long I have it, but you need to go."

"Take care of yourself 'til I get back. I'll send people as I get 'em." Hawke left the room and didn't look back. The game lay ahead now, and he was staking everything on his ability to get the results that would save all of them.

CHAPTER FORTY-FIVE

Six hours later, traveling under a SIN he'd "borrowed" for the day, Hawke debarked from a flight to Louis Armstrong International Airport, met the gypsy cab he'd arranged for, and rode into the major smuggling hub of New Orleans. Goods from foreign countries came through here into the CAS, and other goods went out from every North American country to the rest of the world.

He surveyed the landscape while the cab crawled through heavy traffic toward the French Quarter. He wouldn't get into the neighborhood, but he'd get close enough. He didn't intend to let the Middle Eastern cab driver know what his true destination was anyway. That would be foolish.

Hawke liked New Orleans. He'd worked here often, usually on in and out runs. Work that needed a new face. With his skin color, he could pass as just about any race in the sprawl. He enjoyed the wild times here, the food and the people. The only other place he liked so well was Brazil during Carnival season.

Once the cab let him out on Canal Street, Hawke walked into the Quarter. On the average city street—especially somewhere like New Orleans—he fit in everywhere in jeans, a pullover shirt, and a hoodie.

Outside the Quarter proper, Hawke stopped at a brightly colored food truck with *MR. WIGGLES* painted on the side in half-meter tall letters. The mascot, a pink and purple soap bubble creature, showed a happy grin with big teeth.

Hawke scanned the LED menu board posted beside the serving window, waited for a half-dozen customers before him to get their food, then ordered spicy wings and grilled broccoli.

A matronly woman pushed a credslot toward him.

"Herve around?" he asked.

The woman didn't blink. "No. Herve not here today."

"Too bad. I heard he had a little friend he wanted to show me." Hawke slotted his credstick, knew the total was going to be for a lot more than just the food and drink, and took the bulb and Styrofoam tray the woman handed to him.

The tray was warm in his hand as he walked to the alley behind the food truck. He stood and ate, watching the street and sidewalk traffic, knowing he was being watched. By the time he finished the wings and broccoli, as good as he remembered, a ten-year-old boy on a bicycle rolled past, quickly handing off a pizza box he carried in his handlebar basket.

Hawke took the handoff in a smooth turn, pulling the flat box to his chest and walking on down the alley. He stopped beside an overflowing Dumpster and opened the box. The katars inside weren't as good as his personal weapons, but they'd do. They even came with a holster that fit over his back. He removed the hoodie, pulled the blades on, and slid the Cavalier Evanator into a specially constructed holster at the small of his back. With the loose hoodie back on, everything was nicely concealed.

The people at *Mr. Wiggles* offered a customized full meal deal for traveling mercs. Hawke had used them before.

Not feeling so naked now, he walked toward the Quarter, taking his time so he wouldn't arrive 'til after the sun set and the club doors opened.

By the time he reached Bourbon Street, the nightly party that was New Orleans was in full swing. Crowds of locals and tourists rubbed shoulders along the sidewalks and streets where traffic had all but came to a standstill. Jugglers and dancers performed for nuyen slotted by passersby. Many people wore masks and costumes. Blues music enhanced by wiz synthesizers blared out over everything.

Laissez les bon temps roulez.

Let the good times roll.

In spite of the tension boiling through his belly, Hawke smiled. New Orleans was one of those sprawls where he couldn't help but feel alive. Of course, every time he'd been here, he'd ended up running about two steps ahead of death.

Hawke threaded through the crowd, which was difficult for

someone with personal space issues. He almost had his pocket picked four times: twice by kids, once by a clumsy guy whose fingers Hawke broke when the guy tried pulling a knife, and once by an old woman who was a lot faster than she looked. Hawke didn't take any of it personally. They were just street dips getting by. They'd just picked the wrong mark to lift from.

In one of the alleys off Bourbon Street, not far from a voodoo shop watched over by two unblinking zombie heads mounted on the door, Hawke reached the doorway to an inner courtyard. A sigil in the form of a skeletal snake occupied the space above the solid wood door at the entrance.

Not liking what was about to happen, Hawke reached up and tapped the snake's head. The thing moved swiftly, pulling back and sinking its fangs into the back of his hand. He ignored the pain, didn't move, and let the animated skull drink its fill. If he hadn't, the snake would have pumped him full of a paralytic and sounded an alarm.

When the snake was satisfied, it pulled back and lay along the wall above the door again. Bones clicked into place, and a lock somewhere inside the door *thunked.*

Cautiously, Hawke placed his hand on the door and pushed. The man he'd come to see was careful, and was always changing up the spells that protected his home. Hawke couldn't even imagine trying to live somewhere consistently. That trait alone had almost made him cross the man off the list of runners he did business with.

But Remy "Snakechaser" Bordelon was New Orleans born and bred, and he'd led two lives there, neither one far from the other. He'd joined the police and became a homicide detective, but never strayed from his roots as a voodoo practitioner. When he'd gotten kicked off the force for something he'd done but the internal affairs division couldn't prove, he'd continued his investigations as a private detective, and rose to the rank of *houngan asogwe*, high priest. Now he worked both the mean streets and the astral side of New Orleans.

Hawke continued into the courtyard. Low wattage lights punched holes in some of the shadows throughout the ten-meter by ten-meter space. Flowering plants and shrubs filled the space with pollen-heavy perfume. The stone brick floor lay even and straight, all original materials from more than three hundred years ago. Spanish, French, German, and Italian feet had trod those stones in times past. Sometimes Snakechaser said he could almost reach out and touch the people, back through all those years.

Inside the courtyard, the music playing in the bars and buildings framing the open space was somewhat muted. Hawke walked through the wrought-iron tables and chairs that sat in three different groupings.

The Bordelon family had owned the block for generations, first as freedmen in the 1830s. They'd lived with the city, riding out the good times and the bad, pouring their blood and magic into keeping it safe. Now only Snakechaser was left to carry on that heritage.

Hawke gazed up at the second floor room where the man kept an office and his private quarters. The surrounding businesses rented from him, providing a solid financial foundation.

Soft, yellow lights glowed inside the windows. Hawke followed the wide stairs up to the second floor. As he reached the top landing, shadows shifted in front of the door.

Two large men stood in front of Snakechaser's door. Both were dressed in combat leathers sporting green and black 40Leg Jamaican krewe markings. The 40Leg was a large centipede known for its venomous bite. Legend had it that if someone bitten by the 40Leg didn't kill it, he would feel pain every time the centipede moved.

"What chu doin' up 'ere, waste mon?" The bigger man nearer Hawke stepped forward and reached inside his jacket as he boomed the challenge. His short hair hugged his round face. Gold hoops pierced his eyebrows, nose, and lips. A neon tattoo of a 40Leg flashed a semi-circular pattern around his right eye.

"I jus' lef' a party an' got lost." Hawke blinked blearily, like he was drunk, knowing something was wrong because these weren't the kind of men Snakechaser would have hanging around outside his door. "I was followin' a woman . . ." He blinked and looked around again as if searching. He didn't know if the ruse would work. It was thin, but it was all he had. "'Ave you seen 'er?"

Through the window blinds, Hawke glimpsed Snakechaser lying on his office floor. Three other men stood around the room. All of them wore 40Leg colors, and Hawke was certain Snakechaser had gotten himself sideways with the Jamaican gang—and was a few moments away from getting himself dead.

CHAPTER FORTY-SIX

"'ey." The big ganger took another step forward and drew the silenced Remington Suppressor machine pistol from his hip. "You. Waste mon. 'ey."

Hawke stared at the man as he slurred, "Are you talkin' to me?" and got another step closer.

"Ain't seen no woman. You got turned 'round. Get on now. Get on back to your party. You only be gettin' yourself trouble if you stay 'round 'ere." The man waved his free hand in a shooing motion.

Wired reflexes online now, Hawke grabbed the hand and twisted, torquing it so the man had to roll with the motion or get it broken. He cursed, yelled for help, and tried to bring the Remington into play.

Stepping forward, using his momentum and his body, Hawke caught the ganger's weapon with his other hand and twisted sharply. Bone snapped and the pistol came free, fitting in Hawke's fingers like it belonged there. With his arm thrust forward, one foot behind the first ganger's left foot to keep him off balance, Hawke pulled the pistol into target lock from less than a meter away and put three silenced rounds through the second ganger's head even as he clawed for his weapon.

Thwip! Thwip! Thwip!

The first ganger untangled his feet and set himself, growling curses edged with fear. He fisted Hawke's hoodie and tried to smash his forehead into the runner's jaw. Hawke lifted his head to dodge the blow, then slid back. He cracked the pistol butt against the neon 40Leg tat hard enough to leave a depression in the smashed orbital.

Hawke gave the man cred, because he tried to stay in the

fight. He grabbed Hawke's gun wrist and wouldn't let go. Hawke torqued the captured hand again, breaking bones in the man's wrist and fingers with wet *snaps*. Overcome by pain, the man lost his focus and his grip, allowing Hawke to slip the Remington under his chin and fire two rounds.

Hot blood sprayed over his face and clothing as the bullets tore through the man's brain and blew off the top of his skull. Hawke let the dead man drop, knelt next the body, and removed two fresh magazines for the Remington. He glanced into Snakechaser's office as he dumped the partially-used mag from his captured weapon and fed a new one in.

Wired reflexes making everything smooth and fast, Hawke stepped toward the French doors at the front of the office. He glanced at the lock and saw it was open. Filmy gray curtains presented a flattened, colorless image of the room's interior.

Snakechaser remained on the floor. Hawke detected no wounds or blood, and realized whatever was going on inside the office was on a different plane than the one he was privy to.

He opened the left door and swung it inside, following with his captured pistol raised before him. A long-bladed ceiling fan stirred the air around inside the building, but didn't do much to combat the humidity. A massive teak desk with carvings of old gods and monsters occupied the back of the office, just behind Snakechaser's prone body.

A handful of oil paintings of various New Orleans and Mardi Gras highlights hung on the walls. All of them had been done by Snakechaser. If he hadn't become a cop and *houngan*, he could have been an artist. One of the most striking paintings was of the tarot readers clustered in folding chairs along Jackson Square with Café du Monde in the background. Snakechaser had been working on the painting the day Hawke first met him three years ago.

In the painting, wispy figures drifted up from the readers' cards and Baron Samedi, his feathered top hat in place, his face painted like a skull, and a cigar between his teeth, hovered over the readers with his arms spread wide. Somehow, Snakechaser had caught magic in the oils, and the mocking sound of Baron Samedi's laughter always echoed inside Hawke's head whenever he looked at the painting.

Putrefaction warred with the thick scent of the flowers outside the office. Inside, the stench of death ruled, rolling off two of the gangers in waves. They stood behind the third man, who stood like a statue less than a meter from Snakechaser.

The third man was in his seventies, perhaps older. His withered skin hung loosely on his face, and his hands were scaly and liver-spotted. Thick, gold rings encrusted with jewels glinted in the office light. He wore an expensive suit that might have fit at one time, but now hung on him like a linen sack. Waxy burn scars in the shape of a jawbone hollowed the emaciated cheeks.

The two men at the rear turned to face Hawke, who cursed when he realized what he was up against. He'd seen reanimated corpses before, and even fought briefly against one in a run a few years ago, but he'd never been this close to one before. According to word on the street, *bokors*—and sometimes *houngan* who skirted the dark side of voodoo—used their art to tie spirits of the newly dead they controlled into fresh corpses for a time. The spirits were usually echoes, like badly copied versions of an original program, but they were still dangerous.

Porcelain jesters' masks covered the zombies' faces, putting false smiles on the dead features, but there was no mistaking the stench or the reason for the mottled flesh. They moved more quickly than Hawke expected, and he guessed that was because the spell that bound them was fairly recent, or the *bokor* that had created them was exceptionally strong.

Maybe both.

He leveled the Remington and put three rounds into the head of the zombie on the left. Decayed brain matter evacuated the shattered skull and the thing slowed in its approach, lurching to the side and blocking Hawke's field of fire on the second zombie. Running up the back of the first zombie, the second leaped at him.

Hawke got two rounds off, but both only smacked into dead flesh, not the thing's head. The zombie collided with him, knocking him back and shattering the French doors as they smashed into them.

Landing on his back, Hawke felt the wind whoosh from his lungs. The zombie leaned down to snap at him. The mask prevented any contact at first, but the teeth clacked together behind the porcelain layer. A moment later, the jester face shattered, leaving the zombie's ruined and disfigured face only centimeters from Hawke's.

CHAPTER FORTY-SEVEN

The thing lunged at him again, trying to sink its yellow teeth into his flesh. Hawke had heard some zombies spread infection, depending on how they were created. Virus-born zombies carried sickness and death in their veins for anyone they injured. Even some of the magically generated zombies could infect living beings with the corruption, if they'd been made with magically-enhanced bacteria.

Hawke arched his back and lifted the thing away enough to shove his arm under his attacker's chin. The zombie bit the Remington and tore it from his grip. Heaving again, Hawke pushed the animated corpse off and rolled to his feet.

Just as quickly, the zombie got its feet under it and stood. Without hesitation, it came at Hawke again.

Not wanting to use his own machine pistol because it wasn't silenced and would bring law enforcement, Hawke shucked his hoodie and drew the katars. When the zombie reached him, Hawke sank his left blade into the thing's chest to hold it at bay, then cut off its left arm. As the limb thumped to the floor, he shifted and swung again, taking off the zombie's remaining arm just above the elbow.

The undead creature swung at Hawke with its stump but only succeeded in spreading a little of the stagnant fluid that remained within the body. This corpse must have been taken fresh from wherever it had been found, because the liquid was blood, not embalming fluid.

Yanking the embedded katar to the side, Hawke tripped the zombie. Without arms, his attacker couldn't keep its balance and smacked face-first into the hardwood floor. Teeth embedded in the flooring, standing like a miniature Stonehenge. Before it could get up again, Hawke slashed it across the back of its thighs, cutting ligaments and leaving it crippled.

A quick stab to the base of the zombie's skull returned it to death. Hawke wasn't sure if the interruption of the revitalized neurons disrupted the reanimation spell, or if the second brain death unfettered the spirit that had been bound to it. Either way, it was dead. Again.

Breathing faster, his enhanced lungs a bellows inside his chest as they kicked into action, Hawke turned to face the third man. He didn't know whether to keep the katars ready or try for the silenced pistol lying on the floor a few meters away.

Spinning without a sound, like he was on ball bearings, the old man turned to Hawke. Full-on, he realized the guy was older than he'd first thought. The man might have been in his nineties, or even older. The burn scarring, lighter than the ebony skin it lay on, completed the outline of a skull face, including upper and lower teeth charred into the man's lips.

Hawke lifted the katar, defying the sudden urge to run that rose within him.

The man pointed a bony finger at Hawke, then his mouth opened and blood gushed forth, spilling out in a torrent. Without a word, he toppled to the floor as his sunken eyes registered a brief moment of surprise.

Behind the crumpled corpse, Snakechaser sat up and roped his long arms around his knees, heaving a sigh like he was incredibly tired. He was short and stout, his shoulders broad and thick. His short hair curled tightly to his scalp. A chinstrap beard framed his strong jawline. His slightly rounded face was handsome enough that he was a favorite with the ladies. He wore black slacks and fitted black pullover that showed off his powerful physique. His golden eyes were startling.

"*Hoi*, Hawke. Long time, no see." Snakechaser smiled as he got to his feet like it was a normal day, and he didn't have dead men scattered around his office and outside his door. "Why don't we take this surprise visit somewhere else?"

"From the sound of it, I think you're right about this young woman being possessed." Snakechaser leaned back in his chair and surveyed the partiers on the main floor of the club they'd retreated

to. They had a back booth, away from the main ruckus. Snakechaser had a knack for getting preferred seating. His gold eyes—
natural, not cybered—roved constantly.

Someone who didn't know Snakechaser would have pre-
sumed he wasn't listening or thinking about much at all. Familiar
with enough cops, and with the *houngan* himself, Hawke knew
that wasn't true. He rolled a shot glass in his fingers.

"Can you help her?"

Snakechaser flicked his attention back to Hawke. "*Mon ami*,
you know that is a question I can't answer until I've seen her."

"Would you be willing to try?" Hawke continued before
Snakechaser could reply. "I don't have enough cred to pay you, so
all I can offer is a share of the profits."

"Profits from what?"

Hawke shook his head. "I don't know. Gotta be something
big, though. The Azzies are interested. NeoNET, too. Somebody
else with deep pockets. And I haven't even tried to find other buyers yet."

"No loyalties to whomever your Johnson represented?"

"None whatsoever. I got handed something a lot bigger than
I was prepared to take on."

"But now you're refusing to let go."

Hawke hesitated. "The woman, she didn't ask for any of this
either."

"At least, you don't think she did."

"She got set up by her mentor."

"That's what really bothers you about this, isn't it? That be-
trayal by someone you're supposed to trust."

Hawke didn't want to answer that question because it was
hitting too close to home. When he'd first gotten into the shadows, he'd gotten paired with a man named Hargrove. From what
Hawke had later found out, Hargrove had been with one of the
big corps, a hatchet man for when things got badly slotted or
someone was put up against the wall.

Something had gone wrong, and Hargrove had been tossed
out. A kill squad had been put on his trail. Still in his teens, Hawke
had been living on the streets doing strong-arm stuff when Hargrove found him and brought him into the biz.

"You're a natural at this stuff, chummer, but you have a long
way to go if you want to survive. I can teach you." Hargrove was a
lean blade of a man who'd been vain enough to leave a little gray

at his temples. He'd worn a goatee when he could, but his appearance had changed for every run.

For three years, Hawke had followed the man and learned everything he could from Hargrove and the other runners they did biz with. Hawke had taken in every lesson, every run, and made it his own.

Until the day when a run had gone badly, and Hargrove hung Hawke out to dry. Badly injured, almost dead, Hawke had managed to survive. When he went looking for Hargrove, he found his old mentor had disappeared, sucked into the shadows.

Hawke hadn't ever told Snakechaser the whole story. The man was gifted enough to pick up most of it through a cop's observation skills and his own magical ability.

"If you're going to do this, *omae*," Snakechaser said softly as he watched Hawke from the corner of his eye, "you're going to have to be truthful with yourself. You can't go into this much firepower without being solid as to why you're doing it." He pointed at Hawke with a forefinger. "If you've never listened to me before, youngblood, listen to me now."

Slowly, Hawke nodded. "I'm doing this for her. To get her out of whatever slotted-up situation she's in."

Snakechaser held up that same finger. "And you don't even know if you *can* do it."

CHAPTER FORTY-EIGHT

Bristling with anger and frustration, Hawke glared at Snakechaser. He thought he had the man figured out for the most part, but this surprised him. "You don't think I should do this?"

"That *we* should do this?"

The pronoun made Hawke feel better immediately. "Yeah, *we.* If I'm just wasting your time, let me know."

"I didn't say that." Snakechaser paused while the young male server plunked down fresh drinks and went away. "Those dead men Crazy Mary's cleaning out of my office right now? Do you know how they ended up there?"

Crazy Mary was a crime scene cleaner Snakechaser had used on a New Orleans run that Hawke had been part of. The ork woman was ancient and had limited imagination, but she was wiz at making even trace evidence disappear. She'd shown up at Snakechaser's office as they were leaving, like she'd already had an appointment.

"No," Hawke said.

"A cousin was having trouble, and asked if I could help out. You know I can't turn down family."

Cousin didn't necessarily mean blood relative. To Snakechaser's way of thinking, everyone in the sprawl who had been born into the area was related to each other. He'd even made a case for it once by having Hawke pick someone off the street. If the person had been born in New Orleans, Snakechaser and they had family together no further back than five or six generations. According to Snakechaser, that was close enough to consider them family.

"This cousin," he continued, "she had a baby recently. The father was Champagne Sonnier."

The name didn't ring any bells for Hawke, and he shook his head.

"Oh, you'd have known Sonnier, *mon ami.* He was strictly a low-level street tough waiting to get his ticket punched. A few months ago, one of Mary Jo Doonan's enforcers done for him down in the Lower Nine, when Sonnier tried to hijack a shipment."

Hawke had heard of Doonan. She was a rogue CIA agent who ran a big part of the sprawl's smuggling enterprise. She also wasn't known for her charity.

"The only thing worthwhile that Sonnier ever did was get himself killed and father one of the prettiest little girls you could ever wish for." Snakechaser smiled, the expression genuine. He liked kids, and kids liked him. That ease with those relationships was one of the reasons Hawke wanted him to work with Rachel Gordon.

"That *bokor* in my office was Big Eel Sonnier, a legend in the 40Leg krewes, and Champagne Sonnier's great-great grandfather. Champagne was Big Eel's last living relative, because good luck and common sense seemed to wither up and breed out of the Sonnier family a long time ago. Champagne was being trained to take over the family business once the old man died. Except he liked to moonlight too, which is what got him killed. After that, Big Eel all out of family like he was, he came after that little girl."

"She's one of your cousins, too."

Snakechaser grinned and spread his hands. "Family. You see what I'm talking about, don't you?"

Hawke nodded, knowing it made sense in Snakechaser's view of the world. "You interfered with Big Eel's efforts to get the child."

"I did. All the way up to tonight. And now my cousin and my littler cousin don't have to worry about that evil man anymore." Snakechaser sipped his drink. "A lot of people don't need to worry about Big Eel anymore. It works out for everybody."

"What does that have to do with me?"

"I'm saying you're going to need people to do this. Especially if the corps are trying so hard to find her."

"I'm getting a team together."

"Who do you have?"

"You, if you're in."

Snakechaser nodded. "I'm in. You're family too, *mon ami.* A cousin. But whoever else you bring in, they have to have your interests close to their hearts as well. It can't just be about the nuyen."

That made Hawke uncomfortable. "It's not going to be like that. I keep people at a distance. You know that."

The *houngan* grinned again. "Sure you do. You keep telling yourself that. You came into my office tonight, stepped right into a mess of troubles I had, and didn't bat an eye."

"I batted an eye. I even thought about leaving."

Snakechaser laughed. "It would have been all right if you did. I was in the astral, ready to lower the kibosh on all of them. You just saved me some effort, is all. If I could have been taken by those people, you don't need me." His face grew more serious and the golden eyes brightened. "You need me, and you need more people like me. They're out there, and you know them. Reach out. There are people who like you."

For a moment, Hawke remembered Deckard, and the way things had gone at Tang's. "Not everybody likes me."

"So don't ask those people. Problem solved." The smile returned, and Snakechaser's gaze held steady. "What are you looking for? Maybe I can help connect you."

"I'm going to be moving around a lot, using thin SINs, and some big corps are sniffing around trying to find me. First person I'm going to need is someone to watch my back."

"Muscle." Snakechaser nodded. "Definitely. Who do you know?"

Hawke hesitated. Runners kind of knew of each other in the shadows, but they didn't like their names—real or false—jandered around without real reason.

"I've worked with Hammer Bresnahan and Franchise Klee. And Twitch Liu. All of 'em are good in a bad spot."

Snakechaser shook his head. "I know Hammer. He's good. I've heard of Klee. Also good. But I've worked with Twitch. She's fast and lethal, but she can be . . . arbitrary."

"I know, but I've never known anyone whose gun-fu was so strong. I've only worked with her once, and she leaves an impression."

"Good *and* bad. There's a reason you've only worked with her once."

"I know. She's not my first choice."

"She wouldn't even be on my list, *mon ami*."

CHAPTER FORTY-NINE

"I'm not the first person you came to, am I, mon?"

Twitch hauled in the one-man sailboat's mylar sail with prac-ticed ease, dropping it down the mast to the boom. Wearing only a blue-and-white horizontally striped bikini that accentuated the golden honey of her skin, thin and underweight even for her pe-tite frame, she looked relatively helpless on the four-meter long vessel, but she knew what she was doing. "It's okay. You can tell me the truth."

"No, you weren't." Hawke had spent sixteen hours tracking the others down, only to receive no joy. He stood on the small plascrete dock above the bobbing Sunfish sailboat and watched Twitch batten the hatches. Being on the dock made him some-what uneasy, because it shifted underfoot with the incoming tide. Ocean waves slapped against the rocky shoreline only a few min-utes away.

Farther inland, the regular beach crew hung out along the shoreline. Fishermen occupied other docks and used multiple rods to troll the sapphire waters. Places where the coastline was too harsh and broken had palm trees and brush growing right up to the edge. A few other sailboats and a couple old cruisers cut through the waves along the horizon.

Negril's economy was wobbly at best, fluctuating with the slim tourist trade still hanging on and with smugglers delivering goods to Miami and other ports along the CAS. The illegal trade was strictly small-time, but it remained profitable.

Twitch shrugged, and didn't seem to take offense at Hawke's admission. "I couldn't reach a couple other guys." He was brutally honest. There was no other way to be with Twitch. She could de-tect a lie effortlessly, and her skills were all natural.

Glancing over her shoulder, Twitch shot him a wry grin. She was Chinese by way of Jamaica, so she looked Asian with her small body, skin tone, and ebony black hair that hung past her shoulders. Even her SIN name, if it truly was so, seemed too big for her. Twitch suited her better than Jessie Liu. But her natural accent was totally unexpected: pure Caribe, mon.

"Hammer's been busy lately," she said, "and Franchise got harpooned by Lone Star in Atlanta last week. He'll get out, but not in time if you need him fast."

"They were my first picks."

"They would have been mine, too." There was no animosity in her words. Twitch always spoke the truth, no matter how bad it got.

"I need someone fast, but I want someone good."

"Evidently you didn't want to work with me."

"I didn't go to you first. I'm here now. Nobody's as good at close-in gunfighting as you are." Hawke paused, wishing she would face him, but not really knowing if that would make this any better. After the last time, he'd never expected to see her again. "You scare me, Twitch. I like a run to go smoothly. With you, that doesn't always happen."

"Life is a loose ping-pong ball in a room filled with mouse-traps. I hate it when things are too cut and dried. I like to kick loose. Can't blame me if I like to live in the moment, mon."

"I can if you get someone killed."

Her voice tightened then. "I've *saved* people with you, Hawke. No one has ever died because of me."

So far, Hawke thought. But he didn't say it because that would have been a full step over the line.

"But you're here now." Twitch raked black hair out of her face with her fingers.

"I am."

Squatting to tie the sail to the boom, making sure she was turned so that he took in all her curves and recognized she was a woman, Twitch smiled up at him. She was a tease, and she knew her small stature put people off guard, and in just that moment of distraction that bordered between lust and guilt, she could kill three men. Hawke had seen her do it with a holdout pistol no bigger than her tiny, closed fist. Just *bam bam bam*; a rapid syncopation that had ended lives.

Finished with the boat, Twitch picked up a small bag with

built-in flotation and reached up to Hawke. He took her petite hand and pulled her onto the dock. She was surprisingly strong and athletic. In addition to being a crack shot, she was an incredible gymnast.

"What's the run?"

"I'm still working out the parameters."

"Okay, what's the payoff?"

"I'm still working on that as well."

She took a pair of dark sunglasses from her bag and slid them on, then scrunched up her nose at him in a frown. She looked about twelve. Except for the curves. "I gotta be honest, mon. Doesn't sound like something I'd be interested in, and I ain't sayin' that just to drek all over your day."

"It's dangerous. Kill teams from two corps, including Aztechnology, are after me. Possibly a third corp involved as well."

One of Twitch's eyebrows lifted over the bridge of the sunglasses. "Ooooh, you know how I like danger, mon." Excitement wiped out the look of disapproval. "Have you talked to Jovi about this?"

Jovi was Twitch's wife and the love of her life. She was a fixer, managing goods—legal and smuggled—and runs. She stayed far back in the shadows, and managed Twitch's business affairs.

"I did. Otherwise I would have never found you."

"But you didn't tell her everything."

"She's a fixer. She doesn't *want* to know everything. That's part of her guarantee for anonymity. And part of her protection."

"Wiz." Twitch looked up at Hawke. "I suppose we need to leave right away."

"Chron's ticking on this one. Every minute makes things just a little more dangerous. And I've still got to pick up more people."

CHAPTER FIFTY

Twitch and Jovi kept a small cabin in back of Savann-la-Mar. Standing in front of the bulletproof and soundproof window that pulsed the image of an empty room when viewed from outside, Hawke gazed down the hillside at the sprawl. The metro area was small, and the country's history still showed in the old lighthouse and the stone-and-mortar fort built sometime in the 18th century.

Most of the houses were older, two-story affairs painted in bright colors. Many had been converted into tourist shops with personal quarters on the second floor. People thronged the narrow streets, gathering around markets and street musicians.

Hawke liked the look of the country and the sprawl, but it wasn't home.

"So, Hawke." Jovi's dulcet voice was educated, but there was no mistaking that she'd been born in the islands. "I didn't think our paths would cross again. I wasn't hoping I'd never see you again, mon, but I don't think I would have minded. Yet here you stand."

Hawke turned and reached for the tea his nose told him Jovi had carried in with her. The small cup and saucer almost disappeared in his big hands.

Hawke took no insult over the words. Jovi was as straightforward as Twitch. "I didn't think I'd be here either, but I need her."

Jovi studied him coolly, without expression. She was a person who studied people like she had all the time in the world. When she had the time. And she never once thought she knew everything about someone. People were constantly a source of interest to her.

Where Twitch was small, Jovi Alexander stood almost one point eight meters tall. Her Jamaican ancestry showed in her long limbs, the kinky hair she cut into a short block style, and her flawless, dark mocha skin. She was careful with her makeup, accentuating her eyes and drawing them out instead of burying them in color. Like Twitch, she was in her late twenties, and liked to flaunt her figure. She wore a yellow and black tiger-striped sun dress that cut high across her rounded thighs and plunged between her modest breasts.

Twitch was in the back bedroom, packing, leaving them a few moments to talk.

"How is she?" Hawke asked.

Jovi flashed him a flirty smile. "She keeps me happy."

Feeling a little uncomfortable at the deliberate overshare, Hawke sipped his tea. "Congrats on the wedding. I missed that."

"Null sheen. What we do isn't exactly socially based. Our wedding was small, just for us. You have a private life." She raised an arched brow. "I assume?"

Hawke ignored that. "I need to know if she's solid, Jovi, because the situation I'm getting her into has left a lot of bodies behind already. She's going to be walking onto a battlefield with me."

The flirty smile disappeared. Jovi took her own cup of tea to a small loveseat and sat, crossing her legs. Hawke heard the smooth glide of skin. "Sit. We have a few minutes. She has to say goodbye to her guns."

"You see." Hawke sat and managed not to spill his tea. "That's one of the things that worries me."

Jovi laughed, a delicate tinkling that shouldn't have come from someone so big. "I can't imagine you worried."

"This is what worry looks like on me. After last time, I wasn't going to work with her again."

"Yet again, here you are."

"Because there's no one else I know who's as good. I need her, Jovi. I need her to be the best she can be. I don't want to take her out there just to watch her flame out. Not because she can't help me do what I want to do, but because she's special."

"She is that, mon."

Hawke waited and watched the woman. His deception suite didn't pick up any micro expressions, but Jovi was good with lies when she had to be. "I need you to be straight with me."

"I am." Sighing sadly, Jovi dipped her tea bag a couple times into the hot water, then took it out of the cup and set it on the saucer's edge. "She's solid. She hasn't been out since the last time she went with you. She knew she had problems, and she knew she needed to work on them. We got some help for her. She's gained weight, learned to sail, and hasn't killed anyone since that last run."

Hawke stepped back through that, realizing the last run he'd used Twitch on had been fifteen months ago. "That's a long time to go without work."

"She doesn't have to worry about the financials. I take care of that. She could take off another year and be just fine. Without me helping out."

Twitch had never been one to spend credits. She was a minimalist, a trait Hawke understood. Life came with too much baggage. The trick was to get rid of as much of that baggage as possible.

"But she needs the work. She can live here quiet and small with me, spend her mornings out on the salt, but she needs that excitement. Watching her lately has been like watching a caged bird. It ain't natural for her not to live at least some of her life on the edge."

Jovi locked eyes with Hawke. "I've tried to get her to let go of it. I want her to let go of that life. I'm the only reason she's stayed here this long. That, and the fact that nobody will take a chance on her." She bit her lip. "No, that's not true. There are people who would take her, they've come around, but they would use her. She'd be out there on her own."

"She's going to be out there on her own with me, and I've never been this deep in the drek before. You need to know that."

"I understand what you're saying, mon, but the thing is, you bring people back when they're out there with you."

Not all of them. Maybe that loss showed on his face, or maybe Jovi just knew the score.

"Not all of them. I know that. I'd be a fool to think there weren't some losses. But you don't intentionally leave a chummer out there alone." Unshed tears showed in Jovi's eyes. "I have to let her go because she needs this, but I don't want to. You're the safest bet I can make, Hawke. Don't let me be wrong."

Hawke didn't know what to say to that, and he was saved from having to say anything when Twitch returned. She wore canvas capris and a flowered top, not looking anything at all like the Twitch he usually knew. A small hat sat at a jaunty angle on her head.

She smiled. "Everybody through talking about the crazy girl, hey?"

"No one said you were crazy." Jovi frowned. "And I thought we agreed nobody was gonna use that word around here."

"Hawke wasn't here for the rules. I thought maybe it might have come up while you were talking."

"No," Hawke said.

"When do we leave?"

"I've chartered a plane to Miami. I don't want to wait 'til morning to get out of here."

"So we can leave right away?"

"Yeah."

"Good, because sitting around waiting to go would be hard." Twitch walked over to Jovi, hugged her, and kissed her tenderly. Then she stepped back. "Don't worry about me while I'm gone."

"I won't." Jovi's voice cracked only a little. "I never worry about you. Make sure you drop messages."

"I will." Twitch walked out of the house, and Hawke spotted some of the old swagger he remembered in the roll of her slim hips. She knew he was watching, but she was thinking more about what lay ahead of them.

Twitch was the only person Hawke knew who loved the idea of walking into a fight. He put his tea down, nodded a final good-bye to Jovi while trying not to see the tears in her eyes, and followed the gunslinger to his rental car.

CHAPTER FIFTY-ONE

Although Flicker couldn't see exactly what the *houngan* was do-ing as he sat at the foot of Rachel Gordon's hospital bed, she *felt* some of the power coursing through the room. Or maybe she was only creating the sensation in her mind because the lights over-head dimmed every now and again.

But there was also the *shimmery* movement in the air around the two of them. Flicker had seen that before when dealing with mages. She didn't ask questions. Even if Snakechaser chose to answer, she wouldn't understand how everything he was doing worked.

She didn't know what to make of the man. She'd never heard of him, and wasn't versed in voodoo in any way, but Hawke had said he—and *she*—could trust him with their lives.

At this juncture of everything going on, everyone who got brought into the run was getting trusted with her life.

Flicker had to admit she didn't like that, and she totally un-derstood what Hawke was getting at when he'd dug in his heels about getting more manpower. Every member added to the crew stripped away another layer of concealment.

It has to be done. She told herself that again and again, till she'd lost track of the number of times. *You don't want to walk around with a target on your back.*

That was if she even got to keep walking around at all. There was no guarantee she'd leave their present hideout alive. She had sources out in the world, fixers who watched developments in the corps, and who kept their eyes on the blackboards where run-ner info flowed like a twisting sewer. Runner intel was corrupt; truth and lies and every mixture between, twisted and turned and inflated and conflated. There was no way to know whether some-thing she found there was even true.

But every now and again, a crumb leaked onto the Matrix that a runner could use. Flicker kept watch, but she was looking forward to getting someone really wiz who could peel back the real secrets on the Matrix. Hawke had promised he knew a guy.

The lights darkened for a moment again, and the med decks controlling the equipment that kept Rachel stabilized winked out for a second. The med hardware reset with shrill beeps and chirps that grated on Flicker's nerves. She needed to get out of the room, but she couldn't because there was nowhere else to go.

Through it all, Snakechaser sat singing in a low voice, some tune that Flicker couldn't understand, yet somehow felt she might have known from somewhere. He rocked slightly on his haunches, head back and eyes closed. Occasionally, he shivered and looked like he wanted to back away from the girl on the bed—or whatever had bound itself to her. Then he would dig in again, and another shimmer would pass between him and the girl.

Flicker didn't want to watch, but she couldn't look away.

Rachel ran through the jungle. She had gotten lost in the darkness of the cave until, by chance, she'd found herself back at the entrance. The bloated thing was gone from the cave mouth, no doubt hunting something else to cram into its maw. She wasted no time clambering down the mountainside, following a thin trail worn in the stone that she'd had to look hard for to find in the first place.

The forest floor wasn't any safer, due to the flying and crawling and slithering predators there, but as long as she stayed beneath the thick branches and leaves of the trees, she was hidden well enough. There were also clusters of berries and a small creek of clear water that meandered over the rise and fall of the landscape.

Not knowing where else to go, she'd headed down, hoping to find a civilized place that would tell her where she was. Tall blades of grass came up to her waist, and she gave wide berth to all fallen trees after discovering the nightmarish, fist-sized parasites living within them. She didn't recognize them, was certain she'd never seen them before in her life, but they also looked strangely familiar.

Even now, she couldn't remember what the things looked like because her mind refused to see them again, but she knew they were horrible. A cluster of them had been feasting on the bloody ruin of—something. She hadn't looked closely enough to figure out what it was.

"This is your test."

Rachel stumbled and fell, catching herself on her hands, almost slamming her face into the doughy ground. Her fingers slid through the mud and wetness as she glanced around wildly, searching for the source of the voice.

The ground ruptured as tentacles burst up from the earth around her. Easily as long as she was tall, they whipped around as if searching for her. Viscous liquid dripped from thorn-laden maws lining their undersides, opening and closing hungrily.

Rachel scrambled to her feet even as one slapped around her left ankle and yanked, now long enough to lift her off the ground. She dangled, helpless, as other tentacles homed in on her.

"Escape!" the voice thundered. *"Escape or die!"*

Another greedy tentacle lashed at her, snapping like a whip to ensnare her right wrist. Thorns plunged into her flesh, and the greedy maws began sucking her blood.

Overcome by pain and fear, Rachel screamed and fought to break free, but more tentacles wound around her, enveloping her, growing into a cocoon that threatened to cover her.

"Fight! This is your heritage! Break free of the shell that binds you!"

Rachel pulled and twisted frantically, not following any logical path now, just fighting like a trapped animal. Blood limned her arms where the tentacles had latched on, and the acidic burn grew stronger by the second. A tentacle curled around her neck and she felt her pulse exploding in her head. Another one swept toward her eyes, maws snapping in anticipation, and she knew she'd at least be blinded.

Just before the tentacle latched onto her face, a strong hand reached out and caught it. Instantly, the limb rolled and turned on its captor.

A man Rachel had never before seen stood next to her. Broad and powerful-looking, his skin a dark coffee color, he stared at her with bright golden eyes. He wore a tuxedo jacket with the sleeves ripped off over his bare chest, which was adorned with white paint, and black slacks. Black leather sandals covered his feet. Peacock feathers stood up from the band of his black top hat. A white painted skull lay over his face.

Instinctively, Rachel tried to draw back from the man, thinking he was another threat.

"Nasty things, aren't they, *cher*?" The man grinned, the skull overlying his features robbing that expression of any reassurance. "And powerful, too." He squeezed the tentacle in his fist. "Not powerful enough, though."

Blue flames sprang from the man's hand and the tentacle turned to gray ash in an eyeblink. The ash drifted away, but other tentacles turned toward the man.

He laughed, the big, booming noise coming from deep inside his broad chest. He clasped his palms together, called out in a language she didn't understand, then drew his hands apart. When he did, an ebony walking stick appeared between them. His right hand closed over the handle, which was a black flower with furled petals around a stamen that towered over them.

More strange language poured from the man's mouth as he stood his ground. He waved the walking stick like a sword at the tentacles, and whatever he touched turned to ash. He laughed again, the joyous sound filling Rachel's ears. She didn't know why or how, but somehow, hearing him made her feel a bit better.

Freed from the tentacles, she plummeted to the ground. Immediately, she pushed herself up. More tentacles sprang from the earth and chased her.

The man stabbed the walking stick into the ground and held on with both hands. The tentacles swept over him at once. He lifted his voice in song, and the tentacles blew away as ash in a whirlwind.

"Enough games!" he shouted. "Come out and face me yourself!"

For a moment, nothing happened, then the ground broke open like a suppurating wound. A large caterpillar-looking thing squirmed out of the mud. It wasn't a caterpillar, though. It was covered in chitinous plates that undulated over segments of what looked like gooey mucus. The creature reared several meters tall, dwarfing the man. Its entire body was festooned with tentacles that waved wildly around it.

Standing before the thing, the man held his ground. He took his hat from his head and held it in one hand as he sang more of the strange melody. The creature swayed as though entranced. Grinning, the man gripped his walking stick, then rapped it on his hat.

Immediately, flickering miniature skulls flew out of the hat and headed straight for the creature. They adhered to it and started burning, filling the area with the stench of burned, rancid grease.

Squealing in a macabre, high-pitched whistle, the creature spun and whipped its appendages against its body, but only succeeded in spreading the fire. It tried to dig back into the ground, frantically undulating its body to get traction, but before it could escape, it fell over, quivered a little, and died, curling up into a limp, smoldering, tentacle-covered ball.

The man clapped his hat back on his head and held out his hand to Rachel. "C'mon, *cher*. We don't have much time to figure out how we're going to get you out of here."

Dazed, afraid to trust the stranger, but not wanting to be alone, Rachel took his hand. His flesh felt warm, comforting, and his palm was callused. "Who are you?"

"I am Remy Bordelon, at your service, *cher*." He smiled. "I am a dabbler in the occult, and I was sent here by Katar Hawke to aid you."

"Do you know where I—we—are?"

Bordelon shook his head. "Not yet, but I am confident we will figure that out."

CHAPTER FIFTY-TWO

"*This* is the place?"

Not happy with what he was looking at, Hawke stood across the street from The Pink Cadillac and stared at the small bar shoved in between a Stuffer Shack and a dingy electronics store.

A graffiti-covered, three-story eyesore that had seen its better days decades ago, the bar's flickering sign blinked neon radiance over the Detroit suburb. The failing lights sizzled like frying meat, even above the thrasher metal blasting from inside the venue, but it still created a complete image of a buxom blonde driving a pink Cadillac every third or fourth try.

Stuffer Shack wrappers whirled over cracked concrete, and takeout cups bounced along the narrow two-lane street, propelled by a wind that picked up the foul odor of nearby livestock barns. Like the bar, the neighborhood was well past its glory days.

"Hey, mon." Twitch punched him in the arm. "Rolla's down on his luck right now. I told you that. And as I recall, you've been there a time or two yourself. We all have. At least he's working at something sensible instead of suiting up for one of the corp sec armies. He likes to be his own man. In some ways, he reminds me of you."

Out on the street, draped in the night, Twitch sounded different than she had on the island. She was more confident, more like her old self. Maybe it was the guns. She wore curve-hugging black body armor that fitted her like a second skin. Hawke thought she somehow looked more undressed now than she had in the bikini. Of course, he was looking beyond the guns. People who didn't know her, chances were they wouldn't see anything but the guns.

Two Ultimax 70 slug-throwers were lashed to her thighs in counter-terrorist drop holsters. The heavy-caliber pistols were fairly primitive, with laser sights but no smartlinks. Not that Twitch needed them. She was an all-natural shootist.

A pair of Cavalier Deputies rode in shoulder leather. The pistols were replicas of Old West pistols, but carried seven rounds in the cylinders instead of six. The weapons were deadly accurate at distance, and favored by competition pistoleers.

An Ares Executioner hung down her back in a scabbard. The submachine gun was a favorite of Hawke's when he had to spray a lot of rounds into an area.

Twin black bracers produced by Tiffani Élégance covered Twitch's forearms from her wrists almost to her elbows. Raised images of sea turtles covered the four barrels of each built-in weapon. The small-caliber caseless ammo didn't have much stopping power unless it was deliberately placed for kill shots. Twitch could do that in her sleep, but she had to be close up to use them.

In this burned out suburb, Twitch wouldn't draw much law enforcement attention. Inside Detroit's eight-meter wall, Knight Errant Security Services ran a tight ship. Ares Macrotechnology, KE's parent corporation, had turned the metroplex into a safe place for the wealthy to come and make their fortunes. In the distance, the spires of Ares' global headquarters gleamed as they reached for the dark heavens. A suborbital heading for space looked like a falling star in reverse.

"So?" The gunslinger looked up at Hawke. "You waiting for the chicken to cross the road ahead of you?"

Hawke shook his head. Twitch radiated confidence. It had come to her the moment she'd started strapping on iron.

"This guy better be all you say he is." He stepped off the curb and headed for the bar.

"Or what?"

"Or we're still looking for muscle, and I'll have to take an antibacterial shower for nothing."

Twitch's lips crooked in a smile. "He is."

A sour burn twisted in the pit of Hawke's stomach. They'd spent the last twenty-seven hours tracking down street sams he'd worked with before. Three were dead, not unusual for the job they did. One was incarcerated. And two had gone corp, accepting big signing bonuses to work for the man.

Twitch had been prompting him to take a look at this street samurai, Rolla, since they'd left Negril. Hawke had put her off, saying he wasn't working with anyone he hadn't worked with before. It was a good rule.

Unfortunately, rules got broken when things didn't turn out the way they were supposed to.

Just as he reached the sec door leading to the club, a man stumbled out and threw up on the sidewalk. He was middle-aged, bearded, and wore glasses. He glanced up at Hawke as he wiped his arm across his mouth.

"I wouldn't go in there if I was you."

Hawke paused. "Why?"

The man hooked a thumb back toward the club. "Got a dozen thrill gangers in there, slumming from the metroplex, who thought it'd be wiz to rob the club tonight."

Muffled by the door and the music that continued unabated, gunshots cracked inside. Now that he was listening, Hawke could hear screams and yells, too.

"Is Rolla working tonight, mon?" Twitch asked.

The man nodded. "Yeah."

Twitch grinned. "Bad night to be thrill gangers." She grabbed the door and entered before Hawke knew she was moving.

Unlimbering the Savalette Guardian Twitch had arranged for him when she'd picked out her own weapons from a local fixer she knew, Hawke brought his wired reflexes online and juiced the smartlink to the pistol. A reticle ghosted into view, sitting in the lower right quadrant of his vision until he actively aimed the weapon.

Once through the door, Hawke had to fight through the crowd fleeing the bar. The guests crushed through the hallway outside the main bar area, jostling him against the wall again and again. Somehow, Twitch went through them like a bullet, untouched by flailing arms and driving legs.

Finally, Hawke reached the main room, shouldering through a wedge of street toughs who'd found better things to do than slake their thirst at The Pink Cadillac. He gazed out onto the open floor, where a dozen gangers confronted a troll holding a heavy, round metal table as a shield against their bullets. Divided between male and female humans, dressed in posh clothing and wearing gang colors that announced them as the Carraways, the gang members spread out in a loose semi-circle in front of their target.

CHAPTER FIFTY-THREE

"You all got five seconds to leave the premises!" the troll roared. "The boss here tells me I gotta tell you that first."

He was three meters tall if he was a centimeter, and too big to get complete coverage from the metal table he held effortlessly in his big hands. Thick horns curved back from his forehead and twisted up behind his head. A short goatee framed his chin. His heavy face was mostly unblemished, and considering his occupation, was something a noob wouldn't understand. Someone new to the fighting biz would think Rolla hadn't fought much. To a trained observer, those unmarked looks were a badge of honor, proof that he was good at what he did. He wore a black suit that didn't fit the environs. It was buttoned down, complete with a tie, and made him look professional.

"We don't need your warning!" one of the Carraways yelled back. He opened up with the machine pistol in his hands and tracked a line across the table Rolla held. "Give us the creds, or we'll burn this place to the ground!"

"Rolla!" A small man leaned out from the doorway at the back of the bar. "Don't do anything! I'll pay!"

"See?" the ganger leader taunted. "The old man knows the score. Put that table down and walk away."

The troll didn't move. "Five. Mr. Edgarson, you don't want to do this. You let scum like this walk over you tonight, they'll just show up again. Four."

"It's not your decision!" Edgarson yelled.

Rolla's huge chest rose and fell. "It's more than just your bar, Mr. Edgarson. Three. I've got a rep to protect. Two."

"Rep? What rep? You're a bouncer. I hire you to bounce. And to do what I say. And I'm saying you need to walk away."

"Better do what the old man says, trog, otherwise we're gonna leave you smeared across the wall so bad DocWagon won't be able to put you back together." The gang leader shoved a new magazine into his weapon.

"Like we agreed, Mr. Edgarson," Rolla said in a loud, calm tone. "These null-brains have been warned. One."

The ganger leader glanced at his followers in disbelief.

Stepping fluidly to his left, Rolla turned, presenting his profile to the gangers as they leveled their weapons. Both of his huge hands were now close together on the table's edge. As he turned back, he released the table, then followed it, roaring like a bull.

The flying furniture smashed into the center group of gangers, mowing them down like tenpins. Rolla headed left and raised his left hand up in front of his face. A folding transplas shield had appeared from under his jacket sleeve. It and his jacket took rounds from the gangers' weapons, but the bullets didn't penetrate.

The raucous gunfire filled the club, bullets smashing into the walls and bar furniture, turning them into explosions of splinters and shattered pieces of wood and metal. Edgarson squawked in surprise and vanished behind the doorway.

At Hawke's side, Twitch crossed her arms over her chest and leaned against the wall. She smiled at his tenseness. "Chill, mon. Rolla knows what he's doing. Take a look at what you'll be gettin' when he signs on."

Hawke watched the developing action, but didn't put his pistol away. Even if they didn't take part, which he was loath to do, that didn't mean someone wouldn't take a shot at them. There weren't many neutral parties in a free-wheeling gunfight.

Reaching the knot of gangers, Rolla barreled into them, knocking them off their feet with the shield, reaching out to smack the farthest one into the wall. Dropping into a crouch, Rolla grabbed a dazed ganger's leg, twisted, and heaved the hapless individual across the room into the other group of Carraways blasting away in an attempt to find a target. The flailing ganger missile took down half of the crew there.

Rolla went through the rest like a thresher, popping his big hands out in punches and backhanded slaps, leaving unconscious opponents in his wake as he worked his way across the room.

Getting to his feet woozily, the leader aimed his machine pistol and fired in uneven bursts. Bullets *plonked* against Rolla's suit, flattening against either his underweave armor or dermal plating, and dropped at his feet. The troll grabbed a nearby chair and flung it at the ganger. The chair spun and the legs bracketed the punk's slender body, propelling him backward.

Hawke's commlink chirped, and he opened the channel when he recognized the fake SIN. "I'm kinda busy—"

"Drek! Have they already found you?" Dolphin was the decker Hawke had set up for the team. She was currently in Denver, seeing to the hardware and software she'd need. She wanted everything clean, without history. *"I thought they were still en route. Wait. They are still en route. Who's shooting at you?"*

"They're not shooting at me." Hawke watched as Rolla backhanded another ganger, sending her flying halfway across the room. "Did you say someone's looking for me?"

"Yeah, omae, someone's definitely looking for you. A NeoNET hit squad's been sniffing around your back trail. They found that flimsy fake SIN you used to get down to Jamaica. I told you you should have let me take care of you."

"I wasn't able to reach you until this morning."

Still on the move, Rolla felled gangers like trees. Broken or unconscious, they lay in his wake. Three gangers on the outskirts read which way the wind was blowing and tried to break for the front door. The troll street sam picked up a small table and flung it like a discus. The projectile struck the rearmost ganger and knocked him into his chummers, sending them all to the floor.

"I stay bizzy, omae. You know that. I had to clear my schedule to help you in the first place, and you're lucky I even took your message. I keep a backlog in drops." Dolphin sounded a little put out. Sometimes she wore her feelings on her sleeve, and no one had to ever wonder where they stood with her.

"That's not what I meant. I meant I worked with what I could get."

"Well, what you could get got you noticed. Taking that jet to Jamaica left you too exposed. NeoNET has sniffers on your Matrix trail. I took care of some of them, which should buy you some time in the future, but they have you by the short hairs at the moment."

"How far out are they?" Hawke was thinking maybe he and Twitch could get gone before there was a problem.

"About five minutes out, give or take thirty seconds. Ground vehicles. I've been digging into NeoNET, and picked 'em up right before I called you. Whoever's pulling the strings there, they're digging deep for you."

Not for him. For Rachel. "Thanks for the heads-up. See you in Minneapolis?"

"Definitely." Dolphin sounded excited. *"NeoNET, the Azzies, and some mysterious third party?, You sure know how to slice off a chunk of trouble."*

Before Hawke could reply, the connection clicked dead. Out in the middle of the floor, Rolla stood alone, dusting himself off, surrounded by the scattered bodies of the defeated gangers. Hawke didn't think any were dead, but anyone that had a Doc-Wagon account had been racked up as a medical emergency. That meant a lot of heat was descending on The Pink Cadillac, not counting the hit team on his heels.

Hawke leaned over to Twitch. "A crew from NeoNET is on top of us. We have to go."

"Rolla!" Edgarson emerged from the back room and gazed around at the carnage that now filled his establishment. "Look what you've done!"

"I didn't do that." Rolla glanced over at Twitch and nodded. "I did what you paid me to do."

Edgarson gestured at the shambles he was standing in. The old man looked like he was about ready to cry. "This? I didn't pay you to do this! This is going to cost me a ton of nuyen! This'll make my insurance policy go up!"

"You shouldn't have been so cheap," Rolla said. "You should have paid to have a guy at the door, like I suggested."

"You—*you* were supposed to be on the door!"

"The door. The floor. The storage room to make sure the bartenders weren't nicking your liquor supply." Rolla shook his head. "I told you there was only so much I could do."

"I should fire you!"

"Nope. You're not firing me. That's not going on my résumé. I quit. Keep what you owe me." Rolla smiled at the gangers littering the floor. "This was worth it." He glanced up at Twitch and winked. "Gimme a minute to get my duffel."

"Sure," Twitch replied. "But we need to hurry, mon, because we're about to have some party crashers."

The troll glowered down at Hawke. "Really? You got dogs at your heels? Doesn't make a good first impression."

Hawke didn't know what to say to that, and before he could say anything, Rolla turned and walked to the back room. Edgarson stepped away from him.

"Wait," Edgarson pleaded. "Maybe I was hasty. This neighborhood, it's a lot more dangerous than it used to be. Until tonight, we didn't have any real trouble. Not like this. Please. We can talk."

Rolla ignored the man and kept walking. He returned a moment later with a military duffel over his shoulder. When he reached them, he leaned down and kissed Twitch's cheeks. "Hey, toots. Marriage doing okay by you?"

"Marriage is awesome." Twitch wrapped her arms around the troll's free arm and hung close. "Thanks for the wine chiller, mon. Jovi and I are enjoying it, and the supply of wine you sent."

"My pleasure." Rolla sized Hawke up with a glance as they headed for the front door. "Who's your bald friend?"

"This is Hawke. You'll get to know more about him on the road."

"We'll see. I'm there for you, toots, but I don't owe this guy anything, and it already sounds like he's dangerous to be around." Rolla narrowed his eyes at Hawke. "If I don't like the deal, I'll tell Jovi she doesn't like the deal either. Then you and me will find something else to do."

Hawke didn't know whether to be angry, or to try to deal with the street sam professionally. He understood where Rolla was coming from, but he didn't have to like it.

Before he could make up his mind, he stepped outside onto the street and got hit with bright lights.

"Stand down!" an electronically enhanced voice threatened. *"Drop your weapons and surrender, or we will open fire!"*

CHAPTER FIFTY-FOUR

In a blink, Hawke's cybereyes filtered out the brightness and let him see the eight men in combat armor crouched behind the open doors of the two Rover Model 2072 vans on the other side of the street. Both vehicles were covered in heavy composite armor that absorbed the moonlight and streetlights. Even The Pink Cadillac's neon lighting didn't seem to touch them.

Atop both vehicles, men sat tense and ready behind machine guns and half-shields, making them small targets. All of the gunners had laser sights that left small ruby ovals dotting Hawke and his companions like measles.

Instinct told Hawke to run, to dive back inside the bar and try to head out the back. He couldn't leave Twitch behind, though. That was one of the problems with a team: not everyone moved at the same speed, and only one person could get through a door at a time.

"Twitch," Hawke whispered as he held his hands out to his sides. "Maybe we can make it back inside—"

She chuckled, as if honestly amused. "These clowns, mon? You want us to run from second-tier muscle? NeoNET didn't even bother to send a group of top-flight sec men." She shook her head. "I got this."

That was the old Twitch, the one who didn't back down and didn't know when to quit.

"Glad to hear you say that, toots," Rolla growled, "'cause I only got about half of them."

Holding her hands out level at her sides, Twitch stepped forward, and even though he couldn't see her face, Hawke knew she was wearing that grin she always did before a showdown.

"Stay where you are," the enhanced voice advised. *"Drop your weapons and raise your hands."*

"No, mon," Twitch said. Her hands folded over her chest and plucked the Cavalier Deputys from shoulder leather. "You wannabes need to find something else to do tonight."

The speaker shifted, and one of the laser dots gleamed on Twitch's left cheek. *"This is your last warning."*

The gunslinger grinned. "Got that right—"

Though Hawke had his pistol in hand and his wired reflexes still pinging, he couldn't get his weapon up before Twitch was already firing. Even though he'd seen her in action before, watching her work was beautiful—and it was also hard to see if not reduced to slo-mo. She wasn't chipped, didn't have any magical abilities, and hadn't had any specialized training.

She was just a natural with a handgun.

She was the most dangerous person in a shootout Hawke had ever seen.

The Cavalier Deputies spat fire, roaring and bucking as they unleashed death. Her hands moved only slightly, rolling with the recoil, turning slightly to shift to a new target the moment each bullet left the barrel. The nine shots filled Hawke's hearing like one long drumbeat.

Across the street, the eight sec men dropped in place, each with a neat, round hole at the bridge of their noses between their eyes. The AP bullets had punched through the eye protectors and face shields.

Braced, searching for a target, Hawke stood there, his smartlink reticule jumping from dead man to dead man.

None of them moved.

Coolly, as if she had all day long, Twitch broke the revolvers open and replaced the spent shells with fresh cartridges from the pouch at her waist.

Rolla patted the gunslinger on the shoulder. "Not bad, toots, but you had to shoot the one on the end twice. Wasted a bullet."

Hawke hadn't even noticed that, but now that he was looking, he saw that the sec man had *two* holes in his forehead, spaced less than a centimeter apart.

Twitch shrugged. "I wanted to make sure, mon. It's been a while. I thought he turned his head at the last second."

"Chummer," Rolla said, "none of them had time to turn nothin'." The troll shifted his gaze to Hawke. "You got a ride?"

Hawke holstered his weapon. "I do."

"We'll need to leave it. If those guys found you, they can find whatever you're driving."

Hawke nodded. He'd thought of that, too. "We're on foot 'til we can arrange other transportation."

Rolla shook his head and sighed. "I gotta say, as a prospective employer, you ain't very impressive so far."

Finished reloading, Twitch shoved her weapons back into leather. "We're running right now. This isn't Hawke's best element. He's good on his feet when he's going for the prize, mon. That's when you'll see him all shiny."

Wanting to put as much distance from the impromptu battle-field as possible, Hawke took off walking. He opened the comm to Dolphin. "*Hola.*"

"*I see you're still alive,*" she said brightly.

"We might not have been if you hadn't given me the warning. Thanks."

"*Null sheen, omae. My pleasure.*"

"You said you could see me?" Hawke looked around.

"*I can. I do. I'm tapped into the neighborhood cams, drekky though they are.*"

"Can you wipe the footage?"

"*There's no footage, no record. I got control of the cams before I called you and stopped them.*"

"Thank you."

"*I've also arranged for a Bulldog for you. It doesn't look like much, but I know a rigger there who does top-notch work. The wheels will be wiz. Turn left at the end of the block and go three blocks farther to an alley on your left again. You'll find the keys in it. I'll also have new SINS–bulletproof ones this time, at least more so than the ones you two have been running under–for you and the two people with you.*"

When Dolphin had her game on, she was spectacular. Looking back at Twitch and Rolla as they followed him, Hawke started feeling a little more confident. He didn't allow that feeling to develop much, though. Aztechnology and NeoNET were sure to stack their forces wide and deep.

A few minutes later, Hawke entered an alley and found a nonde-script Bulldog step-van sitting there, its still-warm engine ticking quietly. It was painted a forgettable gray-brown that would blend in anywhere.

The door had been upgraded to include a concealed print lock. Dolphin had relayed the change to Hawke and let him know the vehicle would be attuned to him. When he placed his hand on the door, the locks *thunked* and released.

He opened the door and slid behind the wheel while the sirens of the law enforcement teams closing in screamed around him. The seat automatically adjusted to accommodate him, then a five-point racer's belt reached around him and locked him into place when he cranked the engine over. It growled quietly, low and deep and powerful. The Bulldog had definitely been upgraded.

Rolla opened the rear door for Twitch, then claimed the shotgun seat for himself. The vehicle rocked under his massive weight as he settled in. Although the Bulldog was a standard van, not a larger utility vehicle, the troll was still able to get comfortable. It helped that Twitch was so small in the back.

Engaging the transmission, Hawke pulled the van out into the street. The vehicle handled much smoother and responded more powerfully than it should have.

"So, what's this run you're needing help with?" Rolla asked.

"I'm not quite sure," Hawke admitted.

Rolla craned his massive head over his shoulder and gazed at Twitch. "We're on a snipe hunt?"

"Just listen to him, mon."

Turning back to Hawke, the troll grunted with dissatisfaction.

"We're not entirely in the dark on this," Hawke replied. "I've got something a lot of people want. I just have to hang onto it long enough to figure out what it is and how to make it work for us."

"What do you have?"

"A young woman. An artifact she found in South America."

"Can't she tell you?"

"She's in a coma."

"Wow. This just gets more and more wiz. I can see why you'd be so attracted to it."

"I don't have a choice. I'm carrying a bulls-eye between my shoulders right now. I'm just trying to get the woman out from under. When I do, we'll be in the clear, too."

"You sure about that?"

Hawke tightened his hands on the wheel and looked at the troll. "No. I can let you out at the next corner if you want."

Rolla shook his head and hooked a thumb over his shoulder.

He sighed. "Nope. Twitch has already bought into this. I know her. Given your impressive debut, I'm gonna stick with her and make sure she's okay."

"That works for me."

"So, what am I getting paid?" Rolla turned his attention back to Hawke.

"You're getting a piece of the prize. We share and share alike."

"How many ways are we cutting this thing?"

"If I get everybody I want? Eight ways."

"That's a lot of pieces. To make this worthwhile, the pieces are gonna have to be worth a lot."

"I think they are. Aztechnology doesn't go after small items."

"Aztechnology, huh?" Rolla shook his head. "Is that who those guys back there were?"

"No." Hawke coasted to a stop at a deserted intersection and gazed up at a police helicopter headed in the direction of The Pink Cadillac. The searchlight on the helo's nose flashed through the streets and ripped away the shadows. "Those guys were with NeoNET."

"NeoNET, hmmm." Rolla scratched his goatee-covered chin with black talons. "I owe them some payback for a job I got screwed over on."

"So that means you're gonna pay me for the privilege of sticking it to that corp?" Hawke gazed blankly at Rolla.

The troll stared back at him for a moment, then smiled. "Heh. No. But I'm in." He held out a callused fist.

Hawke bumped knuckles with him, and they all settled in for the twelve-hour ride to Minneapolis.

CHAPTER FIFTY-FIVE

"Got a minute, omae?*"*

Reclined in the passenger seat while Twitch took a turn behind the wheel, Hawke jerked awake as the voice echoed inside his head. Twitch's eyes cut to him and he shook his head, letting her know he were fine. Rolla snored like a bellows in the back seat.

"I do, Dolphin. What have you got?" Hawke rubbed his eyes. Sitting up straighter, he checked the takeout cup of soykaf in the holder between the seats. It was equipped with a heating unit, but it didn't work on an empty cup. He checked his chron and found it was 0418 hours. He'd only been asleep a couple hours.

"I've been looking into your dead Johnson." Dolphin sounded slow and distant, and he knew she was jacked into the Matrix and talking to him from there. *"Want to take a look with me?"*

"How?"

"There's a rig in the glove box."

Leaning forward, Hawke opened the glove box and sorted through the paperwork inside that was all registered to his current SIN. "I don't see it."

Dolphin sighed. *"Of course you don't,* liebling. *I didn't put it there for just anyone to find. There's a print scanner at the back of the unit, opens a hidey hole."*

Hawke ran his hand around the inside of the glove compartment for a moment, then felt something vibrate within. He pulled his hand back as a hidden compartment revealed itself. A light flicked on inside and lit the micro-sized DNI within. The Direct Neural Interface was a rigging harness for Matrix surfers who didn't have jacks.

Dolphin wanted to take him into the 'trix, and he wasn't thrilled about that. Hawke preferred his world three-dimensional, with physical rules he could easily understand. Cyberspace was too fluid, too open to interpretation, and it was never the same thing twice.

Hawke stared at the DNI like it was a poisonous viper. "I don't want to go into the Matrix."

"Don't be such a baby, Hawke," Dolphin chided. *"It's perfectly safe."*

"Maybe for you." Hawke could still remember the crash in '64. He'd been a kid, playing in a game when the system had gone down. Luckily, the game he'd been on had been supported by Saeder-Krupp Schwerindustriesellschaft, the heavy industries corp owned by the great western dragon, Lofwyr. S-K maintained its own Matrix kill switch, and had prevented the damage that had run rampant throughout other systems. Most of the other corps had suffered significant losses.

Since that time, the corps had reformed the Matrix into grids and created the Grid Overwatch Division, called GOD. The Matrix had gotten a lot more dangerous and dodgy nowadays. If someone was going to snoop and spy on people and corporations in the Matrix these days, they had to know what they were doing.

Hawke didn't.

"You'll just be piggybacking off me," Dolphin insisted. *"It'll be like you're not even there. And if I try to just* explain *everything I've found, you won't understand. This is what you came to me for, remember? You need to see this for yourself."*

Reluctantly, Hawke picked up the rig, running his thumbs over the ebony buds. Taking a breath to steel himself, he pulled it on and stared out the bug-smeared windshield. They were on the highway, seemingly locked into a void of darkness the headlights carved a long tunnel through.

"Just relax." Dolphin's voice was a deep whisper inside his skull. *"I've got you."*

Hawke experienced a brief sensation of endless falling, then—

—he stood in a massive room filled with library stacks containing millions of books, scrolls, stone tablets, paintings, scrimshaw, and objects he couldn't even name. Everything was made of wood, the burnished surfaces gleaming from polish and care. Travertine Italian marble tiles the color of old bone covered the floor. The faint smell of spices—cinnamon, cardamom, saffron, and vanilla—hung in the cool air. Elevators and ziplines crisscrossed the endless space. Hawke just stared at everything for a few moments.

"Sorry. I forgot how overwhelming it can be to someone who hasn't been here before."

He turned toward the voice, and spotted Dolphin perched behind a tall mahogany desk covered with books and a large red apple. Petite and blonde, her hair pulled back in a ponytail, she looked like she was in her late twenties or early thirties, slim and vivacious. She wore sea-green framed glasses, an unnecessary affectation in the cyber world, but which complemented her loose-fitting, pale green turtleneck.

"Hi." She waved, her gray eyes shining with excitement.

"Hi." Hawke walked over to the desk. His movement made him aware of his clothing. Instead of the tactical gear he wore in the van—*where I really am*, he reminded himself—he was dressed in a light gray Savile Row suit. He looked back at Dolphin. "Not my usual look."

Dolphin grinned and her cheeks reddened a little. "It's cyberspace. No reason you can't look good while you're here. Skins are free." She shrugged. "Unless you want something special." The mirth left her face as she turned serious. "Do you want anything special? I didn't even think to ask. How you see yourself in cyberspace is important."

"This is fine." Hawke stopped on the other side of the tall desk and looked around at the library. "This is your place?"

"It is." Dolphin smiled with pride. "It's kind of a *Warehouse 13* motif. Stuff from everywhere. I'm still exploring. It's hard to do when I'm getting new acquisitions in all the time, but I can't quit reaching for the new stuff, you know?"

Hawke didn't understand the reference, but let it go. Dolphin had all kinds of interests, and pop culture was only one of them. He'd always felt a little uncomfortable around her because she radiated a kind of innocence he didn't think he'd ever understand. He didn't know much about her other than her decker skills, but he had her true SIN: Adeline "Addy" Jaeger. He'd helped her keep that information off the Matrix when she'd first come to him for help. She was a technomancer, someone who'd evolved after the Crash of '64, and who could link with the Matrix simply with their minds. She'd gotten hacked, and her SIN had almost been turned loose into the wild. Hawke had prevented that.

She was also a constant collector of information. She chased secrets and rumors and gossip on the Matrix, and provided services to people who wanted those things, or who feared those things getting released to the public. If she'd used her gifts for purely predatory purposes, she could have been wealthier than Hawke assumed she already was. Financial motivation wasn't what spurred her on: she just liked *knowing* things.

"Maybe I'll give you a tour and highlight my special projects some other time," Dolphin suggested.

"Sure."

"I know we're facing a time crunch, so we're going to get to what I've discovered so far." Dolphin got down from her chair. She walked forward, and the desk disappeared as the room began changing around them.

When she took Hawke by the hand, her flesh felt warm and vibrant, and he wondered if she was the same in real life. He'd never met her in the flesh. "The first visit is going to be somewhat unpleasant, I'm afraid. How well did you know your Johnson?"

"I met him briefly twice, talked to him once in between."

"Good, then you're not emotionally invested."

As she led Hawke forward, the lights in the library turned dark, then went black. When the lights came back on, he was standing in a morgue, next to a stainless steel table holding Mr. Johnson's lifeless body.

CHAPTER FIFTY-SIX

The chill pervading the room was cold enough to make Hawke's bones ache. He didn't know if it was a programmed virtual reality sensation, or if the feeling was a visceral reaction to seeing the dead man laid out on the table under the stark white lights. He'd seen plenty of dead people before, those who'd been killed quietly in their sleep and those who had been spread all over an alley by explosives, so he didn't think the blood or just the idea of someone being dead was the cause.

There was something unnatural about seeing a once living human being and their parts all spread out in surroundings that were clean and austere at the same time. The impersonality of it all cut like a monofilament blade.

Mr. Johnson lay on the table, arms tucked close by his sides, his various organs floating above his open chest. The heart, lungs, kidneys, eyes, brain, and other pieces were all recognizable, and spun slowly on their individual axes. One of the kidneys had been replaced with bioware that looked both human and artificial at the same time, because it was so perfect.

The brain was a ruptured mass that had expanded once freed of the skull and was now full of bone splinters as well. All of the flesh was devoid of blood for the most part, cleaned by the medtechs who had then cut him to pieces.

A flattened bullet hovered above the dead man's face. As Hawke looked at it, he flashed back to when Mr. Johnson had taken the round through his hand while in the club. The hand at the dead man's side still had the bullet hole in it. The surrounding flesh had turned dark violet and black with postmortem bruising.

Dolphin stepped into the carnage and waved at the bullet. It immediately plopped back into the dead man's brain, which oozed into his skull and left a small diameter hole in the forehead. The back of Mr. Johnson's head was gone, and bits of hair-covered scalp and bone dangled beneath his head. They were sucked back into the head as well, but a few pieces were missing. Some of the smaller bone splinters darted back down to the wounded hand.

"You already know what killed him," Dolphin said, "but I wanted you to know I checked on that as well. To verify things. The one bullet struck him in the brain. Death was instantaneous. Off—" She snapped her fingers. "—like that."

"Are we inside the medical examiner's files?" Hawke felt a little threatened as he gazed around the room. If they were inside a government node and tripped some kind of alarm, he'd never know. Not only that, he wasn't certain he'd know how to escape.

"No." Dolphin smiled at him. "This is a re-creation I set up in my private data storage, totally secure from outside interference. Anyone wanting to get in here would have to follow me in, and that's impossible because the firewall we're behind is something I designed. No one has this software."

Hawke resisted the urge to tell her that she charged clients for breaking into cyber strongholds of people who thought they were as well-protected as she believed she was. "So, you're just doing this from an educated guess?"

"I stole copies of these files from the medical examiner's office and brought them here, then started tracking down who your Johnson really is. It took time. His info was really protected behind black ice."

Ice was decker slang for intrusion countermeasures code written to defend cyber systems. IC came in different protective levels and had multiple uses. White IC was designed to slow and observe a decker targeting a site. Trace IC tracked a decker's location in the physical world and allowed law enforcement teams, or someone more lethal, to find him or her. Gray IC destroyed cyberdecks.

"He was protected by black ice?" Hawke looked at the Johnson again and tried to figure out what made him so important. Black IC was expensive, code written expressly to kill deckers. It wasn't just handed down to shield a wageslave. Not even one who negotiated with shadowrunners.

"Yeah. Quality stuff. Top shelf variety." Dolphin stared at Hawke with raised eyebrows. "This guy's a nobody, so whoever was protecting him was more interested in protecting themselves.

Or in hiding what they're doing. To them, he's just one more piece of the firewall."

"What do you mean?"

"I mean the corporation he worked for, KilmerTek, hired Mr. Johnson four days before they put him onto you."

Four days. Hawke tried to wrap his head around that, but it didn't make any sense. "You found that order?"

"No, but this guy didn't meet you on his own. I checked through his background, which was simple, up to his employment with KilmerTek. You two had no commonalities. Nothing to tie you together."

"Did he do biz with shadowrunners at his old job?"

"Not that I could find, and I think I'd have found it by now. If he had, no matter how deeply it was buried, I would have dug it up. The guy is—was an open book. "

Hawke believed her.

"PCC detectives from Santa Fe are investigating your Johnson from their end, coordinating with Denver cops. I've got datasniffers working both ends, so if they find anything, I'll be the next to know."

"You think KilmerTek hired him just to make contact with me?"

"That's exactly why he was hired: to get you onboard for the run. Being new to KilmerTek, the Johnson couldn't have his fingers in much of the day-to-day biz, so there's not much anyone can track about his time there. He was a name and SIN on their payroll, that's it. I'm running datasniffers back through his files at the corporation, but I already know they're not going to find much. He wasn't wired into the corp." Dolphin looked back down at the dead man. "He was a use and lose interface. For all we know, KilmerTek paid to have him flatlined as well."

"Not before the job was finished," Hawke replied. "I was hired to get Rachel Gordon. I got her. Whoever sent him still needed the Johnson to contact me and receive her."

"Maybe you didn't get Rachel quietly enough, or maybe they thought their profile was running too high, and decided to cut their losses. Once KilmerTek saw how high the stakes had gotten, with the Azzies and NeoNET looking for you and bodies dropping everywhere, they could have gotten cold feet. Just set up the Johnson to meet with you, then whack you both to erase the trail."

Hawke took in a breath and let it out, thinking he would never do someone on his team that way, and then realizing that was

precisely why he'd never had a permanent team. So he didn't ever
have to make a decision like that.

"Who was he?"

"His real name was Christopher Gant." Dolphin reached for
the bioware kidney, tapped it, and spun it. "The med ID on the kidney cinched the identification for the medical examiner. No one
tried to erase it. I followed up on the intel, and came up with the
same result the M.E. did. Null sheen. Before he was hired by KilmerTek, Gant was a number-cruncher at Valeddy-Mortensen. V-M
manufactures low-end electronics for cheap game decks, nothing
special. Gant was just a projects manager, juggling accounts and
massaging buyers."

"What does KilmerTek do?"

"They drill oil fields in Oklahoma and Texas. They're a wildcat-
ter operation that barely gets by, hitting just enough wells to keep
in the black."

"No connection to Rachel?"

"None."

"What about to Guatemalan artifacts?"

"Zilch. They've got a modest museum they fund in Houston,
but that's mostly a public relations effort to make peace with
the Native American Nations. There's nothing to indicate they'd
be interested in whatever Rachel found down there." Dolphin
waved and the morgue collapsed around them, shrinking to a
small, thin line that spread horizontally, then grew back into a
business foyer.

Under the high ceiling and ornate light fixtures, Hawke
stood on a thick carpet. A double-door entrance was on his
left. The transplas doors announced *KILMERTEK CORPORATION*
in gold letters. To his right, three people answered comms behind a long desk. Dark green potted plants with colorful flowers anchored the room. Comfortable chairs and couches dotted the carpet. People walked by and through Hawke, never
paying attention to Dolphin or him. On the walls, a collection
of trideo images of well sites gushed black crude high into ce-
rulean skies.

"This is KilmerTek during its day-to-day operations, as far as
I've seen." Dolphin craned her head around, watching everything.

"Maybe Rachel Gordon or the artifact is a personal interest
of one of the board members. Flicker identified Ayuni Sukenobu,
one of NeoNET's board members, as a possible supporter of the

Guatemalan dig Professor Fredericks proposed."

"There's no one like that here that I can see. The board of directors consists of seven people—five women and two men—all primarily concerned with the bottom line. If it doesn't turn a profit, they're not interested. They don't have hobbies in things remotely like what you and Flicker found."

"Rachel found the artifact."

Dolphin shrugged. "Either way."

Hawke sighed in disgust. "If no one at KilmerTek's interested in archeology—"

"Or whatever Rachel Gordon found in Guatemala," Dolphin said, "because we don't know exactly what that is either."

"—then that corp is a smokescreen, too. Designed to confuse the issue."

Dolphin nodded. "Probably, but I would have checked them out anyway, just to be thorough." She frowned and crossed her arms. "If this is a time suck, it worked. To a degree."

"What do you mean?"

"If no one at KilmerTek is interested in weird archeology, someone outside the corp had to have pushed them to hire Gant and send him after you. There was a plan. This didn't just happen randomly."

"You think KilmerTek is in someone's pocket."

"Yep. Most of these small corps are. A lot of them have to maintain contracts with bigger corps or governmental departments and agencies in order to remain solvent." Dolphin looked pointedly at the holos of oil wells on the wall. "Especially one that's solely dependent on a natural resource whose worth bounces around radically in the stock market. It's feast or famine for these drillers."

"And making a deal on the side helps keep them solvent." Hawke pulled up a stock market report for KilmerTek. "Crude oil hasn't been doing so well lately."

Dolphin touched her nose with a forefinger and smiled at him. "Exactly. A few months ago, a few African nations signed a deal to allow more drilling. Oil prices went into freefall. Seventeen days ago, investment specialists were selling KilmerTek stock like they were having a fire sale. There was talk the corp was going to go under when they couldn't make their lease payments. Vultures were starting to gather to pick over the bones when the company eventually imploded."

"Let me guess—that didn't happen."

"No, because KilmerTek received an infusion of nuyen that saved them. The details of that deal still haven't been released, and it's more protected than Gant was."

"Those two events don't have to be related."

Dolphin grinned as the foyer melted down around them and the library took its place. "Want to bet on that?"

"No."

"Too bad." She walked back to the desk, sat, and lifted a hand over the desktop. A deck window opened in the air. "The information you need is out there somewhere. I'll find it."

"I know you will. Be careful."

"Me?" Dolphin made a pistol of her thumb and forefinger and shot him. "You're the one in front of bullets and blades, *omae*. Don't stand still too long."

The library grayed out and vanished, taking Dolphin with it.

CHAPTER FIFTY-SEVEN

Down on one knee, Rachel peered into the clear water of the shallow creek. To her right, over a hundred meters away, the gurgling stream poured down broken boulders, falling several dozen meters to splash into a large pool that flowed on at the far end. Those splashes had drawn Rachel to the water.

Ripples on the pool's surface glinted in the sporadic sunlight through the towering conifers. Feathered creatures, she wasn't sure if they were actual birds or lizards, flitted around the cascading water, hunting brightly-colored winged insects that glittered like jewels when the sun caught them. The insects fed on large pink and orange blossoms sprouting from plants hugging the rough rock face.

Thirsty and hungry, Rachel bent down over the creek and cupped her hands to catch the water. Small, finger-length fish darted beneath the surface and above the pebbled bed. The water felt cool, almost cold in her palms, in spite of the tropical conditions. As thirsty as she was, she hesitated to drink, thinking something would rear up from the depths at any moment and try to kill her. Or that the water was poisoned.

She didn't know how long she'd been running, but she hadn't stopped because the things hunting her hadn't stopped either. Night hadn't fallen, and she didn't think it was going to. And if it did, she was convinced that whatever lurked in the darkness would be even more dangerous than what she'd seen so far.

As tired as she was, she didn't dare do more than occasionally nap. There had been no food or water since she had arrived. She didn't know how she was finding the strength to keep going.

"Drinking that ain't gonna slake your thirst any, *cher.*" Remy Bordelon leaned on his walking stick as he stood guard a short distance away. He'd stuck beside her and defended her from the stalking horrors stalking her every step. She doubted she would have survived without him. "That water ain't real."

"So you keep saying." Rachel couldn't help voicing her frustration, even though she struggled to keep it within her. She was afraid he'd leave, and she didn't want to be alone. But anger helped keep her awake, and there was no way she could participate in a conversation anywhere near normal. "You keep telling me that none of this is real, but I can't get out of here."

"Oh, this is real, *cher*." Bordelon gazed around the jungle. Drying mud smears left powdery gray residue on his clothes. Fatigue burned in his golden eyes, making them seem more deeply set than they had earlier.

His shoulders were bowed with weariness now. Scrapes showed on his knuckles and bare arms. Dried blood clung to cuts on his face and arms as well. His clothing had been torn again and again, but each time it had stubbornly re-knitted itself. She assumed the clothing was a representation of the protective spells he wore. The monsters they'd faced each time had gotten stronger, quicker, and more clever.

"You make a blunder here, you'll end up dead," he told her. "Make no mistake about that. But this here's the astral. It ain't the real world you know, but it's real enough."

He kept mentioning that too: the Astral. Rachel knew about the astral plane from some of her intro classes in college. Not everyone knew they had magic, and some who thought they had magic didn't have it at all, so the courses were designed to weed those out.

She'd never shown any innate magical ability, so she didn't know much about the subject, but she knew enough to argue the point. "This isn't the astral. It can't be. The astral is supposed to be our world, just rendered in mana form." Mana was a form of energy, and all things—organic and inorganic—had energy that was being used or stored. "I don't know where you come from, but this isn't my world. This looks nothing like my world."

"I've been thinking about that. This looks like Guatemala, maybe from a long time ago. Could be this vision of the world is as much the artifact's as it is yours."

"You think the artifact is *alive*?" The possibility wasn't new to Rachel, but she didn't want that to be the answer.

"I don't know. Could be it's only a conduit to another place." He looked around. "*This* place."

"None of this makes any sense. This place is . . . is *ancient*. It can't exist."

"No, but the memory of it does." Bordelon faced her and smiled gently. Despite his attempt, the skull face painted over his features robbed him of any true sympathy. "I come from New Orleans, *cher*, a place of magic and the past. In that sprawl, you can see many forms of the city. It spreads out over her like layers of an onion. History clings to that sprawl, tainting it with bygone eras even now, if you know where to look. If you're gifted enough, and tied to the history somehow, you can sometimes see some of what has gone before. I have walked along the streets when the Spanish and the French ruled the city centuries ago."

Not wanting to hear any more, Rachel drank the water from her cupped hands. She experienced a chill, wet sensation in her mouth and throat, but her thirst remained as strong as ever. The same thing had happened when she'd sampled some of the berries she'd passed. Cupping her hands again, she scooped up more water and drank, only to feel just as parched.

In frustration, she slapped her hands into the creek. Startled, the fish darted away and water soaked her, plastering the rags she wore to her body. How could she be drenched by water that never reached her stomach? It didn't make sense. It was just so . . . so . . . *weird.*

Before she knew what was happening, she started laughing uncontrollably and couldn't stop. She looked up at Bordelon, who gazed at her with concern.

"You realize how insane this is, don't you?" she demanded. "I'm an archeology student. Not a mage. Not someone people are supposed to shoot at or steal away. I'm just, just . . . no one. I'm *no one!*" She dragged in a ragged breath. "I don't deserve this."

She wanted nothing more than to go back to being no one. At least that person had a future ahead of her. As suddenly as the laughter started, it departed and the tears came, rolling down her face. She touched her tongue to one, tasted the salt, felt the actual wetness, and realized her own tears were more real than the water.

Bordelon crossed and knelt beside her. Reaching into his sleeveless tuxedo jacket, he took out a handkerchief and tenderly blotted her face like she was a child.

"Shh, shh. Everything's gonna be all right, *cher.*" He spoke softly, but the white skull undercut whatever comfort she might have felt. "You got people looking out for you."

"You mean Hawke?" She shook her head. "I'm just a payday to him."

"Maybe you was at first, *cher*, maybe you was. But that was in the beginning. Now you're something different. Now you're someone he wants to save. He's out there right now, risking his life to get you out of this mess."

Rachel made herself stop crying. She focused on his golden eyes and his words, letting his confident tone soak into her. "How can you know that?"

Reaching out to squeeze her shoulder with one of his big hands, Bordelon smiled. "Because I know my cousin, *cher*. Sometimes I know him better than he knows himself. He's gonna find a way to save you."

Taking comfort from the man's touch, Rachel wished she could believe him.

"You can believe me," Bordelon said as if he could read her mind. "I would not lie to you. My cousin can be a determined, inflexible man when he sets his mind to something, and he's set his mind to save you."

"Why would he do that?"

Bordelon shook his head. "I don't think he knows. He spends much time avoiding his true self. He keeps himself isolated and cut off, thinking that an island cannot be harmed." He paused. "But there's something about you that has woken him from his self-imposed quarantine. Even an island is changed when ships pass by."

"I don't even know him."

"No, and he doesn't know you. However, there is something inside you that he feels he knows, or wants to know, and he wants to protect it. Be glad of that. And trust it as I do."

Rachel wiped her face, feeling grime roll across her skin. She wanted a bath, but even if nothing lived in the water that would kill her, she doubted the creek would allow her to clean herself. If she couldn't really drink the water, she wouldn't be able to wash either. All she could be was uncomfortable in drenched clothing. Wherever she was, the land seemed determined to reject her. Or maybe it simply wanted to punish her.

"Do you look like this in the physical world?"

Bordelon laughed in his deep basso voice and pulled her to her feet. "I do, for the most part. My face and my body, sure. My clothing and paint—" He trailed his hand over his face and down to his chest where the bones stood out in bright relief. "—these things are part of me here. I have two selves, as many people on the Matrix do. I'm sure you have an avatar you play in the sim-sense games. Here, I am free to show myself as who I want to be."

Rachel looked at her reflection in the creek, seeing how bedraggled she'd gotten. In the end, though, she was herself. "I don't look any different."

"Many people don't look different, *cher*. The spirits I work with have marked me in their own fashion. I have accepted their gifts. I glory in them, and am thankful."

"Is the voice I hear a spirit?" She had told him about the voice, but he'd never heard it.

"Not to my knowledge." Bordelon's eyes narrowed. "Whatever that voice belongs to is like nothing I have ever seen before."

"Why did the artifact bring me here?"

"We don't know that it did." Bordelon frowned. "We only suspect it did, because you surely didn't do this to yourself. To come here, you would have had to know this place existed."

"What if I can't get out of here?"

"You must, *cher*. You have no choice." From the way he hesitated, she knew there was something he was leaving unsaid.

"What are you not telling me?"

Bordelon nodded. "You must leave this place, because if you don't, you will die."

Rachel wrapped her arms around herself as a large winged shadow passed by above the tree tops. "I know. I can't escape them forever."

"It's not just them, *cher*. You're dying. Slowly, but you are wasting away during every moment you spend here. If you stay in here too long, your mortal body will eventually fail."

CHAPTER FIFTY-EIGHT

A frigid wind blew through Minneapolis, making Hawke pull his long coat tighter around him. Neon lights from Stuffer Shacks, dives, diners, and adult entertainment venues washed over him, and somehow made the night feel colder. The few pedestrians braving the weather looked at him and got out of his way.

The sprawl was much chillier than Detroit. Some said residual Native American magic from the terrorist bomb that had destroyed the Aztechnology arcology in Calgary in 2061 had prolonged the winters here. Other people just said the cold this year was part of a weather pattern. There were other rumors, too. There always were.

Hawke didn't care why it was so cold, because it helped keep him vigilant. He was running on fumes, and he knew it. He wasn't at his best, and he needed to be. His team depended on him.

Lifting his gaze, he stared up at the Ngola Building. Thirty-seven stories tall, the building was dwarfed by several others around it. LED lights tracked up the side of the building, spelling out the corporate name: *NGOLA BIOWARE.*

"Ngola Bioware is the latest owner of the building," Dolphin informed him over his PAN. *"They develop bioware replacement organs for patients whose organs were destroyed by diseases that wrack struggling African nations. They're located here because warlords in those countries try to control the local organ biz, and take lethal efforts to shut down homegrown solutions. Several of Ngola's development labs and production plants have been blown up by drones in the last few years. As a result, they set up shop here. Of course, this is only one of several sites, because their enemies have pursued them here as well."*

"Security's gonna be tight."

"You knew that going in. But they'll be trying to keep their research

and prototype designs safe, as well as their people. We're not here to steal anything, and we're not going to hurt anybody. We just want access to the central computer nodes for a few minutes. We're not taking anything. We're just borrowing."

"We still have to break into the building."

"I'm going to help make that easier. Have faith."

"I'm struggling with that at the moment. Faith's in short supply."

"You have faith in me," Dolphin chided. *"Otherwise you wouldn't have contacted me. By the way, I've patched Javier in."*

Another voice broke in. Hawke recognized the gravelly tone of Javier Paredes Verdugo, and instantly felt a little better about the night's possible outcome. Paredes was the best combat mage he knew. They'd only worked together once, but the run had been against the Draco Foundation on a seek-and-find mission for a client interested in a series of murders in Peru. There had been a lot of magical barriers and some serious muscle onsite. Hawke had gotten the intel and passed it on, but he'd never heard anything about the murders or that Mr. Johnson again. Paredes had been vital in the effort to escape after they'd gotten caught inside.

"I'm late to the party," Paredes said in his smooth, confident voice, *"so I want to know why we're breaking into Ngola. How does it connect with any Aztechnology or NeoNET chasing after you guys?"*

Dolphin looped the video feed into Hawke's PAN so that he saw an overlay of Paredes leaning on a balcony railing overlooking the Minneapolis sprawl. Hawke didn't recognize the view, but he knew where Paredes was because that was where he was supposed to be.

Small and dapper, Paredes looked like a trust fund baby. His longish dark hair, parted in the middle, covered his ears and the back of his neck. Almond-shaped, hazel eyes always twinkled, as if he were constantly amused by something only he knew. A thin mustache covered his upper lip, and a narrow French tickler smudged his chin. He wore an Armante suit, even in his hotel room. Rings glinted on all of his fingers, and all of them held deadly surprises. Paredes was a guy who was always prepared. He held a glass of wine in one hand.

"Hello, *omae*," Hawke greeted him.

Paredes smiled. *"It is good to see you again, hermano. It has been much too long."* His Spanish accent hadn't disappeared since he'd been gone from his home country.

"You know I like my distance."

With a shrug, Paredes dismissed that. *"I know. Your rules."* He shook his head. *"They get in the way of things sometimes."*

"Rules have kept me alive."

"I know, but what use is a life lived without friends? As I have told you before, there is strength in numbers."

Hawke didn't enter into the old argument. He liked Paredes. They'd had a good time when they had worked together. Paredes had a yacht out in San Diego, and had invited Hawke there. "Tell Javier why we're interested in Ngola, Dolphin." Hawke paused at a street corner only a few blocks from the target building.

"Of course," the technomancer replied. *"We're here because the Ngola building wasn't always the Ngola building. Until 2061, it was a UCAS-based subsidiary of Transys Neuronet."*

"I know of Transys," Paredes mused. *"They specialized in bio-ware and cyberware. Supposed to be working on cyber that could be used by the dragons, if you believe the shadow whispers."*

"They are," Dolphin said. *"Very wiz tech. I've seen some of it."*

"Really? Fascinating. I'd love to hear more about this."

Hawke started across the street with the light. "Guys. Focus."

"Sorry." Dolphin sounded contrite. *"More later, Javier. Transys was one of the companies that plotzed after the Crash in '61. They got snapped up by Celedyr, then merged under one umbrella with Erika and Novatech, all of which was rebranded into NeoNET. A few months after the merger, NeoNET built a new building here. The old building changed ownership a few times before finally ending up with Ngola Corp."*

Translucent images moved across Hawke's vision, showing the building as it had been in 2060. *Transys Neuronet* crawled up the side of the structure. Not a lot had changed in the exterior.

"Ngola didn't have a lot of money to put into redesigning the space or upgrading equipment," Dolphin went on. *"They've done what they can, but they don't have a bottom line that allows them to keep on top of cutting-edge tech."*

"Ngola is funded by grants and foundations from other corps wanting a tax write-off." Paredes was a quick study and caught up in short order. In Hawke's image, he studied a translucent screen floating before him. *"The corp basically provides free health care to African nations needing help. I can see this for myself, but I still do not see why we are here tonight."*

"Because NeoNET is one of those corps donating credits and ser-

vices to Ngola," Dolphin replied. *"To be precise, they're providing cyber security. And that's going to give us a backdoor into NeoNET's systems."*

"You propose to hack into NeoNET from Ngola?" Paredes asked.

"Yes."

"How is this any easier than hacking into NeoNET from the outside?"

"Because I've written some shiny sleaze programs that will allow me to mask myself as part of Ngola's protocol. Once I get in—"

"You're very confident." Paredes smiled.

"I'm very good," Dolphin replied. *"Once I get in, I've got sniffers and snoopers ready to unleash. If there's any intel there concerning Rachel Gordon, Professor Fredericks, or that Guatemala site, I'll find it."*

At the corner of the two streets that fronted the Ngola building, Hawke took in the sec men in the armored box at the entrance. He'd walked the perimeter, looking for outlying security and planting wireless cameras Dolphin had instructed him to get so she could watch over the neighborhood with her programs, but he hadn't seen anything suspicious.

They were clear to go.

Only a few windows in the buildings had lights, letting him know where some people were burning the midnight oil. That was to be expected with the seven-hour difference between much of Africa and Minneapolis.

The streets were desolate and empty except for occasional traffic. Loose trash swirled in the wind. The garage across the street flashed *AVAILABLE PARKING*.

"Okay," Hawke said as he stepped off the curb and headed for the garage, "since everybody's up to speed, let's do this."

CHAPTER FIFTY-NINE

On the parking garage's twelfth floor, right below the roof, Hawke joined Twitch and Rolla. Both wore variants of the chameleon armor he'd used in Guatemala. Standing in the shadows as they were, he didn't see them 'til he was almost on top of them.

Twitch was gunned up, and Rolla was heavily armed as well, carrying a pair of Remington Roomsweepers at his hips and a bulky Krime Cannon slung over his shoulder. He also had a double-bladed combat axe with a telescoping haft for easier carrying. Seeing the weapon, Hawke felt instant respect. There was a reason he carried his katars. The way he and Rolla worked, things got up close and personal quick.

"Where's Dani?" Hawke asked when he realized the fourth member of their party wasn't present.

"Up top," Twitch replied. "Says she's preparing the way. Whatever that means."

"Means she's up where a Lone Star flyby can spot her and start wondering what somebody's doing hanging out on a parking garage rooftop," Rolla growled.

Neither of them appreciated what Dani Nighthorse could do. *Yet*, Hawke told himself. Twitch had never worked with Nighthorse. In fact, Hawke had never included her on a run that involved magic in any way. The current job had gone to the magical side of things immediately.

"She knows what she's doing," he said. "I'll get her."

"There's no need. I am here." Dani Nighthorse stepped out of the shadows and approached them.

Like the others, Nighthorse wore chameleon armor, but hers was embellished with barely visible sigils that changed shades with the suit. They also provided another layer of protection.

Hawke didn't know how old Nighthorse was, but she'd been around the shadows longer than he had.

In spite of the UGE that had changed her into an elf in her early teen years, her Norwegian roots still showed in her blonde hair and tall build. She was tall, curvy, and muscular. In addition to shamanic magic, she was hell on wheels in personal combat as well.

Her purple eyes studied Hawke. "It's been a long time, *min venn.*"

"It's good to see you." He hadn't meant to stay away from her for so long, but she'd been the first person he'd run with more than once since stepping out on his own. It was too easy to get close to her, and he thought that attraction would only get in the way, and possibly get one or both of them killed.

Rolla folded his arms over his broad chest. "Maybe you should ask her what she was doing up on the roof."

Hawke wasn't going to do that, but before he could tell the troll that, Nighthorse answered him.

"I was making preparations for tonight." She looked at Hawke, not addressing Rolla. "Those two are too noisy." Her gaze flicked over the troll dismissively. "And I'm not questioning whether your weapons are loaded."

"They're always loaded."

"You still check before you go into battle. So do I." Nighthorse returned her attention to Hawke. "Are we ready?"

"Yeah, we're ready. Perimeter's secure, and Dolphin has extra video points in place if she needs them." Hawke walked over to the opening in the wall that looked out onto the Ngola Building.

The cold breeze whipped into the parking garage. Only a few vehicles were parked in the striped zones. They took care to stay away from them, because they probably had better security systems than the parking garage did. Dolphin had gotten control of the garage systems easily.

The Ngola Building was going to be more of a challenge.

"Are you ready, Dolphin?" Hawke watched the street.

"Yes."

"Javier?"

"I am here," Paredes replied. He'd left the hotel, and even though his physical body was in a vehicle hidden nearby, Hawke knew the mage was with them, but in the astral world. Paredes could "manifest" an insubstantial representation of himself when

not engaged with a spell. For tonight, he was only manifesting his voice. The group could handle the physical threats. Paredes was there to take care of the magical defenses.

"All right, gear up, people." Hawke took the helmet Twitch had been holding for him. Stripping out of the long coat, he pulled it on. A quick touch of the tab on the suit's collar sealed the helmet to the armor.

The others did the same.

Hawke nodded at Rolla. The street samurai reached into a large equipment bag and took out a massive crossbow. He pulled back the tungsten string and locked it into place, then added a matte black quarrel as thick as Hawke's thumb. With practiced efficiency, he slapped a spool of tungsten wire onto the crossbow's forward stock and threaded the other end through the quarrel.

Setting himself, one foot up on the window ledge to brace himself, Rolla took aim at the Ngola Building.

"Ninth floor," Hawke said, watching as a sedan rolled across the street. "Wait for the truck to cover the noise."

"I know," the troll growled. "And I can count." He let out half a breath, then squeezed the trigger as the truck's engine noise echoed between the buildings.

The quarrel zipped across the intervening space and dug into the building only centimeters above the third window from the left. The *thock* of the quarrel biting into stone was barely audible to Hawke, even though he'd been listening for it. He was certain a casual passerby wouldn't have noticed. It quivered for a moment as the head burrowed more deeply into the stone. Faint dust clouded around the window, then disappeared in a gust of wind. The tungsten-steel alloy cable was almost invisible in the darkness.

Hawke let out a breath he hadn't known he was holding. He affixed one of the pulleys to the line, then held it ready. "Dani?"

Nighthorse stepped to the ledge as Rolla secured the other end of the cable to a nearby support pillar. Once the line was taut, she gripped the pulley, stepped up onto the ledge, and took a breath.

"You take out the window. Dolphin's already spoofed the security on that entrance point. Once you land, move quick. I'll be right on your heels."

Nighthorse nodded.

Hawke grabbed another pulley and put it on the line. "Go."

Nighthorse leaned into the fall down the zip-line and soared toward the Ngola Building. The pulley whispered as it rolled, but that faded away in a couple meters.

True to his word, Hawke launched himself after Nighthorse. The line sagged as it took his weight. He weighed twice as much as she did, and together they accounted for a load. Rolla would stress the line even more.

Shoving the possible issues about the infiltration out of his mind, Hawke focused on what he was doing. Wind whipped around him. The helmet's sensors counted down the distance to the wall. *50 meters...40...30...20...10...*

CHAPTER SIXTY

Nighthorse barely slowed her approach, closing on the wall faster than Hawke would have expected. The security system was temporarily offline, due to Dolphin's machinations in the security server, which was separate from the mainframe, but the bulletproof transplas was another issue.

A shimmer passed before Nighthorse when she was less than two meters from the window. She kicked her legs up and braked the pulley. Hawke held his breath, worried she was going to hit the window and be rebuffed back into the street. The armor wasn't enough to save her from a nine-story fall to the pavement.

"Dani—?"

"I've got it." In spite of the situation, with the ground waiting so far below her and Hawke speeding along less than two meters behind her, she sounded calm and unhurried.

Just before Nighthorse's boots touched the window, the transplas smoked in several places, then disappeared in a dim flash. Arching her body, the shaman sailed through the empty space. Her empty pulley banged into the quarrel and stopped short of the wall.

Stunned by how fast things were happening, Hawke almost missed his release. He released his pulley late and flew through the window, hitting his left hand on the frame, then dropping to a crouch in the spot Nighthorse had just vacated. He rolled forward to shed momentum, and came up on one knee with the Beretta 201T he'd selected for tonight's op in his hands. The silencer made it slightly longer, but he had no problem pulling it from his shoulder leather.

The helmet's night vision kicked on automatically, turning the long hallway into a collage of greens and blacks. He hadn't seen anything on his approach, and Nighthorse hadn't issued a warning, but he wanted to be ready.

Standing beside the left wall, Nighthorse held her pistol, too. Their primary weapons were loaded with stick-and-shock rounds, designed to knock down targets and render them unconscious with a jolt of electricity. To Hawke's knowledge, no one in the building deserved getting killed tonight, and he intended to keep it that way.

Twitch flew through the window a moment later, rolled, and came up with pistols in both hands. She moved so fast that Hawke never saw her draw the weapons, but knew she'd couldn't have been holding them and hanging onto the pulley at the same time.

"Take point," he said.

Twitch nodded and prowled forward.

Hawke turned back to the window as Rolla released the pulley. Maybe the wire dipped too far from the troll's weight, or maybe Rolla misjudged his approach, but his feet slammed against the bottom of the frame instead of coming through, and he fell backward headfirst.

Rolla yelped and cursed, waving his arms.

Diving forward, Hawke clamped a hand around one of the troll's big feet and hung on. Suspending nearly four hundred kilos with one arm, even with his augmented strength and reinforced skeletal structure, was difficult. Hawke was pulled halfway through the window before he could catch his knees below the ledge and ram his left shoulder against the wall to halt his movement.

But he stopped Rolla's fall.

"I can't believe you just managed that," Paredes said softly. *"You're going to get yourself killed."*

"Keep on . . . the perimeter lookout," Hawke ordered through gritted teeth. He'd forgotten about the mage in the astral. There were too many players on the op, too many things to keep an eye on. Catching one of his people before he took a swan dive onto concrete had been nowhere in the plans.

Shocked, maybe because he was still alive, or maybe because Hawke had caught him, Rolla cursed in a heated rush. He flailed his arms, nearly tearing himself from Hawke's grip.

"Be still, or I won't be able to hold on to you," Hawke ordered.

Rolla ceased moving and became dead weight that seemed to get heavier by the second. "Okay . . . okay. I'm not moving. Frag, that's a long way down."

"It'll go by really fast," Paredes commented.

"Hey," Twitch said.

"Sorry."

Placing his pistol on the ground, Hawke grabbed the troll with his other hand as well. "I can't pull you up."

"Well, don't fraggin' drop me."

"I'm not gonna drop you if I can help it, but you have to figure out a way up."

"Just you hang on then."

"I've got you."

With astonishing physical control, Rolla bent at the waist and grabbed Hawke's left wrist with his huge right hand. The helmet masked the troll's face, so Hawke couldn't read whatever emotions might be showing. Panic touched him for just a moment when he considered the probability that Rolla would pull them both through the window if things went wrong. *More wrong*, he corrected himself.

Rolla caught the window frame with his other hand and managed some of his own weight, easing the strain on Hawke's arms, shoulders, and back. Getting the troll inside the building wasn't made any easier then, but it was manageable. He came through slowly at first, then more quickly as his balance shifted.

Breathing hard, Hawke stood to one side as Rolla knelt on the floor.

"Gimme a second," the troll said, his voice hoarse. "Head rush from hanging upside down."

"Landing on your head would have been a lot more stressful," Paredes said.

Rolla growled a curse at the combat mage, who only laughed.

"Time's up." Hawke picked up his pistol. "We're behind the clock now." He waved to Twitch, and they started forward again.

"I'm coming." Still a little unsteady, Rolla forced himself to his feet and drew his own pistol. "We get time later, I owe you a beer, *omae*."

"We get outta here in one piece, and I'll take you up on that. Right now, just keep our six covered."

"Done."

Every minute spent inside a place you weren't supposed to be increased the chances of getting caught. Aware of that, Hawke had to clamp down on the impulse to hurry Twitch along. Safe was safe, and safe was preferable to almost any other scenario, except arriving too late to do what needed to be done. Sometimes staying safe meant going slower than he wanted. Beneath the armor, his skin crawled in impatience.

He kept himself focused, and slapped wireless button cams on the walls as he passed. They would serve as a secondary security perimeter and spy eyes if they needed them.

Dolphin had the blueprints routed to the helmets' video feeds. A three-dimensional diagram of the ninth floor overlaid Hawke's face shield. Three turns later, they reached the hallway where the mainframe was kept.

Pausing at the intersection, Twitch waved them back. Hawke cued his helmet, and picked up the feed from the gunslinger's point of view.

Farther down the hall, light emanated from a security office. Cams hung throughout the hallway, keeping everything in view.

"Do you have the cams?" Twitch asked.

"*I have them now,*" Dolphin replied. "*They won't see you until I let them. Or until an alarm is triggered. So don't—*"

"Trigger any alarms," Twitch said. "Yeah, I got that." Moving slowly, she crept forward, ducking beneath the bulletproof glass of the sec checkpoint's window.

Hawke nodded to Nighthorse, who headed down the hallway in the other direction, placing a couple more button cams as she went. The door twenty meters down led to a stairwell. Once in place, she booted a maglock to the door. The barrier wouldn't prevent a sec team from getting through, but it would slow any guards down.

Nighthorse started coming back. The plan was for her to put the guards inside the checkpoint to sleep with her magic. Before she could do that, however, a *click* drew Hawke's attention toward the overhead vent. Through the slits, he spotted a small cleaning 'bot that shifted and peered down at him.

"Dolphin, do you—"

"*I see it! I see it!*" She cursed. "*There's nothing in the files about a maintenance 'bot active tonight. I'm trying to acquire—*"

The 'bot blinked and powered away.

"*I'm too late! It just sounded an alarm! I'm sorry!*"

Hawke looked at Twitch. "Okay, Plan B. We go in hard and fast."

At the security checkpoint door, Twitch folded one of her pistols under her arm, then reached into a thigh pouch for three slap charges she'd readied earlier. She placed the charges on the lock and where the hinges would be inside the metal door. When she was finished, Twitch knelt and nodded at Hawke.

Hawke took a breath. Once the charges went off, there was no turning back. Ngola's sec teams would know they had a problem in the building from the 'bot's warning, and they'd know where that problem was. They had no choice but to get in, do the job, and get out as fast as they could.

He nodded back. "Do it."

CHAPTER SIXTY-ONE

Twitch ignited the charges with a command from her PAN. The thermite charges, a blend of iron and copper oxides, flared and burned incredibly hot. The lock and the other sections of the door turned to glowing, orange molten slag.

Twitch stood and kicked the door, but it didn't move. Inside the checkpoint, shadows moved across the window. Dolphin wouldn't be able to keep them masked anymore.

Fire alarms rang through the floor, adding to the confusion. Hawke filtered the harsh *whoops* out of his audio and ran forward. Stepping back, Twitch held her pistols at her sides.

Hawke slammed a shoulder into the door, shattering the slagged hinges and knocking it free. Following the falling slab of metal into the room, Hawke threw himself forward, landing on his stomach and leaving Twitch's field of fire clear.

Caught off-guard, the five sec men in the room tried to bring up their weapons. Chairs lined one wall, facing a trideo projector displaying combat biking across an area that nearly filled the available space, placing everyone in the middle of the action. The three-dimensional images of the armored biker teams using clubs and small arms was in full gorefest mode. The camera zoomed in on a 'roided ork who yanked a steel dart from his ruined eye, then spat out blood and broken teeth. The image distorted as two sec men barreled through with weapons blazing and their helmets askew.

Twitch's guns fired, but none of the men in the room went down. Surprised, Hawke checked the button cams and saw she was dealing with a crowd of sec guards from farther down the hallway. They boiled out of a locker room with guns in their fists.

On his own, Hawke rolled to one side and gripped the armored door with one hand, flipping it so the line of bullets from the weapons hammered into the impromptu shield. He threw his arm forward, aiming at a sixth sec man coming through a door on the far side of the room. As the door vibrated under the on-slaught, Hawke fired two rounds that struck the man in the throat.

Choked by the impact, the man stumbled, then the electrical charges released in bright blue bursts and rendered him unconscious. He fell in a boneless heap less than a meter from Hawke.

Staying low, spinning momentarily from the other sec men in the hallway, Twitch stepped into the room and fired on the fly. Both her rounds struck men between the eyes, released their charges in blue arcs, and dropped the targets in the tangle of three-dimensional combat bikers.

Still on the move, the gunslinger kept firing, dropping two more targets in rapid succession. The last man was fully armored, and recognized he was facing intruders using non-lethal rounds. More confident, he stood his ground and opened fire. The armor-piercing rounds ripped into the walls but didn't penetrate the thick metal plates enclosing the checkpoint.

Twitch fired a half-dozen rounds that slapped into the man's face shield as she sprinted, but one of his rounds caught her in the shoulder and knocked her off balance. While trying to recover, she got hit again, this time in the side, and got spun around.

Hawke surged up with the door and rushed the man. The guard wheeled on him, helmet covered with blazing stick-and-shock rounds, SMG chattering in his hands.

Ignoring the bullets pockmarking the door, Hawke drove it straight into the man, shoving him back into the wall. Flattened by the door, the man struggled to free his trapped gun arm.

Holding the man in place, Hawke reached around his im-provised barrier and drove a fist into his face shield. The helmet thudded against the wall as if hit by a jackhammer. Probably con-cussed, definitely unconscious, the man sagged.

Hawke stepped back and released the door and the sec man. He turned to Twitch. Both of them stood in the center of the com-bat biker arena match.

"How bad?"

She turned and showed him the deep scars that tracked the armor, but thankfully hadn't penetrated. "I'm wiz."

"Get Dolphin into the mainframe." Hawke shot the trideo projector twice and the resulting electrical charges blew the device offline. He slapped a couple more button cams on the walls.

Twitch ran for the computer room, held back only an instant by a sec door she took out with another slap charge.

Gunfire from the hallway let Hawke know reinforcements had figured out where the problem was. They were running out of time.

"Dolphin."

"*I'm working. I just lost control of the elevators. Fraggers locked me out.*"

Hawke peered out into the hallway and spotted Rolla exchanging shots with a tactical group emerging from the elevators there. Dolphin had hacked the elevators initially, but someone had booted an override protocol. Removing the silencer from his pistol because he wanted the noise to add to the confusion, Hawke leaned out around the door and emptied the magazine. The thunderous *booms* echoed down the hallway. "I need you on the sec computer hack."

"*I've got it,*" Dolphin told him.

"Then hurry up." Hawke pulled back, slapped a new magazine into the Beretta, and released the action to load the first round into the chamber. Reaching into his armor's thigh pocket, he took out a high-explosive grenade. He set the grenade, counted down, and flipped it out into the hallway toward the new sec men, reaching immediately for another.

CHAPTER SIXTY-TWO

In her sanctum sanctorum, knowing she was vulnerable to detection and possible attack now that she was moving in the Matrix, Dolphin watched the feeds streaming from Hawke and his group with a growing sense of urgency. The team was taking heavy fire, and their defensive efforts were restricted by Hawke's insistence on using non-lethal rounds against the sec men.

Seeing the carnage that had opened up so unexpectedly at the Ngola Building reminded her that there were no controls over what happened next.

We're all vulnerable now, she told herself. She considered bailing—she always did when a run went bad, and wasn't ashamed to admit it. Her world consisted of secrecy, hiding, never being physically there when people were getting hurt.

If she hadn't discovered the worlds that lay at her fingertips on the Matrix, she probably would have been content to be a wageslave somewhere. Just putting in her time at a corp. Maybe getting married, having a child. The usual things.

That didn't happen, though. She'd always been a gamer, and that was how other deckers had sucked her into the dark side. They'd hacked into game sites, shown her games in development, and got her started prying into the secrets that were out there. And there were a lot of secrets out there.

Right now, her attention was split between Hawke and Rolla trading bullets with the sec men in the hallway, and Twitch bursting through the door to the mainframe room.

Computer hardware covered the walls, filled with servers, motherboards, coolant systems, and layered redundancies. Two people in anti-static clothing were working on shutting down the mainframe. Two armored guards, their helmets off, were leveling their assault rifles at the entrance.

Panic flared through Dolphin. If the techs shut down the mainframe to protect the files, she couldn't make her run at NeoNET. She opened a channel to Twitch.

"Take out the lab techs first."

Twitch threw herself forward and dropped to her knees, sliding across the floor toward the techs as she shot them in the legs. As the techs fell, Twitch turned her attention to the sec men, and Dolphin's attention turned with it because the gunslinger's point of view was the only one she had access to in the room.

One of the guards unleashed a burst that glanced off Twitch's armor and knocked her off balance. Rolling with the impacts, the gunslinger lay on her side and fired from a prone position. The stick-and-shock rounds adhered to the faces and throats of both men, lit up, and dropped them in quivering piles of unconscious flesh.

"Twitch—" Dolphin said, not knowing how badly the woman was hit.

"Null sheen, I'm wiz." Twitch's point of view shifted as she got to her feet.

Some of the knots in Dolphin's gut relaxed, but her team was still inside, still in dangerous territory. In a sense, working as a decker for a run was a lot like playing a game. But she only had part of the play within her control. If she could have warped them out of the building with a spell or futuristic tech, she would have done it.

Except for Twitch. Dolphin needed her to set up the jackpoint she'd designed to get her into Ngola's cyberware.

Twitch looked down as she holstered one of her pistols and reached into her thigh pouch for the small piece of hardware needed to make the connection. It wasn't anything fancy, wasn't made of anything that would allow people to trace it back later. It looked like a spike, wider at one end than at the other, and was only ten centimeters long.

The program on it was streamlined, some of the best coding Dolphin had ever done. If anything could be tracked back to her, it would be those ones and zeroes.

That's not going to happen, she told herself. *Your hack-fu is strong. That which you write can never be deciphered.*

"Where?" Twitch asked.

Dolphin had told her she'd have to see the hardware first to know where to place the jackpoint. "To your left. On the console. Green light. Do it."

Twitch slotted the jackpoint and released it, waiting as if she was going to see something happen.

This isn't for your eyes any more, gunslinger. We're in my world now. Dolphin watched the code open up around her as she launched her sleaze programs and started cutting through Ngola's defenses like Neil the Ork Barbarian's sword through zombies.

"Go," Dolphin told Twitch. "Get out of there." She was calmer now, her breath coming more evenly, and her heart rate was slowing as she entered her zone.

Twitch drew her other weapon and headed back to the ongoing firefight in the hallway.

Knowing she didn't have a choice, knowing that she had to trust Hawke to take care of the team, Dolphin pushed the screens out of her head and focused on the hack. She looked into the Matrix, then placed her hand on the screen and pulled herself into the Ngola node.

The building wrapped itself around her as her cyber senses assimilated the new environment and translated it into code. Physical objects still looked like physical objects—sometimes. The security programs on the building's mainframe were riled up. Razor-edged simulacrums that resembled spinning Mobius strips leaned threateningly toward her.

The guardian code didn't actually look like that, she knew. That was just her interpretation of the programs. She reached out and hit them with Tinkerbell's fairy dust. At least, that was what the golden powder looked like. In reality it was a compilation of masking utilities she'd written to spoof firewalls.

The dust settled over the simulacrums and glowed for a moment. Then they sat down and ignored her. If they'd been guard dogs, they would have been wagging their tails for her.

Total calm filled Dolphin as she opened her toolbox and layered on the programs she'd readied. She changed her avatar, becoming a sleek black porpoise, a bullet she'd designed to fire through the Matrix.

As all of her programs came online, she became a weapon. An invisible blade that could plunge fearlessly through the Matrix. She set a timer, knowing time worked differently in here. In here, she perceived nanoseconds, not minutes. Everything happened fast.

She floated in the room, watching code pulse through the mainframe and through the peripherals. She could go through all of it, could go through the building—except for the places protected by firewalls. And those she could go through if she hacked them.

Dolphin grinned. The game was on.

CHAPTER SIXTY-THREE

Evading enemy fire chewing at the doorway he was taking cover in, Hawke accessed the secondary array of button cams he'd placed along the walls during their entry.

The HE grenade bounced off the opposite wall and exploded in mid-air, knocking the sec men backward. Since there was no shrapnel, the grenade wouldn't do any real damage, but it would scare the guards into holding back for a moment to assess things.

Hawke threw the second grenade and it detonated in a bright flash, filling the corridor with thick gray smoke. As the cloud eddied, already being sucked away by the air vents, he held his pistol in both hands and waited.

Before the smoke had completely disappeared, Twitch was back, tapping him on the shoulder to let him know she was there. "Dolphin's hardware is in place, mon. Time to go."

Hawke emptied his second magazine, but the sec men shrugged off the gunfire and kept coming forward.

Twitch stepped past him and stopped in the middle of the hallway with her pistols extended. When she fired this time, the basso reports told him she wasn't using stick-and-shock ammo anymore. Brass flew into the air in a steady stream.

The front rank of sec men fell back as the armor-penetrating rounds tore through their protective layers. Cries of wounded men sounded distant outside Hawke's helmet.

Twitch held up her pistols and released the magazines. She tucked one weapon under her arm as she freed an extra mag and looked at Hawke. "Arms and legs only, mon. Nothing vital. They've got DocWagon, I'm sure. Let 'em use it."

Hawke nodded and sprinted toward the corridor where Rolla held his position. The street samurai wasn't visible, though.

Hawke rounded the corner and spotted the troll with his back to him, holding his telescoped axe in both hands, blocking most of the hallway. Like an earthmover, he routed a half-dozen sec men before him, driving them back and down as he cleared the way.

"Well," Paredes said, *"it looks like not dropping him was a good thing."*

Trotting after Rolla, Hawke leveled his Beretta and shot at the sec men trailing them. Twitch was providing most of the cover fire, and wounded guards went down after her.

"What have you been doing?" Hawke asked.

"Your shaman friend and I are dealing with magical threats," the combat mage replied. *"There are some African twists and turns here I haven't before seen. It seems Ngola is preyed upon more by magic-based attackers than physical opponents."*

"Lucky us."

"Trust me, Dani and I are saving you from a lot." Paredes's voice sounded strained. *"It would help if your team hit your extraction point sooner rather than later, however."*

Hawke stepped on the chest of a guy Rolla had left sprawled across the floor with a cracked helmet. Instinctively, the guy grabbed him by the ankle, but the shadowrunner shot him in the throat for his trouble and felt a small tingle from the electrical charge before his foot lifted from the man's spasming hands.

A few seconds later, Rolla stood at the window where they'd entered. Around the street sam, sec men lay unconscious.

"Man, this is gonna suck," the troll said.

"You gotta go first to anchor us." Hawke peered through the window and aimed at the higher end of the zip-line on the parking building across the street. He steadied, targeting the line a few centimeters out from the building. When he fired, two stick-and-shock rounds hit and crackled blue fire for an instant.

Realizing he'd forgotten the nonlethal rounds wouldn't cut through the tungsten, Hawke drew back and reached for a magazine filled with APDS. Before he could switch out, Twitch was there, leaning out to snap off a quick shot. Across the street, the wire parted and whipped toward the Ngola Building.

Multiple bootsteps alerted Hawke that they were about to have more company. He turned and fired at the group of sec men taking a position at the end of the hallway. Their opponents had more cover than they did.

One also had a small rocket launcher that he pulled into place over his shoulder.

CHAPTER SIXTY-FOUR

Reaching into her bag of tricks, Dolphin enabled a trio of sniffer programs that manifested as squid-like creatures equipped with fiber optic cables ending in hooks for tentacles. She called them her Erinyes, after the Greek goddesses of vengeance.

According to legend, no guilty party could escape the Erinyes. She'd crafted hers to seek out any mention of Rachel Gordon, Professor Madison Fredericks, and—on a wider search—anything having to do with Guatemalan archeology.

"Okay, troops, let's go." Dolphin linked up with the Ngola grid, a subsidiary of the NeoNET grid, and flew through cyberspace with her three Erinyes at her side.

The jump from Minneapolis to Boston was a blur of impressions as she followed the gridlink. If she'd slowed down, she could have wandered through the Matrix version of all the sprawls she passed through. She could have hung out in chatrooms, joined in games, or done any of a myriad social or solitary things she wanted to do.

There were so many places to explore out here. Some days she feared her insatiable curiosity, thought maybe her inquisitiveness would lead her into a rabbit hole or a honey trap she wouldn't get out of, or that GOD would pump her full of black ice, and her meat body would die, leaving her mind . . . where? She didn't know. She'd heard horror stories of minds being lost forever on the Matrix.

Maybe that would happen to her one day.

But not today. Hawke and the team were counting on her to come through with something to help them solve the mystery of Rachel Gordon.

Ahead, NeoNET blossomed into being in the center of the

grid. The central node resembled a prismatic, stellated dodeca-hedron that slowly spun on an ever-changing axis. The facets changed colors as well, making it hard for a person to pinpoint an area and keep it marked. A crawler spun around the node as well, advertising *TOMORROW RUNS ON NeoNET.*

Pausing, Dolphin hung outside of NeoNET's node. Security software tingled as it examined her, like spiders crawling on her bare flesh. Then it passed, reading her as non-threatening.

I am so not the program you're looking for, Dolphin couldn't help thinking. She smiled, then whispered to the Erinyes, "Okay, crew, seek. Make Momma happy."

Immediately, the three squid simulacrums darted forward. The wrapper programs she'd put on them got them through Neo-NET's preliminary firewalls. To the corp security, the sniffers were just random inquiries from Ngola, programs looking for updates. The spoof would hold as long as she didn't try to crash any sys-tems or stay too long.

A moment later, the sniffer looking for Guatemalan archeol-ogy pulsed, let her know it had a hit. The other two notified her that they'd found something almost immediately as well.

Opening a small ping program, Dolphin located where the Erinyes had stopped within NeoNET. She went to them, passing through the perimeter firewalls and appearing outside the Ma-trix representation of the NeoNET building in Boston. The Erinyes floated outside an office on the eighty-sixth floor, where another firewall whirled around the building.

Dolphin translated herself back to human form and pulled a snooper program from her toolbox that looked like a soft, pink bubble. She flicked the bubble toward the office and it floated across the distance.

Tension filled her. This was one of the main hurdles she had to clear. If the firewall didn't like the snooper program, even though it was masked to look like Ngola software, the building would go on alert. One thing she had working for her was the fact that the office was protected by deep encryption, but it wasn't as protect-ed as the financial records and research and development.

And she was trying to get into one isolated area of the corp, not take down the whole system.

The bubble bounced against the shimmering silver firewall. A face pressed through the metallic surface and regarded the bubble for a moment, then didn't seem able to see it. The face recessed and the bubble burst against the firewall and spread into a circle.

Feeling more certain, and vibrating with excitement, Dolphin streaked for the pink circle, grabbed its edges, and pulled herself through the firewall into the corp office.

A colorful, intricate Persian rug covered Macassar ebony flooring with a lot of grain. The wood was the real thing, not pulp squeezed through an extruder. A crystal globe of the world as large as a baby elephant, with white continents floating on pale blue seas, hovered in a corner of the room. Beautiful paintings of seashores and exotic landscapes hung on the wall.

A marble-topped desk large enough to hold a miniatures war game of a large seafleet sat in front of a wall of windows offering an amazing view of the city. The chair had a wrought-iron frame, and the back was created by a couple dozen swords that had been welded together. Padding made it comfortable, and even that was covered with real Napa leather.

"Well, well," Dolphin mused. "Somebody has expensive tastes."

She approached the desk and sat in the big chair. Since she wasn't really there, she wasn't actually sitting in the chair, but it satisfied her to emulate doing so. She liked touching people's things, even if just from the Matrix, when she broke into their places.

She waved a hand over the top of the desk and brought the built-in deck online. "Let's see who you are."

The top of the desk was suddenly wreathed in fog, and a large cat's head popped up from the surface. Before Dolphin could pull her hand back, the beast closed its jaws on her wrist with crushing force.

Resisting the instinctive urge to jack out, Dolphin activated programs to shut down the biofeedback the guardian program unleashed on her. But the sec program was powerful—instead of just her hand, her whole body ached with pain. The guardianware was there to protect the deck, but it wasn't true black ice, and couldn't trap her.

She reached into her toolbox and spun out a decryption program that took the form of green powder lying in her hand. She blew on the powder and the small cloud wreathed the big cat's face. It was a jaguar, she noted as she took in the distinctive black pattern spread over its tawny fur. It was also near-sentient.

"Who are you?" Dolphin asked.

"I am Nagual," the cat growled.

Even while fending off the security program, Dolphin's curiosity made her bring up a quick search utility. "Nagual? The being that can change himself into many animals in Mesoamerican folklore?"

The green powder settled over the big cat and searched for weaknesses in the program. Bright points lit up, marking areas she could exploit.

"I am Nagual," it insisted. More of the jaguar emerged from the deck as it surged forward, preparing to attack.

"Well, Nagual, I've got things to do." Dolphin readied a hammer utility designed to smash software, then opened her other hand and hit the jaguar with it. In the Matrix, the utility flashed like a splintered laser beam, striking all of the opposing program's marked weaknesses.

The cat yowled and tried to clamp down harder on Dolphin's arm, but the sec program was already losing power. Angrily, it sank back into the thinning fog disappearing from the desk top. A heartbeat later, it vanished.

Dolphin brought up the computer and pulled up the file index. None of the names made any sense to her. She called the Erinyes into the building, and once they marked the files she was looking for, she started downloading them.

She'd barely gotten started when the building's firewall found her, letting her know the guardianware had a final trick up its sleeve. Keeping calm, knowing she had a little time as the ice started hardening around her, she grabbed the marked files and jacked out.

CHAPTER SIXTY-FIVE

"Twitch!" Hawke yelled as he snap-aimed and shot.

The gunslinger fired instantly, not even bothering to acknowledge hearing him. The bullet struck the rocket launcher operator's left thigh a moment after the rocket's release. The warhead leaped forward, spitting a fire-studded, smoky contrail.

Four meters out from Hawke, a shimmering fog spread out in a thin layer from wall to wall. The rocket detonated against the invisible barrier in front of the team.

Hawke's audio system filtered out most of the blast, but the explosion trapped inside the hallway was still deafening. Enough of the concussive wave came through to knock Twitch from her feet and even rock Hawke back.

"You can thank Paredes for the save later," Nighthorse said. "Right now you need to get gone, *omae*. He about emptied the bottle with that shield. He can sustain it for a bit, but you need to hurry."

Rolla already had one leg over the window's edge. He grabbed the bottom pulley, held on tight, cursed, and pushed himself out into empty space. He zipped down the line, barely controlling his fall with hard braking on the screeching pulley.

Before the street samurai reached the pavement, Twitch followed, dangling from the pulley with one hand and holding a pistol in the other. Sec men charged out from the building. Before they could get their weapons up, Twitch fired around Rolla, who howled a challenge as he dropped to the concrete.

Two sec men went down with wounds to their legs and arms. The others tried to pull back and return fire at the same time, but before they could, Rolla released the smoking pulley and hit the ground a couple meters away, lashing out with his huge fists. Sec men flew in every direction.

With lithe grace, Twitch landed atop the troll's shoulders, looking incredibly small against Rolla's bulk. Pistols in both hands, she turned and twisted like a tank turret as she fired at their opponents.

Hawke turned to Nighthorse. "Go."

She looked like she might object for a moment, then grabbed a pulley and dropped.

The magical barrier blinked a couple times and looked less solid.

Lunging out the window, Hawke grabbed the last pulley with one hand. He worked the controls, freeing the brake, and started to drop. Bullets cut the air around him and one smashed into the pulley, tearing it from its tracks.

Still eight stories above the ground, Hawke fell.

"*Dani!*" Dolphin yelled. "*Above you!*"

Below, rushing up way too fast, Dani Nighthorse turned her attention up to Hawke, who had instinctively tried to assume a parachutist's five-point spread to slow his descent. She raised her arms and spoke something he didn't quite grasp as he passed her, mostly because his mind was still trying to come to grips with the fact that he was falling to his death.

Two stories above the street, Hawke saw a whirlwind rise from the sidewalk and stretch toward him. In the next moment, a cushion of force wrapped around him, feeling like a warm blanket. He didn't stop falling, but his descent slowed appreciably. He landed on his feet and immediately dropped and rolled.

Dazed, not believing he was still alive, Hawke pushed himself to his feet and was even more surprised to find he hadn't released his weapon during the fall.

The whirlwind hovered protectively over Nighthorse, and just for a moment, Hawke saw a large face with ballooning cheeks appear in the spinning debris that had been picked up by the air spirit.

"Thank you, Morshyu," Nighthorse said.

The whirlwind dissipated, and debris flew out from it. Whatever had been there was gone. Hawke felt the vacuum of its passage.

A GMC Bulldog screeched to a halt in the street, its automated side doors and rear cargo door opening. Paredes sat behind the wheel and waved at them.

"Get in!"

Twitch vaulted from Rolla's shoulders and hit the ground running. Reaching the van, she leaped into the passenger seat and brought her pistols to bear on the Ngola sec men, who weren't in any hurry to defend the structure from a departing assault force.

Rolla sprinted to the back of the van and pulled himself inside, making the vehicle rock heavily.

"I still don't know how you caught that one," Paredes called from the driver's seat as Hawke followed Nighthorse into the vehicle's cargo area behind the seats. "He almost breaks the van." The combat mage leaned across Twitch and threw out his arm.

In front of the Ngola Building, a wave of fire bloomed on the concrete and rolled over the sec men. Temporarily blazing, the guards retreated.

Paredes hit a button, and the doors closed as he put his foot on the accelerator. The powerful motor roared, and Hawke rocked against the momentum.

He glanced at Nighthorse. "Thanks for the save."

"Of course, *omae*." She shot Rolla a stern glare. "I was busy finding an air spirit on top of the parking garage. Never question a professional."

Rolla wrapped his arms around his knees and sat with his back against the side of the van. "So, when I almost fell out of the window, why didn't you save me?"

"Because Hawke had you. Be glad."

Leaning back, feeling the soreness from rescuing Rolla sinking into him, Hawke knew he'd be suffering the aftereffects for a while, med suite or no med suite. He opened his comm. "Dolphin? Tell me you got something."

"I do. I don't know what it will tell us yet, but it's definitely about Rachel Gordon and Guatemalan artifacts. I'm going to have to work on the files to break the encryption, but at this moment, it's just a matter of time."

"Wiz." Hawke sighed in relief and didn't allow himself to dwell on the possibility that everything Dolphin had grabbed might be worthless.

He closed his eyes for a moment, just as Flicker reached out to him.

"Hawke."

"Yeah?"

"Whatever we're going to do, we have to do it fast. Rachel's vitals are now in a steady decline. We're losing her."

CHAPTER SIXTY-SIX

Rachel tried to speak, but her voice caught in her parched throat, finally coming out in a weak rasp. "I'm . . . dying?"

"You're under a doctor's care," Bordelon said. "They're giving you glucose and other necessary fluids through an IV. But that's not enough. Whatever's keeping you here is burning through your body's reserves. You're using yourself up just to stay alive here. That is why we must find a way for you to escape."

Trying to focus, Rachel made herself take a breath and let it out. Then she took another one. That was how she was going to stay alive. One breath at a time, for as long as she could keep breathing. "How long do I have?"

Looking sad, Bordelon shook his head. "We don't know, *cher*. A lot of that depends on you. On how bad you want to live. And how fast Hawke can find the answers he's looking for. Time doesn't run in here the same as it does in the physical world."

Dizziness swept through her. She wasn't sure if it was the fatigue, or the sudden knowledge of how dire her predicament was. She swayed, and would have fallen if Bordelon hadn't caught her around the waist and steadied her.

"Careful, *cher*. I got you."

Rachel focused again and tried to remain standing. Her legs trembled and her knees threatened to go out from under her. "I'm just so tired. I need to rest."

"You can't go to sleep," Bordelon said. "Not till you're outta this place." He paused, shifting until he had one of her hands in his. "Let me try to assist you."

"With what?" As soon as the words left her mouth, she felt the sudden connection to Bordelon. Something inside him twisted and turned, trying to escape. But the feeling coming from him was warm as sunlight, and took away some of her weariness. Her senses sharpened and whirled at the same time.

Bordelon sang. The words were melodic and unfamiliar, but Rachel felt like she almost knew them. Energy spread throughout her, and her brain seemed to open up till she felt more connected than ever to the world around them.

As her strength grew, she took more of her weight back until she was standing on her own again. A shadow crossed above her, temporarily blotting out the sun, and she knew without looking that it was one of the winged horrors constantly searching for her.

Glancing up, she spotted the flying lizard streaking down at them. It was three meters long, and had four wings that somehow functioned together, even while being only a little wider across than the thing was long. Pebbled scales the color of bruised plums covered the creature from snout to tail. Three rows of serrated teeth filled the long beak that looked as wide and as powerful as a crocodile's. Its eyes were orange coals, with black rot at their core.

Unable to move, Rachel watched helplessly as Bordelon figured out too late there was a threat. Eyes widening, lips already moving in song, he pushed her behind him, maybe thinking whatever defensive spells he'd woven would protect him from the predator. He held up his walking stick in his free hand.

Ignoring whatever Bordelon was doing, the flying lizard screamed, the shrill cry echoing around the gurgling creek. The mage struck with his stick, shoving it into the lizard's face. Slowed to a crawl but not stopped, somehow hanging suspended in midair, the creature knocked the walking stick aside with its blunt snout and came through Bordelon's defenses. Although it had been slowed, it was still coming, it was still going to tear them to pieces—

"Kill it!" the voice inside her head commanded. "You cannot be the victim in this place! You must unleash the predator within you! Teach these monsters to fear you! You were not born to die in this place if you have the courage and the power!"

Rachel's fear and anger knotted within her, and she felt unbridled energy course through her. Whatever Bordelon had been doing was only a drop in the bucket to what she felt now. There was nothing she could do to avoid this world, so she would embrace her place in it. Instead of running, she chose to claim her ground and fight. At least it would be some kind of end.

Instinctively, she reached around Bordelon and slapped her

hand atop the lizard's head as it came closer, despite the mage's barrier, as if moving through invisible quicksand. The rough, pebbled scales pressed against her palm almost hard enough to cut her flesh. Pain shot up her arm, and she nearly yanked it away, but she felt certain that if she did, she and Bordelon would be killed.

Instead, she pushed back against the lizard and screamed, *"Die!"*

Pale blue fire crackled across the creature's skull. Orange eyes bulging, rolling in fear, the lizard beat its wings frantically and tried to pull back.

But it couldn't break her connection to it.

"Cher!" Perhaps thinking the lizard had gotten hold of her, Bordelon pushed back against Rachel and tried to pull her hand away.

Maintaining contact with her opponent, Rachel used her other hand to push Bordelon aside. The man flew sideways like he'd been hit by a moving vehicle. He lost his hat, but he rolled with the force, and was quickly on his feet again.

"Stay there," Rachel ordered him.

Confused, staring at her in disbelief, the mage obeyed.

The lizard obeyed her as well, quitting its efforts to escape. The creature snarled and trembled as it tensed to fight back. Rachel felt its strength through her touch. If it got away, it would rend her to pieces with its fangs and claws. She picked up those thoughts from its mind.

The pale blue fire continued spreading down the lizard's body like an infection. She realized it was dying only because that thought registered in its small, rapacious brain.

In the next moment, the lizard disappeared in a blaze of blue fire that left a pattern of smoking cinders across the blackened ground. The stench of burned meat filled the air.

CHAPTER SIXTY-SEVEN

Scarcely able to believe what had just happened, Rachel drew back her trembling hand and tried not to be sick. Frightened of what she would discover, she turned her hand over and looked at her palm, certain she would find it charred to the bone. Instead, her flesh was intact, as if nothing had happened. As she watched, the slight cuts she'd received from the scales closed, leaving small white scars.

"*Cher*?" Bordelon called.

"I'm . . . I'm all right." Rachel wrapped her arms around herself, willing herself to wake up, but knowing that wasn't going to happen because she was still here, even though she didn't want to be.

Slowly, Bordelon picked up his top hat and walked back to her. "What just happened?"

"I . . . killed it." Rachel didn't even like saying that out loud, but a small, savage piece of her that she hadn't even known existed was also exulting in that fact.

"How did you do such a thing?"

"I don't know."

Several of the smaller flying lizards suddenly darted within a few meters of Rachel, but none came any closer. None of them dared. One tried to land on Bordelon's shoulder, and he swatted it away with his walking stick.

"Come on," he finally said. "We can't be hanging around here. That smell's gonna draw more of those ill-tempered things." He took her arm and gently pulled her along. She followed, still dazed by what had happened.

Rachel and Bordelon walked along the creek, following it upstream. Negotiating the climb had been difficult, but Rachel discovered her strength was returning. Once they gained the top, Bordelon kept walking, urging her to keep moving. Surprisingly, when they had to stop a while later, it was because he had gotten winded.

The mage leaned against a tree, both hands resting on his walking stick as perspiration dripped down his bare face and arms. "Something has changed for you, *cher*. In you, perhaps. What is it?"

Rachel stood in front of him and looked up at the sky. Winged lizards flew by now and then, but none seemed to notice her. She knew it was because she didn't want them to. Somehow, she was preventing them from finding her.

"I don't know," she admitted. "But I feel better. Stronger. Does that makeany sense?"

Bordelon shook his head. "I don't know. We'll have to wait and see. Usually with magic, there is always a cost. Nothing comes for free."

"Do not listen to him. He knows nothing about you, or what you can become. You cannot allow him to stop you before you become what you were intended to be!"

"I am who I'm supposed to be." Rachel turned, searching for the source of the voice. It couldn't be coming from nowhere. Whoever was speaking had to be somewhere nearby.

"*Cher*?" Concerned, Bordelon came toward her, but she noticed he kept his distance as well.

Closing her eyes, Rachel blocked him out of her mind, ignored the gurgle of the creek, the cries of the leather-winged hunters overhead, the susurrating buzzes of insect wings. Instead, she focused on the voice.

"You are stronger now. Good! You are getting closer! Come . . ."

She searched for whoever was talking to her, struggled to pinpoint where the voice was coming from.

Then she felt a pull. It was gentle but steady, and she was certain the answers she sought lay in that direction. Slowly, she turned in a tight circle until she was certain she was facing the right way.

Rachel opened her eyes and stared into the jungle, at the unending trees and brush. She also saw that the direction she needed to go was farther up the creek. Somehow, unconsciously, she'd been headed the right way all this time.

"Rachel?" Worry chewed into Bordelon's voice.

"It's okay," she replied softly. "I know which way to go now."

She started walking again, still feeling the pull, which grew stronger with every step.

Although she didn't know how much time had passed or how far she'd walked, Rachel knew the day was ending. Finally. It had gone on forever, perhaps waiting for her to get her bearings. Now the sun was setting in the sky behind her, and darkness was spreading in her wake as though it were chasing her.

Panting and limping, Bordelon stumbled along behind her. He'd tried to talk her into taking occasional rests, and sometimes she'd allowed it. She no longer needed those respites. She felt energized, as though she could walk forever. His harsh breathing rattled in her ears.

At the top of the latest rise, she waited for him because he'd started getting panicky when he couldn't see her. Finally, taking advantage of the fact that she wasn't moving, he climbed more slowly, cresting the hill long after she did.

The terrain around them was even more primitive than before. The jungle had grown so dense she knew she'd be hopelessly lost if she hadn't known where she was going. Boulders cropped up now and again, huge, jutting monoliths that soared ten and twenty meters above her, challenging the height of some of the trees.

The stream continued, but it had become soupy and primordial, a sludgy trickle she would never have risked drinking from. *Things* grew in the foul liquid, too. They wriggled and writhed, and every now and again one would tear free of the gelatinous substance and take to the air on dripping, translucent wings. It was like the stream was giving birth to tiny monsters.

A few of the creatures had attacked Bordelon, tearing at him with tiny teeth and razor-sharp, hooked claws. He had sung, and she'd seen the energy in him now—the shimmer that revealed his spellcasting—and knew he was getting weaker.

His spells didn't protect him any more. She did. Their roles had reversed, and now she was the guardian. He was struggling to stay here because the land was fighting him more, resisting his presence.

"I need . . . to rest." Finding a rocky outcrop on a nearby boulder, Bordelon sat. He took off his top hat and placed it beside him. Taking a deep breath, he raked a sweat-slick arm across his sweat-slick face and succeeded only in moving perspiration around.

Rachel gazed up at the night sky, which was still coming, converting more and more of the blue overhead to black. "Not for long. We need to keep moving. Getting caught out here during the night will put us in more danger than we've faced so far."

Bordelon squinted at the sky, then turned and looked farther along the creek. "How far away are we from where you're going?"

"We're close." Rachel sighed in frustration. She knew they were almost where she needed to be, but they weren't there yet, and night was falling fast. They needed to be safe before the darkness was complete. Somewhere out there in the darkened lands, the monsters roared and screamed in bloodlust.

"Do you know where we're going, *cher*?"

"I do."

"Then tell me. Please."

She shook her head. "I can't. I *feel* it, but I can't see it." She waited a few more moments, then knew she had no choice. "Get up. We need to get moving."

Bordelon stood and placed his hat back on his head. "I'll follow, but I don't know if I can keep up."

"If you can't, I'll leave you. I have no choice. My time here is almost up." She knew that was true too, although she couldn't say exactly what she meant by it, or why she was so certain.

CHAPTER SIXTY-EIGHT

"Professor Fredericks' dig was funded by Ayumi Sukenobu," Dolphin said.

Hawke sat in the shotgun seat of the second-hand RV Flicker had waiting for them in Mankato, Minnesota. Outside Minneapolis, even though there'd been no sign of pursuit from Ngola's private sec force or Lone Star, they'd split up and made their separate ways to the rendezvous point.

Except for Dolphin. She was still in Denver, not far from where Flicker and Snakechaser guarded Rachel Gordon, whose prognosis hadn't changed. Her entire body was compromised, nearing full-on medical freefall. From what Flicker could guess, Snakechaser's presence with Rachel—wherever the two of them were— was helping, but he couldn't dam the tide of life leaking out of the woman.

"Who's Sukenobu?" Rolla was stretched out on a sofa in the back of the RV, munching on fare from a Senor Taco they'd stopped at while refueling. He wore shorts and a loud red Hawaiian shirt featuring parrots and troll females in bikinis. He claimed the shirt was a disguise, and Twitch told everyone that Rolla usually wore Hawaiian shirts when not working.

Twitch sat cross-legged, but she wasn't on the floor. Instead she held herself up on her fingertips, swaying slightly as the RV rocked along the highway at just below the speed limit. Her eyes were closed. Bruises along her right arm showed where the bullets had nearly penetrated the armor. Others were on her torso, but none were anything more than inconveniences. Neither she nor Hawke had mentioned any of the injuries to Jovi when they had briefly talked earlier that morning.

Evidently marriage didn't mean Twitch was going to share *ev-*

erything with Jovi. Hawke didn't know how that knowledge made him feel. If Twitch held things back from her wife, it was possible—unlikely, but possible—that the gunslinger might be holding things back from him, too.

Thinking like that was circular, and made Hawke's head throb. It was one of the main reasons he was against taking on permanent partners. There was too much trust involved, too much not knowing everything and everyone involved. Runs were messy, but personal lives were more along the lines of an M. C. Escher painting. Coming and going, everything blending together until nothing was accomplished.

"Sukenobu is one of the chief program designers at NeoNET," Dolphin went on. *"But she's also the granddaughter of one of the corp's founders."*

The RV came with a trideo projector system that displayed images on the windshield in front of Hawke and in the center of the back area. Video footage of the woman at a black tie affair filled the projection area. Sukenobu was in her early forties, tall and thin, with short, dark hair. She wore a necklace of variegated brown and black scales pieced together around her neck. Smiling, she walked to a large, well-lit stage and waved a hand, signaling for a hologram wall to disappear. When the wall was gone, a Tyrannosaurus Rex skeleton stood revealed, frozen in a timeless roar.

"Are those real bones or a trideo printing?" Rolla asked. More interested now, he leaned forward while scooping another overflowing burrito out of one of his greasy fast food bags.

"Those," Dolphin said, *"are real. Six years ago, they were excavated from a site in Alberta by an archaeological team Sukenobu funded after a local professor researching migratory patterns of dinosaurs led him to believe they might find a skeleton in the area. It took them almost three years of digging to locate it."*

"Three years?" Nighthorse sat at a built-in booth closer to the front of the RV. Before her, several small pieces of dark green and yellow rock lay on a large piece of black velvet. During the trip, she'd been concentrating on assembling the pieces. With half of them used now, the construction was beginning to look like a bowl. "She's very serious about her dinosaurs."

"She is," Dolphin agreed. *"Serious doesn't begin to cover it. She's obsessed with the subject."*

Copies of screamsheet pages flicked across the trideo projection area, followed by more images of Sukenobu and dinosaur skeletons.

"But that's only the surface of what she's really interested in."

"She really wants to know more about dragons," Paredes said.

He stood in the small kitchenette, preparing a large salad in a bowl. He hadn't wanted to resort to fast food. Luckily, they were in Nebraska, over halfway to Denver, and there had been plenty of small grocery stands close to the highway.

"Correct," Dolphin said, sounding surprised. *"How'd you know?"*

Paredes carried bowls of salad to Twitch and Nighthorse, both of whom thanked him. "I may know a guy who knows a guy who was involved in a theft of a *Muttaburrasaurus* skeleton in Queensland a few months ago."

The combat mage smiled and picked up another salad bowl, lifting it in Hawke's direction. Hawke got up and met him halfway.

"Thanks."

Paredes nodded. *"De nada, amigo.* My pleasure."

Hawke took the bowl and a fork back to the front of the RV and resumed his seat. The driver's seat was empty. Flicker was driving through a remote connection. She was wired into the traffic reports, and knew where and when to dodge checkpoints and speed traps.

Rolla glanced up at Hawke in disbelief. "Seriously? You're going to eat that?"

"I am." Hawke stuck his fork into a piece of grilled chicken. The salad was simple, but Paredes had embellished it with spices and candied pecans. Some of the condiments had come stocked in the RV.

Shaking his head, the troll took out a handful of *empanadas* and popped one into his mouth. "I don't see how you keep your strength up." He glanced back at the trideo images. "So why does Sukenobu jones so hard for dinosaurs if she's really interested in dragons?"

"Dragons like their privacy," Twitch said. "And their mystery. Even now we don't know much about them, and they like it that way. Everybody knows you never deal with a dragon." She made a pistol of her thumb and forefinger and shot Rolla. "Not if you want to live."

Rolla scowled. "Dinosaurs ain't dragons."

"No," Nighthorse agreed, "but there are some who believe dinosaurs were the progenitors of the great dragons. According to the legends, and shadow whispers among the Awakened, dinosaurs existed in the First World, and were wiped out by a great evil. During that time, the dragons entered the world from wherever they were—assuming they weren't just created during the deconstruction of the First World and the formation of the Second World. Evil, with a capital E, came into the world during that time, and the balance had to be restored."

"You're saying dragons are good?" Rolla smirked at that.

Nighthorse shook her head. "Not all. Balance sometimes only means that opposing powers have to exist. Some believe the dragons took over the bodies of the surviving dinosaurs, and converted them into forms they could use."

"Okay, let's back away from Saturday morning simsense-land and get to the baseline on this thing." Rolla shifted, reached down for his beer, and drained the bulb. "Sukenobu hired—"

"Funded," Dolphin corrected.

Rolla ignored her. "—this professor and the girl to go down to Guatemala and find dinosaur bones?"

"No," Dolphin said. *"According to the proposal presented by Professor Fredericks, he wanted to go to Guatemala and look for an artifact he called the Dragonseed."*

"What's that?" Rolla asked.

"Fredericks found a document that described the Dragonseed as a device that created dragons," Dolphin said.

Only the steady hum of the tires on the highway filled the RV for a moment.

Nighthorse glanced at Paredes. He shook his head. "I've never heard of such a thing."

"Neither have I," she replied. "But the corps would pay dearly for any scrap of information that would enlighten them about dragons. Of course, the dragons would be just as happy eliminating any chance of that."

Nighthorse turned back to Dolphin's image in the lower left of the projection area. "Are there any drawings of the artifact in those documents?"

Dolphin shook her head. *"No. All I've seen is its mention in Fredericks' papers. I've swept the Matrix and found lots of rumors and myths, from Greek mythology–they were called dragon's teeth, and Cadmus and Jason used them to grow warriors–to anime and online game references."*

"Where did Fredericks' info come from?" Rolla asked.

"He translated a document the University of Virginia has had in their collection, acquired and donated by Thomas Jefferson himself. Supposedly, it was found during the Corps of Discovery's mapping of the Louisiana Purchase. The knowledge of exactly where it was found has been lost."

Rolla grunted derisively. "Or got lost on purpose. Even back then, people lost information they didn't want other people to have. Probably happened back in Neanderthal days, too."

"How did Fredericks translate the document?" Paredes frowned. "I find it unbelievable that a professor who has been his position as long as he has would suddenly have an epiphany on a scale like this."

"That's because he didn't have the epiphany," Hawke said. "Rachel Gordon did." Then he started telling them what Fredericks had revealed to him while they'd been traveling toward Distrito Caracas.

CHAPTER SIXTY-NINE

When Hawke finished his tale, Nighthorse looked up at him with her dark eyes. "Rachel is bonded to the Dragonseed." She glanced at Paredes, who nodded as if he understood what she was alluding to.

"What do you mean?" Hawke didn't understand any of what they were talking about. He felt a little better that Paredes and Nighthorse had a handle on the magical knowledge they might need, but he still wasn't happy about them getting deeper and deeper into this magical quagmire.

"The artifact—call it a Dragonseed, or whatever you wish—it's possible it was designed only for certain people to find." Nighthorse seemed certain of her declaration.

"That's why she was having the visions, *omae*," Paredes added. "Maybe only a handful of people could have translated those documents—which I highly suspect are *not* Mayan in origin—and perhaps they were intended only for one individual."

"Rachel."

Paredes nodded. *"Exactamente."*

Hawke frowned. "That doesn't make sense. I saw the dig site. That underground cave system had been buried for thousands of years."

"So?" Paredes pursed his lips.

"No way anyone could plan that."

"You're thinking too small. Technology, *history*, even—all of that is too short when you start thinking about Old Magic. Especially when you're talking about the dragons. They've been around for a long, long time, and they've spun plots and machinations and campaigns since they've first drawn breath. Perhaps this is only one more. Or perhaps this is something they wanted to remain forgotten."

Hawke looked at his team, and thought about all they had gone through, the blood they'd already shed to get this far. He tried to guess how much more they'd have to risk if he continued being involved with Rachel Gordon and her problems.

Maybe . . . maybe it was better to just let her slip away.

Even when he thought that, though, the part of him he tried to keep from making decisions about biz didn't like the idea. He focused on his companions, thinking about them and a way out of getting slotted up.

Finally, he shook his head. "We can't do this. It's too big. Way bigger than anything I'd imagined."

Sympathy showed in Nighthorse's liquid eyes. "We're already in it, Hawke. Up to our ears. There's no way out now except to go through it. You know that."

"We can let them have the woman." Stubbornly, Hawke refused to name her because he knew it would weaken his resolve when he needed to be strong. "Once they have her, there's no need for them to come after us."

"Except to hose us and make sure we don't tell anybody what little we do know," Rolla growled. "The Azzies and NeoNET, they'd be all about that." He took a breath. "Personally, I'd rather take a chance on getting my hands on a big stick to whack 'em back with."

"More than that, you don't leave a chummer hanging," Twitch said softly. "You never have. That's why I came. So *you* wouldn't get left hanging on this."

Dolphin broke the uncomfortable silence that followed. *"We don't have much breathing room anyway. Aztechnology and NeoNET have stepped up the search for us. I'm doing everything I can, but the run on the Ngola Building attracted their attention. They're getting closer. I don't think they're going to back off no matter what."*

Hawke pushed his breath out and tried to think, but it was like his head was filled with congealed Stuffer Shack grease. The thoughts, the ideas were there, but he couldn't reach them.

"We're whole pot committed then," he finally said. "We stick with this thing and see where it leads. Hope we can find a jackpoint on this somewhere, and bail with our skins still intact."

"There's also the possibility we can help the girl," Nighthorse stated. "Don't forget that."

"Do you have a plan to do that?" Hawke demanded. "Because I'm fresh out."

"As a matter of fact, I do." While they'd been talking, the shaman had been working on the bowl. All of the dark green and yellow rocks had been used to construct the dish she now held in her hands.

The object was irregular in shape, but the seams between the pieces had almost vanished. The surface caught the light and reflected it, but the bowl's interior absorbed all light that entered it. Nighthorse could have been holding a black hole in her hands.

"Nice." Paredes came closer and held his hand over the bowl, taking care not to touch it. "Very good work." He pulled his hand back and stepped away.

"I need to do more to make it stronger." Nighthorse held the bowl in her fingertips and examined it with a critical eye. "But I think it will be ready by the time we reach the girl."

"What?" Rolla frowned again. "You think an arts and crafts fruit bowl's gonna fix her?"

"It is *not* a 'fruit bowl,'" Paredes said.

"Then what is it?"

"If I told you, your head would explode." Paredes grinned at him. "As large as your head is, it would make quite the mess."

Pinching his eyebrows together, Rolla turned his attention back to his bag of Senor Taco. "You can get slotted."

"I discovered something else while poking around," Dolphin said. *"Despite her interest in dinos and dragons, Sukenobu wasn't an easy sell when it came to Fredericks' dig proposal. She'd initially turned it down because the professor hadn't been able to thoroughly substantiate his claims on the translation. Guess who tipped her to the possible legitimacy of the dig?"*

"No clue," Hawke answered.

"Deckard," Dolphin replied.

Rolla looked up. "I knew a street sam named Deckard. I heard he got chilled in Santa Fe a couple weeks back."

"He did," Flicker said over the RV's PA. *"Hawke chilled Deckard when he tried to bust into this run."*

A savage grin twisted Rolla's visage. "Couldn't have happened to a more deserving guy. Deckard was bad news for most everyone who did biz with him."

"You're sure it was Deckard?" Hawke struggled to fit all the pieces together. They fit, but he had no idea why. That explained how the troll had magically "known" about the run the Johnson had brought Hawke in for.

"*I am,*" Dolphin said. "*And I'm just as certain KilmerTek sent Deckard after the Johnson who recruited you.*"

"His own corp?" Hawke hated when things got this twisty.

"*Yes. KilmerTek had Deckard on retainer doing sec work for them down in Guatemala. The corp is currently negotiating some oil leases there. Deckard kept the exploration teams safe while they were in the jungle. From what I'm looking at, those leases are all around the dig site Fredericks chose.*"

Even though he was surprised, Hawke wasn't shocked. When it came to corp biz, it was always like Matryoshka nesting dolls. Open one doll and another lay inside. Layers and layers of plots were hidden within each other.

"Are we certain the Dragonseed is the true objective in all this?" Hawke asked. Getting fooled again at this point was going to be costly.

"It's the only thing that makes sense," Nighthorse said.

"But it's linked to Rachel."

"That's one of the things we have to work on, *omae.*" Nighthorse gazed at her creation. "We'll know more after we see this young woman."

CHAPTER SEVENTY

The last ascent to the cave set in the mountains was at least ten meters straight up, with verdant growth all but covering the craggy opening. Instead of being daunted by the difficult climb, Rachel felt even stronger as she grabbed a rocky outcropping and pulled herself higher. She was so close to her destination that the awareness darted around inside her like a striking snake. The thought of getting there consumed her.

"Rachel . . ." Bordelon called to her. "Can you give me a moment, *cher*?"

She looked down and saw Bordelon clinging to the rock face as well. His chest heaved, showing how the difficult climb had strained him. He looked like one more shadow on the rough stone. "All right."

Irritated at the delay, but not wanting to leave the mage behind for fear of what might happen to him, Rachel found a crevice in the wall and tucked herself in. The way their roles had reversed, with her the protector instead of the one needing protection, surprised her, but she held back for him, even when all she wanted to do was sprint the remaining distance.

Wind scourged the heights now, plowing through the trees and raking the mountain with greedy fingers. Its chill cut into her, but she barely felt it. Puffs of scree, gravel, and dirt swirled around, scouring her face and stinging her eyes.

Darkness filled the sky, the sun just a fading orange smear against the western horizon. At least, Rachel assumed the sun had set in the west.

After a few minutes, she felt the compulsion to arrive at her destination rising again, and this time it wouldn't be denied. She looked down at Bordelon. "It might be better if you climbed back down and waited."

The man shook his head as he gazed up at her, the white planes of his skull face standing out against the darkness. "I cannot, *cher*." Stubbornly, he reached up and found one hold, then another, hauling himself up with difficulty. "I must stay with you so you don't become more lost."

More lost? Rachel was certain she was as lost as she could be. She turned her attention back upward and resumed climbing, pushing herself into the teeth of the wind.

After several more meters, the climb summited at a small ledge that led to a cave. A nearly flat spot of bare stone only a couple meters square gave her a brief respite.

The cave opening was twice as tall as her, and almost that wide. A fetid stench came from inside, making her wonder if some *thing* lived there. She approached the black entrance, hesitated, then ventured inside, but the darkness was complete and she couldn't see anything. Wariness prickled the back of her neck, and a sudden chill swept over her.

"Rachel?"

Rachel left the cave and walked back out to the ledge as Bordelon attempted to clamber up the last meter. Thin rain began falling, spitting from the darkness shrouding the mountain. With only a dim moon showing behind a layer of clouds, not much light was available. If not for his skull paint, Rachel didn't think she would have seen him.

Bordelon reached up to another hold, but his fingers slipped. He swung away from the stone wall, holding on by his remaining hand.

Dropping to the ground, Rachel grabbed the collar of his tuxedo jacket, hoping it would hold. Even braced as she was, his weight nearly pulled her over the ledge. She skidded a few centimeters and managed to stop herself, with only her head and shoulders hanging over the edge.

At the end of her arm, Bordelon struggled to find a new purchase. He fought back up to the top, using his elbows to lever himself onto the ledge. The sharp stone cut his forearms, spilling his blood in uneven tracks.

Finally, he lay safely on the ledge. He breathed deeply for a moment, then rolled onto his back. "Thank you."

"I'm glad you're okay." Rachel pushed herself up on her knees and looked back at the cave.

"What's in there?" Bordelon asked as he sat up.

"I don't know. Something. I have to go inside, but it's dark." She stood. "Do you have a light?"

Bordelon put his hands together and materialized his walking stick between his palms. Holding it with his right hand, he sang briefly and struck the ferrule against the stone. A flame wavered to life around the blossom at the top of the stick, the light gleaming in his golden eyes.

"Now I have a light, *cher*." He looked at the cave with trepidation. "You're sure we have to go in there?"

"Yes." Rachel reached down and pulled him to his feet. His arms shook with fatigue, but he stood.

"Then let's see where it takes us." Bordelon walked at her side as they approached the cave. His light penetrated the darkness to reveal a sloping stone floor with a worn trail.

Pausing, Bordelon pushed the walking stick forward. He traced the definite path with his right foot. "Something's been through here plenty before us, *cher*. We'll want to be careful."

"We will be." Rachel stepped forward and entered the cave first.

Bordelon tried to follow, but a sudden, powerful gust of wind hammered into him. Lifted from his feet, yelling and flailing, the mage was blown back over the mountain's edge and dropped like a stone.

"No! This is not for him!"

Galvanized by the voice, Rachel ran through the rain to the edge of the cliff and peered out over the top of the jungle. Clutching his fiery walking stick, Bordelon looked like a firefly falling among the forest.

Then—he winked out, either lost behind the trees or smashed against the ground. Rachel couldn't tell which had happened. Either was horrible to comprehend.

"Come. Turn from these weaklings. It is time for you to become who you are supposed to be."

Shivering in the spitting rain and bone-chilling cold, Rachel turned back to the cave. The voice came from inside, somewhere in the darkness.

"This is your destiny, child. You have no choice in this."

Slowly, her fears quieted, and curiosity about what lay beyond filled her. Walking to the entrance, she peered into the darkness, wishing she had a light.

"Make one. All you have to do is will it."

Rachel shook her head at that. She wasn't one of the Awakened. She didn't have magic.

But she needed a light to show her the way.

With a soft *pop*, a spinning ball of flame manifested in front of her, floating in the air. The light was bright enough to hurt her eyes, but she blinked a couple of times, and the discomfort went away.

"Come, Rachel Gordon. Enter, and know your legacy."

Drawn by the voice, lulled by the command in the words and the curiosity that fired her, Rachel stepped into the cave. The floating ball of light moved just ahead of her, illuminating the ragged stone passage. Her footsteps echoed in the confined space, and she heard water running ahead of her as she walked deeper inside.

CHAPTER SEVENTY-ONE

Flicker controlled the RV remotely, downshifting as the big vehicle started climbing the mountainous range of the High Plains east of Denver. In another hour and twelve minutes, eighteen seconds, they would arrive at their destination.

In the passenger seat, Hawke sat with his arms folded, his eyes closed, and his chest gently rising and falling as he slept. Nearly all the RV's other passengers slept as well. Only Dani Nighthorse stayed awake, her attention focused on the object she was working on.

Flicker knew the shaman was working some kind of magic. There were vague shimmers around the table, and the rigger felt the mystical force like an uncomfortable itch all over her skin, even though her body was in the Denver safehouse. The feeling was one she was creating in her own mind, and she was aware of that, but she still couldn't shake it. Whatever Nighthorse was doing, she was using some powerful juju.

While Flicker was "in" the driver's seat, she was also maintaining a watch over existing road conditions and other vehicles, monitoring the RV's performance, accessing local law enforcement communications, looking over the files Dolphin had uploaded to her from the NeoNET datahack, and keeping an eye on Rachel Gordon and Bordelon.

Multi-tasking kept her from worrying. A little.

Rachel lay on the bed. Flicker didn't have to access the med monitors to know her body was failing. Blood pressure was down. Respiration was down. Chem levels were barely above the minimum to keep her body fed and hydrated. The IV fluids were going straight through her into the Foley catheter and the urine collection bag. Whatever Rachel was getting from the additional nutrients wasn't enough.

Snakechaser still sat on the floor by the bed. He'd been hooked up to an IV and med equipment too, because he hadn't come out of wherever he'd gone four days ago. Flicker didn't know if he even could anymore. Maybe he and Rachel were both trapped in whatever magical nexus the artifact had created, and everyone else's efforts were just going to be a waste of time.

Feeling guilty, knowing she shouldn't be thinking like that, Flicker glanced at Hawke. She wanted him back with her because then she wouldn't have to make decisions, but she was afraid of that, too. What would he feel like when Rachel Gordon died? Flicker didn't know. Hawke didn't let himself get close to people, but he also wasn't as hard as he pretended to be.

Something about Rachel Gordon had gotten to him. Flicker wondered about that. The only thing she'd come up with was the fact that Rachel had been doing okay with her life until the rumble in Guatemala, when the corps had made their play for her. She wasn't damaged goods like many shadowrunners. Flicker had her own issues, too.

Rachel Gordon was . . . normal. Until her life had taken a sudden shift in Guatemala. She'd had something precious: ignorance of how slotted life could really be, and Hawke wanted to try to get that back for her—try to steal back her innocence.

The thought made Flicker laugh, but there was no humor in it. It was just . . . sad. There was no way Hawke could ever return the woman to what she'd had, and no way he wouldn't feel responsible for what was going to happen to her.

In the safehouse, Snakechaser's vital signs suddenly plummeted, triggering alarms that screamed for attention. Something had happened. He was crashing, bottoming out.

"Hawke," Flicker called over his comm because she didn't want to deal with the others.

He woke at once and his hands reached for his weapons.

"Take the wheel." The rigger didn't give any explanation. As soon as he slid into the driver's seat and took control of the RV, she rushed back to her body.

In the safehouse, Flicker stood and started for Snakechaser, only to be pushed back by the med team streaming into the room. They lifted the man toward a crash cart they'd rolled into the room, but he woke and pushed them away.

"I'm fine! I'm fine!" Snakechaser pulled the IV out of his arm and got up. His attention was riveted on Rachel Gordon, who was now more pale than Flicker had ever seen her. "See to the girl!"

The stench of the grave suddenly filled the room, thick in Flicker's nostrils. That was a side effect of Snakechaser's magic. He'd warned her about it, and told her not to worry when it manifested, but his description hadn't touched how rank the stench really was. Trying not to gag, she breathed through her mouth instead of her nose.

"What happened?" she asked, echoing the question Hawke was asking at the other end of the commlink.

"Something in that place shoved me out, *cher*." Restless, Snakechaser laced his hands behind his head and shifted from foot to foot as he watched the med techs. "I tried to go back in, but it wouldn't let me."

Helpless, Flicker watched the trauma team working, feeling Rachel Gordon slip away through the link she had to the medical equipment trying to save the young woman's life.

Feeling less and less connected to herself, growing increasingly numb to her fear and the cold, propelled only by the voice and her need to see what lay at the end of her journey, Rachel followed the floating ball of light into a large cavern, where an artesian well fed a small, round pool occupying the center of the space. Stalactites hung from the roof high overhead, and the cavern spanned several dozen meters in an irregular oval.

"Come to the pool so that you may see."

The floating light led the way, and Rachel followed it to the pool's edge and stopped. Somewhere in the dim recesses of her mind, she realized a predator might be lurking in the water, awaiting its next meal.

That didn't concern her, though. She felt light-headed and relaxed. Not at ease, but uncaring. *Disconnected*—that was the term she was looking for. Like she had drunk too much wine and hadn't gone to sleep yet. Either the voice was protecting her, or she was in danger and it didn't matter.

"Sit."

Obeying the command, Rachel sat cross-legged on the stone bank only centimeters from the water. The chill of the pool rose and enveloped her, but she felt the cold at a distance, like it was there, but it didn't touch her. On one level, she knew it was too cold for her body, and part of her seemed panicked about that, but she didn't care.

The ball of light hovered beside her, its mirror twin floating on the pool's surface, only that version of the light was cold and dead. The light beside her face warmed her cheek. At least it gave her that.

"Watch."

Bubbles erupted in the pool's center. The urge to flee brushed against Rachel's mind for an instant, then went away, smothered by the overwhelming *need* to see what happened next.

A few seconds later, amid the roiling ripples that looked as if something was fighting its way to the surface, the blue gem she had found in Guatemala—or it had found her?—floated up from the depths and hung in the air. Lighted by the ball of flames, the artifact looked like a full moon as it slowly spun on its axis.

"What is this?" Rachel stared at the jewel as the facets caught the light and winked. It was so pretty . . .

"This is the shadow of your legacy, and it is your beginning, Child. You must accept it if you want to live. It will nourish you and give you the knowledge you need until you are able to reach the true Stone."

"Why didn't you guide me to the Stone first?"

"Because you could not reach it on your own, and you were not strong enough to embrace the Power you will find there. You have to make this journey inside the Dragonseed as well as in the physical world. There were many things I had to do in order to assure your success in this matter. Chief among those was assembling a group that could help you. There are others who are hunting the Stone, and if they discover that you have claimed it, they will hunt you as well. I have had to be careful while . . . managing this."

"A group to help me? You mean Hawke and Flicker?"

"Yes, and others you have yet to meet. Gathering them and keeping them on the trail while not informing my enemies has been arduous."

"Did you kill Remy Bordelon?"

"That man still lives. He is part of the group that will protect you."

Still staring at the artifact hovering over the water, Rachel realized how badly she wanted it. They belonged together. She raised her hand and called the artifact to her. Silently, still spinning, the jewel sped across the water, leaving a small wake in its passage.

"Do not touch the Stone!"

But Rachel couldn't help herself. She couldn't bear being separated from it any longer. She leaned forward, reaching for the artifact.

"Stop! You are not ready!"

For the first time, Rachel thought she saw a face in the darkness. It looked regal, handsome, and alien all at the same time. She thought the illumination from the floating light glittered across a haze of glittering scales that burned like beaten gold, or maybe it was a face framed by long steel-gray hair. She couldn't be certain.

Then her fingers touched the artifact, and the world exploded.

CHAPTER SEVENTY-TWO

All of the med monitors were inert and zeroed out above Rachel Gordon's body on the bed. No warning alarms sounded, though Hawke was certain they must have when they'd dropped below safety levels.

Shocked by how frail the woman looked, hammered by the guilt of knowing he'd gotten there too late, Hawke stared at her. He didn't know how he felt. He didn't know her, not really, so there was no attachment of a personal nature. But he remembered how innocent she'd been when he'd talked to her on the *Scorpionfish*. Although scared, she'd still been feisty and had stood up to him, in spite of being a prisoner. He respected that.

And now, after everything, after all the secrets he'd discovered and the dangers he'd faced, the possible deaths he'd asked his friends to risk, he was too late.

He gripped the bed rail and stared down at her, feeling even guiltier because a part of him wondered if her corpse would be enough to get Aztechnology and NeoNET off him. Maybe he could still save his friends. He would accept that.

Snakechaser walked over to Hawke and put a hand on his shoulder. "Now is not the time for mourning, cousin." Snakechaser looked old and worn, graying around the edges. Wherever he'd been with Rachel, the way had been hard. "She's not dead."

"What are you talking about?" Hawke asked, swinging around in disbelief. His anger flared again, and he tried to hold it back. Snakechaser didn't deserve his wrath, but he felt it threatening to spill out of him all the same. He glanced over at Flicker, who stood with her arms around herself. "She's dead."

"No, she's not."

Hawke dismissed the hope the man offered. This was done

and over. He'd rolled the dice and lost. He focused on Flicker. "When did her vital signs disappear?"

"Thirty-eight minutes ago." She didn't look at him. The loss had hit her hard too, or maybe she was thinking they were good and hosed as far as corp attention went. "Nobody flatlines that long and comes back."

Snakechaser smiled and shook his head. "That's just science talking. This here?" He waved at Rachel. "This is *magic*, cousin. She may look like this, dead to us maybe, but this is like a co-coon for her. She is in a process of change. All we need to do is provide a spark to start the chrysalis that will bring her back to this world. She's not finished with whatever she has to do. Trust me on this."

Even though common sense told him dead was dead, Hawke did trust Snakechaser, but there was still that doubt. He refused to be tempted.

"He's right," Nighthorse said. "Rachel's still in there. We've got to go get her, find out what she needs, and help bring her through whatever she's facing." She sat in the middle of the floor, crossed her legs, and placed the bowl she'd constructed from dark-green and yellow rocks in front of her.

"Ah." Snakechaser's golden eyes widened in pleased surprise as he studied the bowl. "You have an inkling of what's taking place here, *cher*?"

"Yes. This is a focus." Nighthorse replied as she made herself comfortable. "Whatever's in there, it has to be powerful. Rachel isn't trained to deal with magic. She needs somewhere to place it. I thought maybe this would help her get some semblance of control. If we can get it to her."

"You're going to need help," Paredes said as he took a seat across the bowl from Nighthorse. He looked up at Snakechaser. "You've been there. You can guide us." He held out a hand.

Doubt clouded Snakechaser's eyes. "Whatever is in there, or is working through that place, it didn't want me there. It threw me right out. I couldn't stop it."

"You'll be with us this time," Nighthorse said. "Three of us will be stronger together." She held out her hand, too.

"I have little energy left," Snakechaser said. "I was inside too long."

"We'll do the heavy lifting," Paredes said. "You just get us into the game."

Nodding, Snakechaser lowered himself to the floor and took their hands.

Nighthorse looked up at Hawke. "You should come with us, too."

"Not me." Hawke shook his head. "I don't want anything to do with magic." And if Rachel was somewhere else, he didn't want to go there to see her dead either.

"You're the one among us who has spent the most time with her, *hermano*," Paredes said. "You're the one she has the strongest relationship with. You need to come."

"She doesn't like me," Hawke pointed out. "She thinks I kidnapped her." Which, in reality, he had.

"Hawke," Nighthorse said, "if this is going to work, I think you need to be there. We should be able to reach her, but you're the best chance we have at getting her to listen."

Twitch walked over to Hawke and nudged him with a shoulder. She looked up at him with her gamine grin. "They're telling it true, mon, and you know it. Go. Save her if you can."

Certain that even if the others got into the dream or whatever Rachel was having that he wouldn't be able to cross over with them, Hawke sat on the other side of the focus facing Snakechaser.

They all held hands, and he felt the itchy blanket of magic wrap around him. A bright shimmer fogged his vision. He was just about to ask if it was going to hurt when—

—he stood on a stone ledge high in a mountain range. Lightning seared the black, starless sky, leaving white-hot scars that lingered for a moment before cooling and fading. Cold, hard rain drenched him, and a basso peal of thunder rolled over him, striking him with physical force.

Snakechaser, Nighthorse, and Paredes stood around him, all of them looking astonished at what they were seeing.

"This place is big," Paredes said, sounding awfully impressed in spite of himself. "I can't even guess how much energy it takes to hold this together."

Nighthorse held up her hands. "There's a lot of power here, a lot of ancient spirits as well." She smiled in pleasure.

"Hawke," a deep voice called.

Turning toward where the voice had come from, Hawke spotted the cave mouth and knew this was the ledge where Snake-chaser had gotten tossed out of this world. Or whatever it was. The place was certainly large enough to be another world, and it looked like nothing he'd ever seen.

"Who are you?" he demanded.

"There will be time for that later. You need to help Rachel. You'll find her inside."

Saving Rachel was the mission focus. Hawke emptied his mind of everything else except the woman. He strode to the cave mouth, waiting for something to happen, and reached for his katars because his pistol hadn't crossed with him. He was surprised when they filled his hands. He tried to bring his wired reflexes online, but got no response. His vision suite—infrared, thermal imaging, and low-light—wasn't working either.

"Your cyber won't work here, *hermano*." Paredes halted beside Hawke and flicked a ball of light into being. "Neither will percussion weapons. Your knives are a part of you. Like my sword." He drew a katana from his side. "Things that exist here must be things that are close to you."

"My cyber's part of me."

"Not here." Nighthorse popped another light into existence and telescoped the staff she wore at her side. "Here it must be personal." She looked up at him. "Rachel is inside. Are you ready?"

Hawke took a fresh grip on his blades. Instead of voicing an answer, he stepped into the cave. The lights floated just ahead of him as he followed the dark, curving tunnel deeper inside.

CHAPTER SEVENTY-THREE

The tunnel widened and turned down, gradually opening into a large cavern where Hawke spotted a blue glow that grew in intensity. Harsh crackling and the buzz of ozone filled the muggy air. An uneasy feeling crawled across Hawke's neck and slid down his spine. He regretted his lack of cyberware and firepower, and consoled himself with the knowledge that his three companions were in their element.

"Hurry!" The voice didn't sound so calm and certain now. Frenzy worried at the edges of it.

Moving faster now, Hawke found Rachel sitting at the edge of a pool. Her arms were outstretched, her hands wrapped around the artifact she'd found in Guatemala. Blue fire lapped over her while her hair danced wildly.

"Save her!"

Keeping an eye on the shadows, Hawke holstered the katars and ran toward Rachel. He reached for her, intending to pull her away from the artifact, but Nighthorse rammed her staff between his feet and tripped him. Unable to keep his balance, Hawke hit the ground, rolled, and shot back up to his feet.

"What do you think you're doing?" he demanded.

Nighthorse held up a hand. "Saving your life. If you touch her, you'll be crippled or dead." She pinned him with her dark eyes. "Wait, and let us see what we can do."

Hawke growled a curse. Everything in him screamed to get Rachel away from the artifact.

"Are you listening?" Nighthorse demanded.

". . . Yes."

Nighthorse lowered her hand. "Good. Everything's going to be fine." She turned her attention to Rachel, but didn't try to touch the woman. "Rachel, do you hear me?"

Rachel continued holding the artifact, only now her image was thinning, like she was losing mass and becoming more transparent.

"Rachel?" Nighthorse sat beside the other woman without touching her. "I'm a friend. I'm here to help you, but I need you to listen to me." She plucked the bowl from thin air, like a sleight-of-hand card trick done by a street performer. "Do you see this?" She held the dark-green and yellow bowl up. "This is malachite. The stone has attributes that help focus magical power. I've fashioned it so it can help you hold that power without it hurting you. This is a focus. I can show you how to use it."

Without warning, Rachel spun with a feral look and superhuman quickness. A bright blue blade appeared in her hand, and she drove it straight for Nighthorse's throat. Before the shaman could move, probably before she even knew the knife was streaking for her, Paredes parried the blow with his sword. Blue sparks flared from the contact.

"Rachel!" Hawke spoke before he knew it, and he caught himself just before he grabbed her.

She spun on him then, wildness gleaming in her eyes as she drew back her blade. It lengthened in her hand, growing thicker and longer.

Hawke held his hands out. "Look, we're not here to hurt you. We're here to help." He kept his words soft, but speaking was a strain. "Rachel?"

"Go away!" she snarled in a ragged voice. "You don't belong here!"

Keeping his empty hands out in the open, Hawke sat in front of her, knowing that if his cyber hadn't translated to this world, his subdermal armor probably hadn't either. He hadn't felt this vulnerable in a long time. "I want to help you."

"I don't need any help." Rachel glowered at the others. She didn't release the artifact. Or maybe it didn't release her. Hawke wasn't certain which was the truth. Perhaps the bond worked both ways.

"Dani," Hawke said, "tell me what to do."

"The Power she has found is Ancient," Nighthorse said. "I've never seen anything like it."

"Nor have I," Paredes echoed. "I have only heard stories about such things."

"Whatever it is," Nighthorse said, "it has to be contained."

"No!" Rachel whirled and stepped into the pool, so she was standing behind the artifact. Her left arm was wrapped around the jewel, while she held the sword in her right hand. The stone pulsed, growing brighter, then darker, and each time it did that, there seemed to be less of Rachel there.

"You have to have a place to put that power," Nighthorse insisted. "Your body is too frail to hold it. You'll only destroy yourself."

"You're trying to trick me!"

Ripples crossed the pool's surface, but they weren't caused by Rachel. Hawke watched as the ripples passed *through* the woman.

"Hurry!" the voice demanded inside his mind.

"Rachel, you've got to listen to me." Hawke leaned toward her.

She turned toward him, holding the long knife at the ready.

"Do you remember what you told me when we were on the *Scorpionfish*? About how you liked history and culture?"

Rachel shifted in the water, but her movements didn't stir the pool. It was like she was no longer there. Wisps of her pulled away and sank into the artifact, like it was feasting on her.

"She must listen to you. Make her listen."

"I . . . do," she said.

Hawke kept his arms wide, thinking desperately. "Then tell me about the artifact."

"It's powerful. It makes me . . . stronger than you."

"Where did it come from?" Hawke asked gently. "Don't you want to know? Who made it? Why did they make it?"

She tilted her head and looked at him. "I . . . don't know."

"But you want to know, don't you? You're curious. You've always been curious." Hawke saw his three companions waiting pensively. The blue glow brought their features into sharp relief. "Why did it pick you?"

"Because . . . because I'm supposed to be with it."

"Why?"

Rachel hesitated and looked at the artifact trapped under her arm. "I . . . I don't know."

"There has to be a reason," Hawke said. "Sometime in the past, that artifact was made so that it would pick you. No one else. Just you."

"Yes."

"You want to know why." Hawke stared at her, barely able to make out her outline now because she had faded so much.

"It is . . . part of me."

"All right, but how could it be made for you thousands of years ago?"

The ghost of a troubled frown turned Rachel's mouth down as she looked at the artifact. "I don't know . . ."

"We can help you find out, Rachel," Hawke said. "We're here to help you, but to let us do that, you need to trust us. Let us help you find out where that artifact came from, and why it's doing what it's doing now."

The knife disappeared from Rachel's hand. She wrapped her arm around the stone, and she was almost gone now. Hawke was certain the stone was holding itself up because there wasn't enough of her left to support it.

"You can . . . help me?"

"Yes." Hawke hoped that was true. He meant every word, but he was afraid it was already too late.

"How?"

Nighthorse handed Hawke the bowl-shaped focus. Hawke didn't want it, but he took it, feeling the buzzing energy within it. Holding the bowl, forcing himself to move, he turned toward Rachel and held it out to her.

"Put the artifact in here," Hawke said. "Then we can study it and figure it out."

Rachel didn't move.

"Is it Mayan?" Hawke asked, trying to appeal to her curiosity. "You told me you didn't think it was Mayan. If it's not, what is it?" He pushed the bowl closer to her. "Let's find out together. All you have to do is put it in here."

For a moment, he didn't think she was going to give up the artifact, or maybe she wasn't strong enough to make it let go of her, then she dropped the stone into the bowl. When the artifact met the focus, all noise and light evaporated from the cavern for a heartbeat.

Vision clearing as quickly as it had vanished, Hawke watched Rachel fall into the water and sink beneath the surface, disappearing like sugar paper.

CHAPTER SEVENTY-FOUR

"No!"

Hawke threw the bowl back to Nighthorse and jumped into the water before he saw her catch it. The bottom of the pool dropped off quickly, and he was up to his chest within two strides. Ducking beneath the water, no longer able to see Rachael, Hawke reached for where she'd last been.

He swept his arms wide and found no trace of her. Shoving forward through the cold water, he reached out again. This time his fingers grazed flesh that was only a shade warmer than the pool. He stretched out again and found her arm.

Wrapping an arm around Rachel, Hawke kicked to the surface and swam toward the pool's edge, pulling her after him. When he got her to the bank, he pushed her up. She rolled limply across the stone, water dribbling from her mouth and nose.

Paredes knelt over Rachel as Hawke kicked up from the pool. The mage put a hand over her lips, then shook his head at Hawke. "She's not breathing, *hermano*."

Hawke dropped to his knees, turned her head to the side and checked to make certain her air passages were clear, then started CPR. "C'mon, Rachel. Don't give up on me now. *Breathe!*" He stopped the chest compressions, opened her mouth again, and breathed into her.

Rachel still didn't respond.

"Hawke, let me." Nighthorse came forward and shoved him aside. She placed her hands over Rachel's chest and shimmers fell across her. A moment later, Rachel's body convulsed, then fell back. Limp and unbreathing, she lay on the wet stone.

Nighthorse looked at Hawke and tears glimmered in her eyes as she shook her head. "I can't reach her."

Hawke started back toward Rachel, unwilling to give up. Before he could touch her, a shadowy figure knocked him aside.

"Enough! You are going to let her die!"

Bruised and aching, his own breath gone for a moment, Hawke watched as the shadow of a man stood above Rachel and spread his hands wide. Shimmers so silver and pure Hawke was certain he could have reached out and touched them danced over Rachel. Her body twitched in response.

"Live, Child! Live so that you may Become!"

Rachel's eyes snapped open, and she took a hoarse, ragged breath. She stared up at the shadow. "Who are you?" she gasped.

"You already know me–I am the Shadowman. I breathed life into you, and now you will complete your Journey. You still have one more task to accomplish."

Hawke got to his feet and moved toward the shadowed figure, intending to put himself between Rachel and whatever threat the being might offer. The shadow waved an arm at him, and Hawke flew a dozen meters away, landing in a bone-bruising sprawl.

"Stay back! I will not kill you unless you try to challenge me again!"

Hawke got to his feet and reached for his katars.

"Hawke, no!" Weakly, Rachel got to her feet and addressed the shadow. "You did this? You sent me after that artifact?"

"Yes, all that and more."

"Why?"

"For you. So that you may Become."

"Become what?"

"You will know when you have finished the final task."

"This is over right now. No one is going to make me do anything." Rachel stood facing the shadow.

For a moment, Hawke saw a gleaming patch of scales, then he was just as certain that the shadow belonged to a tall, handsome man with long, steel-gray hair. Then there was only darkness again.

"If you stop now, you will die. And there will be nothing I can do to prevent it. Your fate rests in your hands alone, Child. I will not take that away from you, not after giving you life."

As Hawke leaped forward, the shadow waved at him again. He came to a sudden stop, suspended a meter above the stone floor. He tried to move and couldn't.

In the next instant, a wall blocked Nighthorse, Snakechaser, and Paredes off from Hawke and Rachel. Snakechaser slammed his walking stick against the barrier, scattering shimmering sparks in all directions. The barrier also proved impenetrable to Paredes's sword. Nighthorse's eyes gleamed with a greenish glow, but the wall stood.

"All of you will do as I say. This remains unfinished." The shadow turned to face Rachel. *"If you do not do as I say, you* will *die."*

"I don't believe you."

"Then believe this: if you do not do as I say, I will destroy this man."

The shadow closed his hand. Immediately, Hawke felt iron bands tighten around his body. Everything hurt, and he was certain every bone in his body was about to shatter. Even though he tried to hold it back, a cry of pain escaped him.

"All right! Stop hurting him!"

The shadow unclenched his fist, and Hawke dropped to the ground, gasping for breath and unable to move.

"All of you are in great danger." The shadow walked to the pool. *"Aztechnology and NeoNET are set on taking the true Artifact. That which you have found is false, placed there to trick my enemies and to start you on your Journey, so you could come here. Now you must find the real Dragonseed."*

The shadow waved his arm, and the pool erupted as water shot up. When it stilled, a three-dimensional image of a ruined city hung there. Made of stone, once-proud towers lay broken across broad stone steps. Walls had holes that earthmovers could be driven through. Columns lay in crumbled pieces. Images of unimaginable creatures stood out in bas-relief among the remains.

"This is Gharyn. Once a powerful trading city, it was lost to the sea millennia ago. But it still protects the Dragonseed."

The three-dimensional image shifted and changed as the pieces twisted and turned into new scenes, new places, new wreckage. Finally, the rushing water stilled to reveal a building partially crushed under a mountain. A glowing gold marker hung in a chamber within the tumble-down ruin.

The shadow turned to face Rachel. *"This is the Dragonseed. Retrieve it so that you may be safe. If you do not, you will all die."*

Hawke finally drew a deep breath, grateful that his ribs no longer felt like jagged glass, then a massive force slammed into him and his senses spun away. He thought maybe the shadow had decided they weren't going to live after all. Then he couldn't think anything at all.

CHAPTER SEVENTY-FIVE

"Hawke!"

Groggily, certain his head was about to split open, Hawke opened his eyes and looked up at Flicker.

"You still with me, *omae*?" She smoothed a hand across his brow.

"Yeah . . . yeah, I'm still here." Hawke discovered he was lying on the floor in the safehouse. Med techs surrounded him. "I'm wiz. Get off me." He sat up as the med techs drew back.

"His vitals are all stable," one of the techs said, glaring at him. "Except for the lack of gratitude, he appears to be fine."

"It's okay," Flicker told the woman. "I got this."

With one more grudging look, the woman and her team left the room.

Hawke looked around and saw Snakechaser, Nighthorse, and Paredes all seated in chairs against the wall. None of them looked worse for the wear.

Best of all, Rachel Gordon sat on the bed with a cup of what smelled like chicken soup. She looked a little confused. "I guess a lot has happened here since I've been away . . . *there*."

"Yeah, I'd say so." Hawke forced himself to his feet and tried to ignore the dizziness spinning up inside his head. "Why am I the last one to recover?"

"You were the only one in there who wasn't Awakened, *hermano*," Paredes said.

Flicker blew out a breath. "Maybe it was that, and maybe it was because you've been running on fumes for days."

"Whatever." Hawke nodded at Rachel. "You okay?"

She stared back at him for a long moment, then nodded.

Flicker folded her arms. "She's lost some weight. She's a little rundown. Nothing she can't come back from." She glared at Hawke. "If this 'Shadowman' doesn't decide to kill us all."

"It's not gonna come to that. We can run."

"It's too late for that," Nighthorse said. "You, me, Rachel—all of us—we've been Marked. Whoever that was in the cave, he's got our number. And he's powerful. If we don't go after his little trinket, we'll all be hosed."

"That's just a smokescreen. If he was so powerful, he'd go get the artifact himself."

"He can't," Rachel said.

"Why?"

"Because it's mine. It's tied to me."

Hawke looked at his Awakened teammates. They all nodded without hesitation. "Then why does he want it?"

"He doesn't want it," Rachel said. "He wants me to have it."

"Why?"

She shrugged. "I don't know."

Hawke wanted to slam his fist through the wall. None of this made any sense. He took a deep breath and let it out. "We don't even know where it is."

"We do," Rachel said. "*I* do. I've already shown them."

Hawke tried to catch up. "Where is it?"

"Off the coast of the Diego Ramirez Islands, it seems," Flicker said.

Shaking his head, Hawke said, "I don't even know where that is."

"Off the coast of Chile," Flicker said. "About a thousand meters down." She touched her deck, and a trideo projection manifested in the center of the room around Hawke and Rachel. The coastline of what he assumed was one of the Diego Ramirez Islands butted into the sparkling green of the Pacific Ocean.

"Underwater?" Hawke couldn't believe it.

"Yeah. A sunken city no one's ever found before. It's supposed to be in a cave system that survived the flooding. But it was still destroyed." Flicker pursed her lips. "There's no reason this Shadowman would make anything easy." She cursed the man—or whatever he was—under her breath.

"Gharyn sank during the Fourth World," Rachel said. "Apparently the city came under attack by some . . . things. Huge, grotesque creatures that laid waste to it before the ocean finished it off."

"Hey, glad to see you've recovered, Hawke," Dolphin said over

the commlink. *"But you don't have time for a celebration. Aztlan and NeoNET both know where you are, and have sent sec teams to intercept you."*

"Let's go," Hawke said. All his confusion and anger vanished as he focused on getting gone. "How'd they find us?"

"They received an anonymous email from KilmerTek."

"From whoever sent the Johnson?"

"That's what I'm guessing."

"Start backgrounding everyone attached to that corp."

"I already have. I'm looking for who's Awakened, has a lot of nuy-en to throw around, and is exceedingly devious." Dolphin sighed. *"If he's connected to that corp–"*

"He has to be," Hawke interrupted as he grabbed bags of gear and led the way out of the room.

"–then he's devious enough that I haven't been able to find him yet."

"Find him."

"He can't hide from me forever."

"If he's as good on the Matrix as he is at magework," Night-horse said, "finding him may sign your death notice."

"It's already been signed," Dolphin said. *"I got an email from an anonymous sender that said if you guys don't find the artifact, I'm go-ing to die with you. So . . . I'm motivated to find him, and to help you guys on your treasure hunt."* She paused. *"Get moving. You've got six minutes before the first Aztechnology sec men hit the safehouse, and NeoNET's right on their heels."*

The medical people were headed out as well. The last two out the door set off incendiaries that would reduce the building to ash as Hawke led his team into the street.

CHAPTER SEVENTY-SIX

"Well, *amigo*, I didn't think I would ever see you again."

An easy smile on his face, Captain Joaquin locked eyes with Hawke as he came aboard the *Scorpionfish* at the prearranged rendezvous off the coast of Cabo San Lucas.

Hawke ignored the man. Arriving at the resort city in the early hours of the morning, they'd easily gotten lost amid the constant partiers haunting the beaches. Once at sea, they'd boarded the submarine and, for all intents and purposes, disappeared.

Flicker had set up the transport, and Joaquin had "hijacked" them on the coast. Of course, Joaquin knew Aztechnology and NeoNET were still breathing down their necks, making them hot property, and he was putting himself at risk as well. Hawke was certain the captain wasn't just doing it for the credits, though. His friendship with Flicker mattered to him.

"*Hola*, Flicker." Joaquin took her into a fierce hug. "I am glad your friend hasn't gotten you killed."

Flicker hugged the man back. "You only think that because you don't know Hawke like I do, Joaquin. He's all about saving people, not getting them killed."

"I hope that is true," the smuggler captain said.

Silently, Hawke hoped so too, but this run was way out of his control now, and that bothered him because he didn't have an end game in mind. Too much depended on what they found in that sunken city.

It's just water, Hawke told himself while leaning on the observation deck railing below the *Scorpionfish's* prow. *A beach, a beer, and some well-filled bikinis, this could be a good place.*

But the observation deck lacked all those things. There was just water, water, and more water all around, and that filled him with barely controlled dread.

According to one of the sailors, the submarine was cruising at something short of two hundred meters underwater. Well above crush depth, he'd assured Hawke That news was unsettling, though, because he hadn't even known there was a "crush" depth. That immediately led to thoughts of how people found out if a submarine went deep enough to get crushed in the first place. He tried not to concentrate on that, and wished he could sleep like the rest of his team.

The large transplas window looked out into the seemingly endless blue-green sea. He spotted mostly marine creatures he couldn't identify, but every now and again he would spot a shark or a whale or a manta ray.

"Can't sleep?"

Turning, Hawke saw Rachel Gordon enter the observation deck chamber. She looked better, more rested, than she had when they'd left the safehouse twelve days ago.

They'd been on the run ever since, constantly harried by Shadowman, who—whenever he evidently thought they were taking too long—set the Aztechnology and NeoNET hounds on them again through his anonymous emails. Despite nearly round-the-clock hacking, Dolphin hadn't gotten any closer to finding out who he was.

"I can't," Hawke admitted.

"I can't sleep because my sleep cycle's all wrong right now. I've been sleeping too much, and now I'm out of sync with everyone else." Rachel studied him. "That's not really your problem, I suppose."

"I'm fine. My mind's just been busy."

Rachel smiled and walked over to the railing near him. "That's not true. You're afraid of the water."

Hawke didn't say anything.

"I know that," Rachel said, "because knowing if people are telling the truth or lying is something I just know now." She shrugged. "I talked to Dani and Snakechaser about it. They think it has to do with how I'm coming into my Awakened powers." She snorted, and for a minute Hawke thought she was going to cry. Suddenly uncomfortable, he realized he didn't know what he would do if she did.

She rubbed a sleeve over her face. "This isn't anywhere near how I imagined my life would go."

"How'd you think it would go?"

For a moment, she was silent. Then she shrugged. "I don't know. Maybe I'd get to travel around the world, see things nobody's seen in hundreds or thousands of years."

"Well, that's kind of what you're doing."

She glared at him, then smiled, then started laughing, hard. Tears welled in her eyes, and she wiped them away. "Doing all that while running from corp assassins is *so* not how I pictured it."

Hawke grinned. "I don't know. I kind of like the running. Keeps the adrenaline spiked."

"Seriously? You're crazy."

"That's not crazy. Crazy is the Shadowman and his little shell game. Until he came along, I figured I had everything handled pretty well."

Her good humor disappeared. "If I could, I'd take it all back." A haunted look filled her eyes as she turned to the window.

Feeling guilty, Hawke looked at her. "Listen to me for a minute, *omae*."

She tore her gaze away from the ocean and looked back at him.

"This isn't your fault," Hawke told her. "You and I are here because of the Shadowman. We're all pieces on his game board at the moment. Until we figure a way out of it."

She wrapped her arms around herself. "Do you think you will?"

"I do."

Tentatively, she smiled at him. "You do remember I can tell when you're lying?"

"Unless you can predict the future, I can lie about it all I want. Otherwise, we might as well put a bullet through our own heads. I'm not gonna do that. I'll go down with a blade in my hand and somebody's blood in my teeth."

"Not exactly a winning game plan."

Hawke smiled. "No, but it's how I live." He leaned on the railing again and looked at all the water, trying to think of it as merely window dressing. A few minutes passed, and a large turtle glided into view.

"That's a leatherback turtle," Rachel said, pointing. "You can tell because they don't have a bony shell like most turtles do. Their carapaces are just thickened skin."

The turtle swam languidly in the distance, growing closer as the submarine got nearer.

"How long can they hold their breath?" Hawke asked, curious because he hadn't ever thought about it before.

"On a long dive, anywhere from thirty minutes to over an hour." Rachel looked at him. "So, why did you stick around and try to save me in Guatemala? It wasn't just to get paid. If that was the case, you would have sold me off to Aztechnology or NeoNET long before now."

"Shadowman—"

"No," Rachel interrupted, "Shadowman is a recent development. Why did you do what you did?"

Hawke hesitated.

"Remember, I can tell when you're lying."

He stared at the turtle a long time before replying. "I don't have a normal life. I don't know if I could ever have one. That decision got taken out of my hands a long time ago." He looked at her. "But I thought . . . maybe you could still be whoever you wanted to be if I could get you out of the drek storm you were in."

"And now?"

"Now?" Hawke thought about that. "Now, I'm just hoping we get to the other side of this thing alive."

"Me, too," Rachel said quietly. "And thank you."

Hawke nodded.

"I think I can sleep now," she said, "so I'm going back to bed. You going to be all right?"

"Yeah."

She turned and walked away, leaving him there. "Don't worry about the ocean, Hawke. I don't think any of us have to be concerned about drowning."

Hawke tried to take some comfort from that, and for a moment or two, he almost managed to.

CHAPTER SEVENTY-SEVEN

Three days later, Rachel told them they'd reached the site where Gharyn had gone into the ocean, and that it lay below the *Scorpionfish*. Joaquin's radar techs confirmed the existence of a large, hollow space under the seabed about seven hundred meters below the ocean's surface.

According to Flicker, that put the distance a hundred or so meters short of the collapsible—she called it collapsible, not crush—depth of the deep sea submersible she'd brought out of her stable of vehicles for the meet in Cabo San Lucas. Hawke hadn't even known she owned a submarine.

"It's not actually mine," Flicker admitted. "It's more of a time-share I have with five other riggers. We all use it to recover lost salvage we get hired for. I had to call in some favors to get it now, *omae*, and if I don't bring it back in one piece, the other people I share it with aren't going to be happy with me."

"I'd rather bring it back in one piece, too," Hawke agreed. "Uncollapsed."

Flicker was jacked into the controls as the *Scorpionfish* opened the moon pool—which had nothing to do with anything lunar, and was the name for an airlock, Hawke discovered—and dropped the *Helldiver* into the open Pacific. The submersible, to his way of thinking, was aptly named because it streaked right for the bottom.

He sat in one of its seats and tried not to think about crush depths or drowning. Occupying himself with thoughts of what they might find in the sunken city didn't help, because he couldn't stop wondering what it would take to flood the air-filled chambers with seawater. Getting shot by NeoNET or Aztechnology sec teams seemed a distant threat, despite the fact that both corps' forces were closing in.

There were no windows to peer out of, and Hawke was glad of that. If there had been, he would have been looking, and that would have only made his anxiety worse.

The submersible's control center was compact, smaller than he expected it to be. He didn't understand any of the controls or readouts he saw floating around Flicker. Rachel sat next to the rigger, watching everything with avid interest. Nighthorse, Snakechaser, and Paredes talked in low voices in the passenger seats. In the compact cargo space barely large enough for him, Rolla snored, and Twitch slept quietly sitting against the wall near him, both of them resting for what was to come.

Hawke wished he could do the same.

"Scorpionfish *to* Helldiver," Joaquin called over the comm.

"We read you, Scorpionfish," Flicker replied.

"We're clearing out as agreed, but I wanted you to know that the pursuit we've been dodging has shown up. They've marked our location, but aren't following us. They know you're in the sea, however." Silently, Hawke cursed the Shadowman. They were at the site. They were going to get the trinket. He didn't have to keep the pressure turned up like this.

"Looks like they're preparing to drop deep sea fish into the ocean after you. They've got big cargo planes headed this way."

"I can confirm that," Dolphin said. *"I just hacked into one of Neo-NET's auxiliary servers and found out Ayumi Sukenobu put in an order for four deep sea submersibles. I can only assume Aztechnology is doing the same."*

"Understood," Flicker replied.

"I'll be there for you, mija," Joaquin told Flicker, *"if I can do it without risking my boat."*

"I'm counting on it. Helldiver *out."* The submersible shuddered as Flicker increased the acceleration of the screwdrive powering it through the ocean.

Hawke made himself breathe and tried not to grip the armrests so hard. Flicker would probably never let him hear the end of it if she returned the vessel with damaged seats.

Finding the opening to the underwater cave system was easy. The *Scorpionfish* hadn't been able to locate it with all her drones and systems, and Flicker couldn't with her drones, either.

Rachel, however, seemed to have a map in her head. She watched the video feed from Flicker's deep sea drones and gave the rigger directions.

Within forty-one minutes of departing the *Scorpionfish*, they were following a channel that Rachel assured them led to the cavern. Hawke just hoped the air-filled cavern actually existed, and that they wouldn't have to go in while wearing ADS. The *Helldiver* had atmospheric diving suits on hand if it came to that, but it would make the expedition much more difficult.

Three minutes after that, Dolphin let them know the first of NeoNET's submersibles had plunged into the ocean overhead.

As Hawke climbed out of the *Helldiver*, which was tucked into a small underwater cove in the sunken city, he took a deep breath. His olfactory suite told him the oxygen content was three percent greater than the surface air, but it smelled metallic and salty.

"Air's good," Flicker called over the commlink. *"Better than what we normally breathe."*

"I know," Hawke replied.

"It's because that air is thousands of years old," Dolphin said.

She was tied in through a satellite relay Flicker had set up inside the *Helldiver*. As the sub had entered the sunken city, the rigger had laid a monofilament comm cable attached to a miniature unit floating on the ocean's surface. Despite Flicker's assurances to the contrary, Hawke worried that the sec teams from Aztechnology and NeoNET would track the device. But that hadn't mattered because—thanks to the Shadowman—both corps already knew where the *Helldiver* had gone in, and didn't need to search for the entrance.

He still couldn't figure out why the man—or whatever he was—was running the operation so closely.

"I just wish I was there with you so I could see everything," Dolphin said. *"The video and cyber version of that place doesn't do it justice. All I'm getting is sonar bounce-back from Flicker's drones."*

"Trust me," Hawke said as he looked around, "it feels a lot different when you remember you've got an ocean sitting on top of you. It loses some of the appeal."

Thousands of years ago, Gharyn had apparently been a port city. Remnants of stone docks and pilings led out into the dark water, disappearing into the green-black depths. Stalactites hung from the ceiling and stalagmites pushed up from the ancient harbor like teeth in the mouth of some gargantuan beast that might close it at any moment.

Huge and deep, the cavern held at least a square kilometer of breathable space from what Flicker's drones had mapped so far. They'd also found a passageway to the west, but Rachel had already informed them they'd be going that way.

"Look over here." Rolla used a laser light to point at the bones of some monstrous creature lying on a section of the walkways that stretched between the docks and led deeper into the passage. "That wingspread had be fifty meters across."

Dressed in a hardsuit and covered in gear like the rest of them, though she looked dwarfed by her load, Twitch stood beside the big troll. "If we have time later, mon, maybe we can grab some of those bones. I'll bet a lot of collectors would pay plenty for them."

"Focus," Hawke said. "We get in, get the Dragonseed, and get out. That's what we're here to do."

"Hey, I can dream." Twitch grinned at him.

Hawke grinned back, thinking it was good at least one of them was confident about surviving the potential looming confrontation.

With Rachel at his side, he took the lead, following the walkways as he headed west. He cradled an AK-97 assault rifle in his arms, locked and loaded, safety off and smartlinked. All of them—except Twitch, who carried no rifle—were equipped with the same model so they could swap ammo easily. And because the 97 was so reliable.

Even under harsh conditions, Hawke reminded himself.

Flicker remained in the *Helldiver* so she could operate the horde of drones mapping the area and doing recon. She was also there to defend the vessel and make sure they maintained an exfil route.

If any of them survived to exfil, that is.

"How do you think this city got buried?" Rolla asked.

No one had an answer.

Hawke stopped at the top of a rise and looked back at the harbor area. He couldn't see the *Helldiver*, which made him feel better. Flicker had the sub masked, hardened against electronic detection as well as she could. According to the rigger, their pursuers would have to be right on top of the submersible to find her.

"C'mon," Rolla said, "you look around this place, you gotta be curious. I am. I mean, whoever built this city didn't build it in a cave. All that rock overhead had to come from somewhere."

Nighthorse directed her infrared beam at the ceiling. "Part of the strata above us is igneous, probably spewed out by a volcano, which might have destroyed the city and maybe the original coastline. Later, other debris—silt from the seabed, erosion from other landforms surrounding the city to the west—all filled in around the original damage. There are a lot of places underground that used to be on top of it. Seattle has the Underground. Same thing, only not as deep."

Rolla grunted in acknowledgment. "When you're down in the Underground, you don't think about all that."

"The next time Mount Rainier starts quivering and quaking, maybe you should think about it a little. Could be one day Seattle ends up on the bottom of the Pacific, too."

"Maybe we could think happy thoughts for the time being," Snakechaser suggested.

Hawke silently agreed. "We need to pick up the pace, people. We only had a forty-four minute head start on Aztechnology and NeoNET, and we're twenty minutes into that. They'll be here soon."

Truthfully, though, he was less worried about what was coming behind them than what might lay ahead of them.

CHAPTER SEVENTY-EIGHT

Past the harbor area, which had survived intact to a large degree, clear lanes ran in straight rows between fallen buildings. The sea had crept in here, and they waded through thigh-deep water that would have caused hypothermia if the hardsuits hadn't come with built-in heating. As it was, compensating for the cold was going to drain the suits' power faster than Hawke had planned.

Thousands of years ago, the narrow areas between the buildings had been wide thoroughfares. On the edges, above the waterline, Hawke spotted broad steps led into the crumbled ruins. Down the middle of the streets, broad-based columns stood under the cavern's ceiling. Many lay crushed beneath the stalactites, but several remained, though a bit shorter now.

"Flicker," Hawke called over the commlink.

"Yes?"

"Find anything yet?"

"If I did," she responded tightly, *"you'd be the first to know. I don't like you walking into the unknown, and I sure don't like you doing it with sec men dogging your every step."*

"I know." Hawke let out a breath and glanced at Rachel. "How close are we?"

"Close." She shook her head. "I just can't tell exact distances. I just know we're headed in the right direction. The pull is stronger."

Again Hawke cursed the Shadowman. If he was so powerful, why wasn't he here now? He kept his anger to himself and kept moving, slowing a little because the water covered heaps of rubble and made footing uncertain.

A klick farther on, the cavern widened into a chamber almost as big as the sunken harbor. Shipwrecks mingled with the wreckage of large buildings that had probably once been some kind of public places.

The main structure still had three walls standing, but they were all broken, not running in straight lines. The building had been three stories or more tall, with huge, arched windows and walkways that would have allowed trucks to easily pass through. Ribbed metal arches spanned part of the space where the roof had been.

"Whoever these people were, they knew metallurgy," Rachel said.

"So?" Hawke asked. Unimpressed by the architecture, he was more consumed with the fact that all but seven minutes of their head start was gone. He didn't doubt that whichever corp sec group reached them first would make better time than they had.

"It must have been lost or forgotten. Everyone assumed metallurgy was learned during the Fifth World." She looked around. "Some of these ships had to have gone down after the city sank."

"Why?"

"They're more modern. Old to us, but not as old as some of these other ships. Maybe people were searching for the city. Legends or myths must have existed about it for a while."

"Let's just hope none of them found what we're looking for."

Rachel shook her head. "They didn't. It's still here."

"Hawke." Flicker sounded tense.

Hawke figured he already knew what she was going to tell him. Standing on a small rise, he stared at the land bridge spanning a canyon at least a thousand meters deep, if his estimation of the fall time of the pebble he'd dropped over the edge was correct.

"Yeah."

"NeoNET just arrived. They're sending out drones now. I'm going to have to scramble my guys and try to keep them hidden. As they progress, I'm going to temporarily lose your six."

"Understood. Just make sure they don't find you."

"Oh, that's the first thing on my to-do list."

Adjusting his backpack, Hawke studied the bridge. At least eighty meters long, the formation widened onto a ledge holding dozens of stone houses perched on a long hillside. All of the homes had fallen into a state of disrepair. Maybe they'd been destroyed by whatever fate had overtaken the city, but some of the damage had been done by houses higher up the hill tumbling down onto the others.

"Think it'll hold?" Rolla asked.

"It has to." Hawke started across. "NeoNET's in the harbor. Going back isn't an option." His boots crunched on the broken rocks covering the stone span, and he kept expecting to feel it quiver as they passed.

"Here," Rachel whispered as she stared up at the massive building that filled the latest chamber they'd found.

The structure resembled a ziggurat, ten stories tall, each one stacked on like cake layers, each one slightly smaller than the last, so that a wide rim was left on all sides. Looking at the design, Hawke thought the empty space on top of each story might have been for pedestrians. Smaller stone-walled areas suggested meeting places, maybe pergolas over common grounds, or garden areas.

The cavern roof was two hundred meters overhead, almost invisible in the darkness.

"You know what this is, don't you?" Excitement rang in Rachel's voice.

"The building holding the knickknack we're looking for," Rolla rumbled. "At least, it better be."

Rachel ignored him. "It's an arcology. People lived here separately from the rest of the sprawl. Maybe it was a racial divide, or maybe it had to do with religion or finances."

"Or maybe it was just for people who thought they were better than other people," Rolla said. "That's the way the world still spins, you know. We didn't invent that. Had to come from somewhere."

Staying alert, Hawke strode toward the building. Piles of debris, fallen rock and sometimes fallen buildings lay in the open area before the massive structures. To the right, he spotted a trio of huge stones at least thirty meters tall that had been carved into the likenesses of skulls. He knew they were skulls from the familiar hollows for the eyes and the noses, as well as the curved fangs, but the dimensions were all wrong for anything human.

"Hawke," Dolphin said.

"Yes?"

"I peeled back another layer of those files I got from Sukenobu. She's been investigating the legend of an artifact that's supposed to be magical in nature."

"What Rachel found certainly fills that bill."

"The artifact is also supposed to have some history of the dragons. How they work their magic and other things."

As mysterious as the dragons continued to be, Hawke knew that would be valuable, maybe even priceless, to any corp. Even those headed up by dragons had members who wanted to better understand their CEOs.

Or possibly usurp them.

"Nothing else?"

"I think I've got everything Sukenobu has."

"She doesn't know much then."

"She knows enough to have come this far. She was gambling on whether it would pay off. Guess where she got the intel on the artifacts." Dolphin's tone held bitter irony.

A sinking feeling big enough to drop a city twisted through Hawke's gut. "KilmerTek?"

"The very same. All information roads lead to KilmerTek. Of course, they were cleverer this time, and used a lot of shell companies to disguise their machinations. Sukenobu didn't figure that out, but I did because I'm getting a feel for the person who put this together. We're dealing with one crafty slot, *omae*."

The Shadowman. Hawke hadn't thought he could hate the man more, but the feeling still had growth potential. "You still don't know who he is?"

"No, but I haven't given up."

Hawke led the way into the building's first floor. The structure was surprisingly sound overall, only tumbled down around the edges. As he walked, he stirred up small clouds of dust. Looking back, he saw their footprints in the fine gray powder. There was no way they could hide the signs of their passage in the time they had left.

He looked at Rachel. "Which way?"

"Up," she said, raking her infrared beam along the stairs to the second floor.

Turning to Rolla, Hawke said, "Mine the room."

The troll hesitated and scratched the back of his neck. "Aren't you afraid that might bring the whole place down on us?"

"Flicker," Hawke called. "How many sec men has NeoNET fielded?"

"I counted eighty-two. Aztechnology is here now, probably at the same troop strength. They're busy destroying NeoNET's subs. Listen."

A steady chorus of gunfire and explosions came over the commlink.

"Both sides are backing off," Flicker said when she came back online. *"I think they realized if no one has a way back to the surface, no one wins. Lots of small unit action has spread thoughout the area, but both corps have now established beachheads. Everybody seems more or less happy with that. At least some of the numbers on both sides will be cut down. If you get lucky, NeoNET's sec teams will turn back to save their evac vessels, or at least post a rearguard."*

"Sukenobu and whoever her counterpart is at Aztechnology want the Dragonseed too much not to pursue it." Hawke looked back at Rolla. "Figure about two hundred to seven. Now, you wanna try to cut down the numbers coming for us, or you wanna let them come ahead?"

Rolla dropped his backpack and began rummaging around the explosives inside it. "They're gonna try to blow us up when they find us. If we're in the building, they'll blow that up too, and search the wreckage for what they came for." He shrugged and held up a block of plastic explosive. "If they hesitate and try to do it the hard way, we might as well blow them up before they get to us. That's why you had Flicker outfit some of her drones with explosives."

Hawke smiled grimly. "I'll leave you and Twitch to it. When you're finished, catch up." He turned and headed up the stairs.

CHAPTER SEVENTY-NINE

"Okay, NeoNET has stepped up their game," Flicker said. *"They're on top of your twenty."*

A window opened in Hawke's vision as he reached the eighth floor landing. The view came from a drone scanning from high ground as the corp sec force arrived. Clad in matte-black hardsuits, the sec teams looked like efficient, heavily-armed beetles moving through the ruined city.

Five hundred meters away, NeoNET scouts advanced through the passage Rachel had led Hawke and his group through. Showing professional chops, the scouts broke off from the main force and invaded the large cavern, taking up spotting and support positions to observe the building.

"They're going to find us pretty quickly," Paredes said. "They've got thermal imaging that will allow them to see through the structure, and they've got combat mages."

Hawke turned to him. "How much can you sense about this place through the astral?"

Paredes shook his head as he looked around. "Surprisingly little. I can see the overall structure, but I can't pass through it."

"Neither can I," Nighthorse confirmed. "Whoever built this place, they had magical blocks in place."

"You could have mentioned this earlier," Hawke said.

"If it had been a problem, I would have. As it was, you've been busy thinking about things from your perspective. You have Snakechaser, Paredes, and myself for this. We've got your back, *omae.*"

Hawke relaxed a little. He knew what she was saying was true. The little he knew about magework wouldn't help. "So, what we have is a magical bunker."

"To a degree, *oui,*" Snakechaser said. "But it's a bunker with limitations. Perhaps they can't attack us with magic here, but neither can we attack them while we're inside."

"Well," Hawke said, "it's a good thing you all brought weapons." He turned back to Rachel. "Let's go. Faster."

"Up," she replied, and ran up the stairs. "We're almost there."

Wired into the drone array through military-spec AR glasses, Ayuni Sukenobu clicked through the feeds from the various units buzzing around the building in the distance. She cycled through each, gaining more information with each picture. Excitement thrummed inside her as she thought about how close she was to her prize.

For over a year, she'd chased the shadow whispers of the Dragonseed. She'd known others were searching for it too; Aztechnology and a few other lesser corps had been researching the artifact, but she was certain she would be the one to find it.

And once she had the Dragonseed, her grandfather would take even more pride in her. She would stand even taller in the eyes of her family and the executive board at NeoNET. After all, she would be the first one to break into the secrets the dragons protected so viciously.

Her hand strayed to the necklace of scales she wore. All her life she'd coveted the dragons' majesty, their power and wealth and mystery. Dunkelzahn himself had taunted her over the years, ridiculing her efforts at hiring people to discover everything he'd hidden away, with every one of her failures delivered to her. After he'd died, the great dragon had left her the necklace of his scales in his will—to continually remind her of the things he'd told her she would never know.

The necklace was anathema to her, but she wore it to remind herself not to give up seeking the knowledge she wanted. It was the spur she needed to continue her quest. The dragons weren't as omnipotent as they pretended to be, and she intended to prove that.

Unconscionably, the drones' views didn't penetrate the walls of the building except to show seven blurry thermographic images proceeding up a set of stairs. Two of the shadowrunners lagged behind, perhaps injured during a fall or other accident, but they were catching up.

Clicking out of the video array, Sukenobu turned to the colonel leading the troops she'd hired. "Why can't I see into the building?"

He shook his head. In his forties, heavily-cybered, scars from past campaigns showed on his face and cyberlimbs. "The drones' video arrays can't penetrate the walls. Could be the bricks they're made of contain a lot of lead."

Angry, scarcely containing her frustration, Sukenobu wheeled on her combat mage leader. "Can you see them?"

The woman shook her head. She was old and wizened, gray and sharp-eyed, looking out of place in her combat suit. Taking a fresh grip on her staff, she said, "No, Director Sukenobu, I cannot."

"Why not?"

"It's the building, ma'am. It's warded against astral interference."

Sukenobu drew a breath and thought about the situation. It stood to reason that the building would be magic, even magically resistant, to protect anything inside. That only proved what was inside was valuable.

She returned her attention to the colonel. "Send a team into the building. Flush those people out and let's deal with them."

"Yes, Director."

Almost immediately, twenty men in five groups closed on the building.

As Hawke reached the tenth floor landing, explosions erupted on the bottom floor. Rumbling detonations filled the structure, and his audio dampers filtered the noise to a tolerable level. Vibrations ran throughout the building, dropping loose stones and scree in small dust clouds.

Hawke held his position, thinking maybe the whole thing was about to fall on their heads. Here he'd traveled to the bottom of the sea only to die in a collapsed building. The thought almost made him smile, but it wasn't humorous. Not really.

The echoes of the explosions died away, and the quaking stilled.

"Well," Rolla announced in a tense voice that cracked only slightly. "We survived, but those guys who came in after us just had one of their worst days. Armor-piercing anti-personnel munitions will slot you up quick."

"They still haven't given up, though," Flicker said. *"You may have destroyed that passageway, but there's still three other sides of the building. More teams are entering now."*

Rachel started running without being told. Hawke followed her, his thoughts dizzy with trying to figure out how they could get past all of the incoming sec troops on their way out.

Assuming they survived whatever waited ahead of them.

Filled with ornate statuary, the passageway ran straight, wide and deep. Arched doorways to other chambers lay on either side, but Rachel passed them all, heading for what appeared to be a blank wall at the end.

She stopped and studied the barrier, and Hawke fell into position beside her. Button cams they'd left in their wake showed sec troops in armor charging up the stairs. He knew other groups would be coming up other passageways, too. At least four stairwells led to the top floor.

"Rachel?" Hawke looked at the wall, seeing only raised images of humans and elves warring against improbable monsters.

"Are those . . . what I think they are?" Nighthorse stepped closer and tentatively ran her fingers over the grotesque, tentacled monsters frozen in stone. "I've heard vague rumors here and there—the merest whispers of whispers—but I never thought I'd see anything like this."

"History lesson later," Hawke said. "Find the goods and go now." He turned back to Rachel. "We need—"

Lunging forward, Rachel placed both hands on the wall and shoved. Her back arched with the effort, her breath hissing out between clenched teeth.

For a moment, nothing happened. Hawke slung his rifle over his shoulder, getting ready to help. Then the wall split down the middle with a crackle of blue lightning. A shimmering haze draped the opening like a spiderweb, then gradually faded away.

"Magic?" Hawke asked Nighthorse.

The shaman nodded. "Guardian spell. Old magic. Very powerful."

"What would it have done?"

"I don't know. Be glad it didn't get the chance to do it. The spell went away after it scanned Rachel. Evidently it recognized her, but that doesn't mean the way will be safe for the rest of us."

"Cheery. Then we should probably be—"

Rachel stepped into the dark room.

CHAPTER EIGHTY

Certain Rachel was about to die in some bloody fashion he'd never seen before, or that one of the tentacled monsters engraved on the wall was lurking inside, Hawke slid the assault rifle from his shoulder and stepped in behind her. He swept the room with the rifle, intending to stop Rachel in case she wasn't really herself again.

Instead, she had frozen a few steps in, staring at the large dragon in the center of the room.

Covered in dark-green and yellow scales, it stood at least thirty meters tall, resting on three huge, clawed feet and holding the other claw in front of it. Enormous wings were folded along its back. Thorny projections covered the wedge-shaped face, some a meter long, but still small in relation to the immense head. Two huge horns curved back over the dragon's head, above the large, almond-shaped eyes that glowed with red fire. Another curved horn stood out on its nose. Below its cruelly curved mouth showing a hint of the massive fangs inside, another horn poked straight down.

Rolla whirled around the door and opened fire on the dragon. Bullets bounced from the statue's scaled chest in a flurry of yellow sparks that died in the darkness.

"Hey!" With a glare, Paredes gestured and a shimmering barrier protected them from ricochets.

"What?" The troll glared belligerently back. "If it was alive, I wasn't gonna give it a chance to strike first."

The dragon never moved.

"It's not alive," Nighthorse said as she stepped into the room.

"Good thing," Rolla said as he replaced his spent magazine. "If it was, I woulda flatlined it."

"More like," Snakechaser said as he approached, holding his walking stick in front of him, "you would have only annoyed it and probably assured our doom."

Hawke played his infrared beam around the room, expanding his cybervision. Along the walls, bas-reliefs of the dragon or others of its kind were rendered in stone and stood out in various poses. In some of the images, the dragon battled the tentacled monsters as elves sheltered at its feet.

"Flicker?"

A small cloud of drones flew into the room and fanned out. Their video feeds ghosted across Hawke's helmet visor.

"The only things living in this room," Flicker said, *"are you guys. But not for long. You're out of time."*

Rachel slowly walked forward, her gaze focused at the dragon's outstretched claw. Nestled inside the curled talons, the blue stone artifact lay in the dragon's palm. As she drew closer, it started glowing, brighter and brighter.

"Maybe we should take a minute," Hawke suggested.

But his words were lost in the rumbling of rock created by the dragon's talons opening to expose the artifact. Rachel hesitated, her hand only centimeters from the stone. Hawke knew she was probably remembering what had happened in the pool, remembering how she had almost lost herself. He knew he was.

"Rachel," he said softly. "We need to know more before you do anything rash."

"I know." She drew her hand back slightly.

"Not to sound pushy, *hermano*," Paredes said, "but hesitation at this point may be as detrimental as doing something rash."

A shimmer filled the space near Rachel and the Shadowman stood beside her.

Rolla fired at the new arrival immediately, but the bullets stopped in mid-air before they reached their target. He flicked his wrist, and the troll street samurai was knocked off his feet and slammed into the wall behind him. After he crashed to the floor, Rolla got up slowly.

"Take the Dragonseed, Child. This is your destiny."

"What if I choose not to?" Rachel pulled her hand back and wrapped her arms around herself.

"Then you will be Unborn, and you will die."

Hawke shifted slightly, but he didn't aim his weapon toward the Shadowman. This close in, with the blue glow of the artifact stripping the darkness from the man's features, he saw the Shad-owman's strong jaw and piercing golden eyes that were much brighter than Snakechaser's.

"You know I speak the truth. You can read that in me."

"I can see the truth in others," Rachel said. "You, I just hear."

"Do not doubt yourself or your power, Child. You are strong. This is your Destiny. Now is the time to embrace it."

"Tell me who you are," Rachel said. "What is your connection to me?"

"I gave you life. I created you. And I would see you Become all that you are supposed to be." The Shadowman stepped closer and gen-tly took her hand. *"These people have brought you this far, Rachel. As have I. But the last choice is yours alone to make."*

"I'll die if I don't take the artifact?"

"Yes."

"Then it sounds like I don't have much of a decision."

"We all must choose life or death, Child. And those choices are of-ten made in times like these. Sometimes it is not so clear-cut."

Slowly, Rachel reached for the artifact. As soon as she touched it, a blinding blue flash filled the chamber, and thunder pealed so loud the concussion knocked Hawke from his feet. When his vi-sion cleared, he saw Rachel standing there bathed in a blue aura. A deeper blue fire burned within her, reaching from her head to her feet and spreading outward.

"Rachel?" Hawke pushed himself to his feet. *"Rachel?"*

Calmly, she looked up at him. "It's okay. I'm fine."

Hawke looked past her at the now-empty talon. "Where's the artifact?"

"She is *the artifact. She is the Dragonseed."* The Shadowman stepped back from her, and now he spread his wings, definitely looking more reptilian now. *"Now she is truly Born."*

The golden eyes, surrounded by scales, cut to Hawke. *"My enemies still pursue her, however. You must protect her. Get her out of this place and back into the world."*

Anger flared within Hawke. "That would have been a hell of a lot easier if you hadn't told NeoNET and Aztechnology where we were. You're the reason we've got two armies standing out there ready to flatline us."

With a deep basso growl, the Shadowman stepped forward. His wings flared, a tail whipped behind him, and his jaws elon-gated, showing an impressive amount of sharp, curved fangs.

"Do not choose to be so reckless, Hawke. You are very close to making a life and death decision of your own in the next few seconds."

"If you could have done this without me and my team, you'd have done it." Hawke expected to end up smeared across a wall at any second, but he couldn't hold back the furious fire burning within him any longer. "Rachel is at risk—*we're* at risk—because of the games you've been playing."

The Shadowman drew back a hand that became a fistful of curved talons.

"No!" Darting in front of Hawke, Rachel held up both hands to the Shadowman. She spoke again, calmly and with more authority. "No. You will not harm him. Not any of them. If you do, you'll have to kill me with them."

"You presume too much, Child."

"Hawke's right," Rachel replied. "You've used all of them." She paused. "You used me as bait for the two corps here now. Why?"

Letting his arm fall back to his side, the Shadowman shrank down, becoming more human in appearance again. *"Because I did not just want to celebrate your Birth. I wanted you brought into your Life with a victory. In ancient times, a Dragonseed would be birthed in the blood of my enemies who fell in battle. Today, in this world, I choose to celebrate by putting my foot on the throats of two of my enemies."*

"How do you figure on doing that?" Hawke demanded. "They're both here. They'll kill us to get Rachel when they find out she's the Artifact. Then they'll kill each other 'til one of them has her."

"No, they won't. Each of them will believe they have succeeded in their endeavors instead." Turning to the dragon statue, the Shadowman gestured, and suddenly the blue stone talisman was clasped in the stone talons again.

Hawke looked at Rachel. The blue glow around her was gone, but she still seemed changed somehow. He could feel the difference in her, even though he couldn't see it. There was something edgy and dark about her now.

"Each of those corps will be allowed to find a Dragonseed." The Shadowman's fanged smile gleamed in the shadows. *"Each will believe they have found the only one, never knowing that both possess the double-edged sword I am leaving them."*

"You couldn't have done that in Guatemala?" Hawke demanded.

The Shadowman shook his head. *"The artifact discovered in Guatemala was only a shadow of this one. A bread crumb trail that started you all on the journey that ended here. It was the starting point that allowed Rachel to take the path she needed to travel in order to Become. She had to be prepared to meet her Destiny. While she was in that coma, her body changed so that she could handle her Growth."*

"He's the one who owns a controlling share in KilmerTek," Dolphin said over Hawke's commlink.

"Who is he?" Hawke asked, watching the Shadowman closely.

"I still don't know," Dolphin admitted. *"I'm still searching for his name."*

"That is a fruitless enterprise." The smugness in the Shadowman's tone was galling. *"You will never find proof of my manipulations."*

"Nobody's that good," Dolphin said defiantly.

The Shadowman chuckled. *"So you say."*

"Why do you want the other corps to find the Dragonseeds?" Rachel asked.

"Because they will get more than they bargained for."

One of Flicker's drones swept in over the Dragonseed and hovered there. A diagnostic spreadsheet opened in Hawke's view. He didn't understand any of it.

In the next heartbeat, the drone exploded in a flash of orange and yellow fire. Gray ash fell to the floor like snow.

"Did you get that, Dolphin?" Flicker asked.

"It was code—like nothing I've ever seen," she replied. *"He's trapped the fake artifact with some kind of . . . virus."*

"I have. One that will allow me certain . . . liberties within both Aztechnology and NeoNET when they attempt to decipher this replica. I will strike a blow at my enemies, and my Child will come into her own. A Birth and twin victories to mark its occasion. This is a good day."

"Not if you don't get out of there," Flicker said. *"NeoNET's knocking on the door, Hawke. You've got to leave now."*

Scanning the images relayed by drone, Hawke saw NeoNET's lead sec teams were already on the ninth floor landing.

Rolla cursed as he set up by the doorway. "You figure this is as good a place as any to die?"

CHAPTER EIGHTY-ONE

The Shadowman laughed, the raucous, otherworldly noise filling the chamber, echoing all around them.

Hawke turned on him. "What's so funny?"

"Do you truly believe I would bring you this far, make certain this Child was Born, only to have you lose her?" The shadows of his face parted to reveal the fangs again. *"I have not. If you are strong enough and sly enough, a way out is still available to you."*

Rachel turned and stared at the walls. "There's a hidden passageway."

"How'd you know that?" Rolla demanded. He popped around the entrance long enough to fire a burst at the first sec men at the other end of the passageway.

"Because she does," Nighthorse said. "I can see it, too."

"I thought you couldn't see through the walls in this place."

"I can—now." The shaman followed Rachel to the wall. "The magical barriers protecting this building have dropped."

Placing her hands on the wall for a moment, Rachel backed away as an entire section, covered by another bas-relief of a rearing, fire-breathing dragon, slid aside. Beyond the false wall, a black passageway stood.

"Now go." The Shadowman's command filled the chamber.

Hawke dropped his pack to the floor and slid his rifle onto his shoulder. Head spinning with questions about what had been done to Rachel and what it meant for them, he focused instead on the approaching enemy troops.

He glanced at Rolla while Twitch picked off sec men trying to approach down the passageway. "Got any plastic explosives left?"

Rolla grinned. "I never empty the cupboard unless I know I'm not coming back."

"We're not coming back." Hawke brought out his own blocks of plastique and equipped them with detonators. By the time he had his ready, Rolla was waiting. "On three."

The street samurai nodded and gripped the explosives. On Hawke's count of three, they threw the explosives down the hallway. The bundles skipped down the debris-strewn floor, tumbling end over end.

"Flicker, they're keyed to your command." Hawke pulled his rifle into his hands and ran for the secret exit.

"I've got them," she replied.

"Detonate them when we're clear."

"Happily."

Hawke followed Paredes into the passageway. Rachel, Nighthorse, and Snakechaser had already entered. Rolla and Twitch brought up the rear.

The passageway was seven or eight meters in diameter, providing plenty of room to run. Hawke paused just a moment to look back and see what the Shadowman was doing.

"Fire in the hole!" Flicker announced.

The blast spread fire and destruction the length of the passageway leading up to the chamber. A wave of flames burst into the chamber and washed over the dragon statue, but didn't do any damage. When the flames extinguished, the Shadowman had vanished with them.

Hawke cursed the man, knowing he'd never been there anyway. He hadn't risked anything.

On the drone view, he saw several sec men down, dead or wounded, in the hallway outside the chamber. But reinforcements were already arriving to take up the slack.

Rolla dropped a big hand on Hawke's shoulder. "Let's go, *omae*. Nothing here to see any more."

Hawke nodded and pulled back. Rachel paused beside him and closed the entrance, blocking the scene of the dragon and the false Dragonseed nestled in its talons.

Together, they ran into the darkness.

"Director Sukenobu, I have the Dragonseed."

Watching the scene inside the temple through her smart-glasses, Sukenobu accessed the man's hardsuit cam.

He stood there in front of what looked like a dragon statue covered in soot. But he held the artifact in one hand. Its blue glow tinted the video display.

A thrill of joy filled her. She had spent a fortune and over a year pursuing the device. Now it was hers.

"Bring it to me at once," she ordered.

"Yes, Director."

Shifting to another sec man's commlink, Sukenobu commanded him to scan the room. He began turning in a complete circle, revealing all the artwork on the walls.

"Slower. I want every millimeter recorded so I can recreate it." Just in case there was something they'd missed.

"Yes, Director."

"Where are Rachel Gordon and the shadowrunners?" Sukenobu didn't think they would just leave the Dragonseed. But maybe they'd been afraid to take it. The artifact was supposed to be exceptionally dangerous and hard to acquire.

Yet, she had it.

"There's no sign of them, Director."

That troubled her. Leaving the Dragonseed behind was one thing, but for the group to disappear completely was unsettling.

"The explosion might have taken them out, Director," the colonel said. "It killed a lot of my men."

Sukenobu considered that, didn't immediately reject the possibility, but she didn't like it when things weren't neatly tied up. Complete closure when the whole truth wasn't in hand was sloppy, wishful thinking. She liked hard facts. Knowledge was always better than guesswork. Guesswork was intolerable.

"I see them," the combat mage said.

Turning to the old woman, Sukenobu asked, *"Now* you see them?"

"Yes, Director. Whatever magic was protecting that building is now gone."

That bothered Sukenobu as well. If the magic was as powerful as the woman had indicated earlier, its absence was a definite clue that something was not as it should be. Sukenobu's grandfather had taught her to be not only aggressive and merciless, but thorough.

"I want to know why the magic is missing," she said.

"Of course, Director."

"In the meantime, I want to know where Rachel Gordon is."

The old woman pointed along the side of the cavern roof high above them. "She's there, Director. With her friends. They're in a concealed passageway above us. The Awakened among them seek to block my sight, but I am too powerful."

Sukenobu didn't question the woman's answer. The truth would be revealed quickly enough. "Colonel."

"Yes, Director."

"Send three of your teams—" Sukenobu grabbed the old woman's arm and pushed her toward the indicated side of the cavern, "—with her to get Rachel Gordon. I want her alive if possible, but above all, I don't want her leaving this area."

"At once, Director." The colonel turned and relayed orders to his men over his commlink.

Sukenobu stayed where she was. The Dragonseed was the most important thing. She would see to Rachel Gordon and the shadowrunners later.

None of them would live. Except maybe the woman. And then only until she was of no further use.

CHAPTER EIGHTY-TWO

"Can you tell how far this passageway goes?" Hawke ran beside Rachel, leading the team away from the building. He'd scattered button cams behind him so he'd know when and if the sec team in the dragon chamber found the hidden door.

"I think it goes down to the harbor. I can't see that far, but that's the feeling I get. I think this was another level of the city."

Hawke agreed with her assessment. Crunched up into the sides of the tunnel, the remains of small houses and buildings sat vacant and broken. Several sections lay across the passageway.

Muffled gunfire sounded on the other side of the corridor wall. Or maybe it was coming up through the floor. Hawke thought it was possible the passage ran across the cavern's roof, at least in sections.

"NeoNET got their Dragonseed," Flicker said.

Images from the two drones inside the dragon chamber ghosted through Hawke's vision. The sec team bolted from the room with their prize locked in an armored box.

When the view shifted out into the passageway, Hawke saw the firefight shaping up between the NeoNET sec team and the Aztechnology warriors. Small arms fire and shimmering spells covered both groups. He was very glad they hadn't been caught in the middle of it.

A moment later, one of the Aztechnology squads reached the dragon chamber. When they did, Flicker's drones, silently floating up near the chamber's ceiling, recorded them taking the false Dragonseed again.

"Well, whoever played us got what he wanted," Flicker said. "Both corps got a Dragonseed."

"Yeah," Hawke growled. "We know what they got, but we still don't know what Rachel got."

"She's alive and you're alive, omae. *I'll settle for all of us getting the same deal at the end of the day."*

Spotting a pile of broken rock partially blocking the passage ahead, Hawke veered left while keeping his AK-97 ready. So far none of the sec teams had found their way into the passage, but that didn't mean there might not be other threats along the way.

"Can you track us?" Hawke asked.

"I'm pinging your armor."

"Where are we?"

"On the outside edge of the big cavern where the last building is. You're about halfway across the cave. You've got NeoNET troops over to your side. I suppose you can hear the gunfire."

"Yeah."

"They're still engaged with Aztechnology."

"Works for me." Hawke skirted the pile of debris, thought he spotted a shifting shadow, then realized it was only dust settling due to the vibrations from below coursing through the passage. "Can either of those teams ping us?"

"I've hardened your shielding as much as I can. We'll have to see. In case things get ugly, I still have explosive-equipped drones along the cavern wall above NeoNET and Aztechnology."

Watching the sec team bring the Dragonseed out of the temple, Sukenobu controlled her impatience. She shifted her attention to the team following the combat mage's direction. They were in position.

"How thick is the passage floor?" the lieutenant in charge of the squads asked.

"No more than two or three meters," the combat mage answered.

"Director Sukenobu," the lieutenant called over the commlink.

"I am here, Lieutenant." Through the relayed feed, Sukenobu studied the craggy cavern roof above and in front of the sec team.

"I don't see any way up into the passage the mage says is there. If those people do have a clear path to run, I don't know how much farther they have to go to get away."

"Do you have a suggestion?"

"I can open that passage from below, maybe take out some of those

people in doing so. Once we get an opening, we can send in drones to take the rest out."

"Do it."

The lieutenant called up one of his men, who approached at a run, leveling a big missile launcher over his shoulder. *"We've got a guaranteed wall-opener here, Director."* Kneeling, the sec man aimed it at the passageway. *"Just tell me where to put this."*

The combat mage pointed at a section of the ceiling and a red dot manifested on the rough surface. *"There."*

Fire and smoke belched from the rear of the weapon as the missile screamed toward its target.

CHAPTER EIGHTY-THREE

"Hawke!" Flicker yelled over the commlink. *"A NeoNET team is right below you! I think they're track–"*

The rest of the rigger's words were lost when the ground beneath Hawke's feet suddenly surged up and his hearing went out. Time slowed as his wired reflexes automatically came online to help him deal with the situation.

Propelled by the sudden blast, he flew upward, pounded again and again by debris that blew upward with him as well. Somewhere in the back of his mind, he realized the passageway floor had gotten hammered with some kind of warhead or explosive. He slammed against the ceiling as a large hole opened up below him.

As gravity reclaimed him and he started on the inevitable downward trajectory, more of the rock floor around the gaping wound in the cracked stone gave way and tumbled, falling into a two hundred meter drop.

The rest of the group was far enough back that they were able to stop their forward momentum and remain on stable ground. Rolla flung out a big arm and caught Twitch, shoving her back from the edge, then stopped Nighthorse and Snakechaser as well.

Near the hole's edge, Rachel lay on her back, barely moving and looking dazed as lime-green tracer fire cut through the air. Then the ground beneath her gave way and she fell, preceding Hawke through the opening by a meter. The sudden sensation of weightlessness tightened his stomach as he tried to position himself to reach any kind of stability.

Ahead of him, in free fall, Rachel tumbled and spun, arms and legs flailing. Her scream shut down Hawke's helmet audio, and he couldn't even speak to her. A plummet from two hundred meters would take something over six seconds. Hawke knew that because he'd jumped that distance before while learning parachuting, but during those times, he'd had a parachute.

Despite the battlesuit's hardening, it wouldn't survive the fall. Neither would he.

On the ground, below Rachel, a squad of NeoNET troops tracked them and fired. Several rounds struck Hawke. He didn't know if the armor deflected the bullets or not, and he didn't waste any time wondering about it because nothing was going to make a difference once he struck the ground. Dead or dying didn't matter. Once he hit the ground below, it was all over.

For a moment, when Rachel's combat armor came apart just short of impact, he was certain she'd gotten hit by another missile and ripped to shreds. Then she emerged from the ragged hardsuit, suddenly growing in size and changing—getting longer—becoming inhuman—covering over with golden scales—sprouting wings—

Just before she hit the ground, Rachel—now a dragon—stretched her wings and caught the air. Incredibly, she stopped her fall. Then she arrowed up at once and grabbed for Hawke with her back feet. One of her taloned claws missed him, though it struck with incredible power, but the other claw caught his left arm and jerked him up. For a moment, the sharp pain that cut through Hawke nearly made him pass out. He was certain his arm had been torn off.

It hadn't, though, because Rachel—if she still *was* Rachel—had him and slowed his fall, though they were still headed to the ground.

Amazed to still be alive, astonished at what Rachel had become, Hawke knew they were easy targets for the sec team only a few meters away. Bullets ricocheted off his armor and from Rachel's scales. Instinctively, Hawke fired the AK-97 one-handed, hitting most of his targets. They went down, dead or wounded or terrified of him or of Rachel.

Not fully in control of her flight, Rachel crashed into the nearby wall and went down in a flurry of wings. Bouncing off the cavern wall himself, breath knocked from his lungs, Hawke hit the ground, swapped out magazines in the rifle as he rolled, and came to a kneeling position firing at the sec team.

A few meters away, Rachel struggled to get up, flapping her wings and kicking her rear legs. She had to be twenty meters long from nose to tail, and she was a huge target. Rounds peppered her, and she was bleeding in a few places now.

"Get down!" Hawke roared.

For a second, the dragon looked confused. Then she ducked her head to take cover behind a low hill. A rocket from one of the men's launchers struck the top of the dirt mound and blew debris into the air and over Rachel's new body.

When the rifle's receiver locked back empty, Hawke reached into his thigh pocket for the grenades he'd brought. Grabbing a couple, not taking time to figure out what they were, he popped the activation rings and threw them at the NeoNET team.

Above, Twitch was at the edge of the hole, firing her pistols systematically, accurately hitting targets even at that distance. Rolla added his own rifle fire. Snakechaser, Nighthorse, and Paredes threw spells to increase the confusion among the sec team. Waves of fire and explosions swept over and detonated in the corps muscle even before the grenades Hawke had thrown dumped more misery into the mixture.

The NeoNET ranks broke, scattering to find defensive positions. Instead of being in control of the firefight, they found themselves hard pressed just to stay alive.

Autofire, the *whumps* of rocket launchers, and the heated rush of flames fought for top position in the cacophony of hellish noise that filled the cavern.

"Hawke."

Rachel's voice sounded different inside Hawke's head, not coming over the commlink now. Behind him, she staggered to her rear feet, rocked uncertainly for a moment, then got her balance.

"I'm here," he told her as he found and fed a new magazine into the rifle. "Are you okay?"

"Yes."

"Are you still . . . *you?*"

"Yes." Rachel stretched her wings and stood taller. *"This is . . . different. But it also feels . . . familiar."*

More rifle fire struck Rachel, but there wasn't as much any more because a good portion of the sec team had gone down under the combined attack. Bodies, some burned black or torn apart, jerked as more explosions tore through them. Rolla still had a few grenades, and was making the most of them.

Rachel draped a scaly wing in front of her face to block the small arms fire. A rocket streaked toward her and she brushed it away with her other wing. When the warhead struck the cavern wall behind her, it exploded, spreading a cloud of dust that almost hid her from sight.

"We can't stay here."

"Well, we can't march across this cavern." Hawke emptied his magazine, firing three-round bursts of suppressive fire.

A four-man squad of NeoNET sec men charged from the left side. Hawke swung his rifle over to them, fired a three-round burst that put one of their attackers down, and cursed when the receiver locked back again. He dropped the rifle and reached for his pistol. Even as his hand closed around the weapon and swept it from its holster, Rachel stretched her neck forward and breathed a stream of flames over the men, setting their suits on fire.

"Hawke," Flicker said, *"NeoNET's sending reinforcements."*

Already aware of the troop movement, Hawke picked up his rifle and slapped another magazine into the weapon. "Blow the drone mines in front of them."

"Blowing them now."

Immediately, the explosive-equipped drones that had attached themselves to the cavern roof between Hawke and the reinforcements detonated in rapid succession, chewing a ragged line amid the stalactites. Several of the stony spears dropped among the sec force, killing some of them outright and trapping others. Then large sections of the roof came free, falling in a spread of boulders and chunks that formed an impromptu wall.

Hawke picked off a couple more targets. "Snakechaser, how much nylon line do you have?" he asked, even though he was certain of the answer.

"Not enough to reach you, cousin."

Cursing, Hawke knew there was no way he could climb up the cavern wall. Even if he could find purchase points to make the ascent, he'd be picked off by sniper fire before he could reach the passage.

"Rachel, you need to get out of here. Join the others and get to Flicker."

"I'm not leaving you."

"Yes, you are. I can't fly. You can. Get gone."

She didn't say anything, but a moment later she spread her wings and took to the air as if she'd been doing it all her life.

Staying behind cover, Hawke kept up bursts of suppressive fire until his rifle ran dry for the last time, thinking that at least they'd saved Rachel's life, even if she could never go back to the innocence she'd once had.

Above him, Rachel wheeled and glided back down. Before he knew what she was doing, she closed her talons around his shoulders and lifted him from the ground.

"I've got you. Just be still."

Although he felt certain Rachel was being stupid about the whole situation, Hawke wanted to live. So maybe he was stupid, too. He held his pistol in one hand and reached up with the other, grabbing one of the talons gripping him.

Rachel struggled to get the altitude she needed, but—after veering around a couple times—she folded her wings and just barely flew into the hole in the bottom of the passage.

Inside, she dropped Hawke to the floor and crashed to the ground next to him.

Rolling to his feet, Hawke noted the NeoNET drones speeding toward them. "Paredes, block that hole!"

The combat mage turned and gestured at the hole. An instant later, a shimmery surface spread over the opening. The drones smashed into the barrier and shattered, falling back to the ground in pieces.

Hawke crossed to where the bloody dragon lay on the stone floor. He dropped down beside the large head and peered into one of her eyes.

"Rachel, can you . . . can you turn back?" he asked.

She flopped her wings helplessly. Then her body started shrinking and she became human, naked and vulnerable, still bleeding from a few wounds that had become much smaller as well. Her eyes rolled back up in her head as she lost consciousness.

Hawke picked her up in his arms and ran. The others followed as drones beat against Paredes's shimmering shield like hungry insects.

Long minutes later, winding through a series of passages, with Flicker's drones mapping the way, Hawke reached the harbor area where the *Helldiver* was anchored.

Flicker popped the hatch and Hawke carried Rachel into the submersible. He put her in one of the seats, took the blanket Nighthorse got out of a supply locker, draped it over her, and strapped the safety belts on.

Returning to human form had undone or healed some of the injuries Rachel had received. Hawke wasn't sure which it was. Nighthorse sat beside her and started singing, healing the wounds that were left.

Hawke glanced at Flicker. "Can you get us out of here?"

The rigger nodded. "Dolphin and I have been working on it. She hacked the other subs, crawled into their commlink arrays, and loaded a virus that will keep their engines offline for a few hours." The screwdrive engaged, propelling them out into deeper water.

Hawke strapped himself into his seat and watched the trideos Flicker put up, knowing she'd done that for him. Schools of fish swirled around the dark water in front of them. Tentacled things crawled along the seabed, then vanished as the bottom dropped away, rendering them too far away to be seen.

Making himself breathe, Hawke waited and watched as they sped back through the passage toward the open sea.

EPILOGUE

Hawke walked along the beach with his hands in his shorts pockets. Along with the cargo shorts, he wore a Hawaiian shirt Rolla had picked out for him. He'd gone along with the selection because it helped him blend into the tourist crowd. Maybe the look wouldn't have worked in daylight, but it worked well enough at night, because the darkness blunted his features and disguised some of the bruises that were still fading.

Moonlight kissed the white rollers coming into the beach. In a few places, partiers had bonfires going. They were young and innocent, and there weren't nearly enough of them these days. Other vacationers would be in the resort hotels, planning their next headhunting coup or insider trading, anything to claw just a little closer to the top of the heap.

Hawke was walking to think because thinking by himself in his hotel room was scary.

Soft footsteps fell in behind his. Sand crunched underfoot, then the steps quickened a little, closing the distance to him. He didn't reach for the pistol holstered at his back—he wasn't completely touristy, and the Hawaiian shirt concealed the weapon quite well.

"Are you just gonna follow me all night?" he asked.

"Do you mind some company?"

"No, I suppose I don't." He paused and turned around, allowing Flicker to catch up to him.

"Good." Dressed in a black and white patterned bikini and wrap that accentuated her dark skin, the elven rigger pulled off touristy with ease. She smiled at him. "I figured I'd find you out here." She took his arm, leaned into him, and pulled him back into a stroll.

Hawke didn't say anything, knowing she'd get to it soon enough.

"So . . . Rachel's a dragon. That's something you don't see every day."

"Not and live," Hawke agreed.

"Nighthorse and Snakechaser are working with her, getting her used to the idea of not being exactly what she thought she would be. They think she's going to be okay."

"That's good."

"It's going to take some time. They don't want to leave her right now."

Hawke had already gotten that feeling about them. Nighthorse and Snakechaser liked taking care of people.

Flicker stopped him and turned to face him head on, because that's what she was all about. "What I want to know is how you're doing."

Uncomfortable, Hawke shrugged. "I'm fine. Why wouldn't I be? We're alive. NeoNET and Aztechnology are satisfied that we don't matter, and they got what they were after. Rachel's 'father' has his virus probably installed in their systems by now, and hasn't killed us either. On top of that, we got a fortune from him for pulling this off."

"But even with all that, you're still not satisfied."

Hawke just blinked and didn't say anything.

"I know you, Hawke. You wanted to save the girl . . . and you didn't get to."

He smiled wryly. "Turns out she isn't exactly a girl."

"No, she isn't, but you—and *we*—saved her. She's still got an opportunity for a good life. An *amazing* life, in fact. After all, her father is filthy rich."

"Her father," Hawke said with some disgust, "may not care all that much for her. He used her as bait in a scheme that could have gotten her killed."

"Maybe that was part of what she had to go through to finish becoming who she truly is. He told us that."

"He also lied about a lot of things before he got to that part."

"He got us out of the sunken city." Flicker stared at him with those aquamarine eyes. "He didn't have to do that."

"As I recall, we made our own way out."

Flicker raised her shoulders and dropped them. "That's because we're that good." She looked at him. "Are you hearing me?

We're that good. We've got a good team here, Hawke. These are good people. They know what they're doing, and they trust each other. Especially after all this. You should trust them, too."

That was what Hawke was dreading. It wasn't Rachel's adjustment to being a dragon that bothered him the most. It wasn't that her father was probably Lofwyr, as Dolphin suspected, and that her heritage carried an immeasurable amount of trouble and grief, if it didn't get them killed outright.

He sucked in a breath and let it out. "I do trust them. It's just that if we try to stay together in the shadows, we're gonna be a big target. We can't hide as well. We can't move as fast."

"They—*we*—want to stay together, Hawke. And we want you to be a part of that."

A cool wind pushed in from the sea. Hawke stood there and let it roll over him, still trying to figure out things.

"We can't go back to the way it was," Flicker said. "This run got too big. If we try to stay on our own, we'll be even more vulnerable alone than we are together. If one of us is found out, the others will be at risk, and they'll take us all, one by one. We all believe that."

Hawke had been thinking about that, too.

"Do you want to know what I think really drove you to help Rachel?" Flicker asked, taking him by the arm and starting along the beach again.

"Not really."

"I think you wanted to help her because you believed she was going to have a good life, and have a family. Be a happy citizen. But that's not going to happen because she's a dragon. The rarest of the rare. So if you want Rachel to have any chance at a family, you're going to have to help make one for her."

When it came down to it, Flicker was right. And Hawke knew she wouldn't take no for an answer.

"It's going to be hard to make it work," he finally said.

"So there are some risks. That's nothing new in the shadows."

"I know."

"But it'll be worth it." Flicker tugged on his arm and smiled up at him. "Say it like you mean it, Hawke."

Knowing she wouldn't give up, he said, "But it'll be worth it."

And Hawke thought it might—it just might at that. They lived in the shadows, after all, where every day hinged on the roll of the dice.

ABOUT THE AUTHOR

Mel Odom is the bestselling author of several novels, including *Preying for Keeps*, *Headhunters*, and *Run Hard, Die Fast* in the *Shadowrun* series. He's also working on the *Makaum War* trilogy, which includes *Master Sergeant* and *Guerilla*, and several other projects. He currently lives in Oklahoma.

SHADOWS DOWN UNDER
BY JEAN RABE • COMING SOON!

DEATH STALKS THE CITY STREETS...

Someone—or some*thing*—is killing nightclub entertainers in Kings Cross, Australia. Striking from the shadows, methodical, heinous, the murderer has wrapped the bawdy, colorful neighborhood in a suffocating blanket of terror.

Ninniniru "Ninn" Tossinn, a troubled private investigator on the run from her past, joins forces with Barega, an elderly Aborigine shaman, to uncover the truth behind the malevolent force—and put themselves on the Cross Slayer's list. But can they defeat the darkness, survive Sydney's powerful mana storm, and reach the true heart of the evil threatening the city? Their search takes them from gritty alleys filled with gang symbols and worse to beneath the squatter-filled harbor bridge over shark-infested waters.

As their investigation deepens, soon the Cross Slayer isn't the only foe stalking them. Ninn and Barega have to put all their trust in each other if they're going to bring the Slayer to justice, uncover the conspiracy behind the murders, and stay alive long enough to do both.

PROLOGUE

The storm came before sunset on a Christmas Eve long ago.

Birthed over the Outback from a single, nacreous cloud at the top of the sky, all milky blue and opalescent gray, shimmering, beautiful, shiny, with a hint of rosy pink, it invited the original people—the Aborigines—to stand beneath its pulsing strands in wonder and appreciation.

And later in terror.

And then in understanding.

And finally in appreciation again.

First the cloud darkened, roiling as if it seethed with a righteous anger. A mean wind grew with it, escalating to such a gale force that even the original people had to seek refuge. Fingers of lightning arced down to spear those who had harmed the once-fair Earth. Thunder made the ground leap and dance.

The devastation was awesome, wiping away small towns, slaughtering dozens and injuring hundreds. It wreaked havoc on the astral plane, too.

When the tempest eased, all but the original people relaxed and considered it a freak of nature and magic; a mana storm. They went back to their lives, started rebuilding their small towns, and then gaped in disbelief when the terrible cloud returned weeks later and expanded, and the rain came at them sideways, driven by winds the land had not seen in long, long memory.

Then came another storm.

And another.

And the time between downpours became shorter, and the winds that came after each one were fiercer.

Thousands died.

It was as if the Awakening was waging war on Australia. Clouds churned across the island continent, and the magic that hammered down drove all but the original people into the sprawls, which were mostly unaffected. The Aborigines had found safe places and a more appropriate name for the weather: The Great Ghost Dance. It had chased the white men back to the cities, where they belonged.

The continent-wide deluge eventually, mercifully, subsided—though scattered mana storms appeared from time to time, they stayed only briefly, perhaps to remind everyone to leave the Outback to its original occupants.

Only one big cloud persisted.

A mother-of-pearl beauty all milky blue and opalescent gray, shimmering, shiny, with just a hint of rosy pink at the edges. Frightening on some days when it darkened like a great charcoal smudge. Wholly terrifying when it turned the world blackest-black and wicked magic coursed down from it.

That cloud had settled over Sydney and stretched out into the bay.

That isolated mana storm had remained.

For more than sixty years.

ONE
ELLA'S LAMENT

The room was long and narrow, the walls shot through with sections of corrugated metal, giving it the feel of a big, antique boxcar that had been canted so one end was higher than the other, descending to the stage down front. Fog clung to the ceiling—or rather what looked like fog, the dense sort that rolls into the harbor and up the pilings of the ruined bridge. The fog was tobacco smoke; the nightclub, unlike many establishments in the city, had no restrictions on that particular vice.

"Welcome one and all on this rare, stormless night!" the announcer boomed through hidden speakers. *"Our extravaganza opens with a damsel fair who creates her own thunder, the one—the only—Miss Ella Gance!"*

The crowd erupted with applause and catcalls as the house lights dimmed. An alto saxophone wailed; the first of many notes lost amid the cheers. Then the crowd quieted, and the sax's seductive melody rose, joined by a muted trombone. The curtains parted, and a single, bright spotlight bathed her.

Ella's coral lips edged up into a suggestive smile, and her perfectly manicured hands smoothed the red silk dress hugging her hips. The slender torch singer swayed gently on her rhinestone-studded heels and crooned.

"Love is where you find it, find it.
And if you find it, keep it, keep it.
Keep it close to your heart, where it's yours alone.
'Cause if someone else finds it, they'll steal it, steal it."

Ella's voice, tempered by expensive vocal range enhancers, trilled as she stepped to the edge of the stage and reached a finger up to brush a single strand of shiny, raven hair off her face. Her liquid brown eyes scanned the crowd as she finished the chorus and waited for the English horn's nasal notes to slice through the strains of the rest of the woodwinds. It was real music, played by actual musicians; finely dressed elves and humans on fourteen instruments comprised the small orchestra. The dwarf who played the cello was absent tonight. Some people came just to hear the ensemble, a rarity in the neighborhood . . . *real* music becoming a rarity in the entire city.

She blew a kiss to an elderly ork sitting to the left of the stage, staring at her in rapt fascination, and rolled her shoulders.

Cadigal's Corner was packed tonight, and Ella knew it was because of her. She was perhaps the most popular singer in Kings Cross, and she drew them in every night—all kinds.

Purists captivated by the neighborhood's outmoded atmosphere that was still mostly stylish, yet slightly going to seed.

Businessmen passing through Sydney who came out of curiosity, or because they could still appreciate a good act.

Craggy-faced laborers from the surrounding blocks who drooled when she gave them a sexy pout.

A few women were wedged here and there between the men; Ella believed they secretly envied her. A pair of choobs she recognized; sometimes they caused trouble, but the pair looked subdued tonight; an obvious Azzie in the middle of the second row; a stage manager from a joint downtown. Several tourists were here too, mostly Americans and Japanese, and mostly young—they stood out like that proverbial sore thumb. She could effortlessly tell the locals from the foreigners, the regulars from those who were here for the first time. The latter were always marked by the expressions on their faces. They hadn't known what to expect from the old-fashioned Australian tawdry-house.

Ella vowed to give them a show they wouldn't soon forget.

"Lover won't you find me, find me.
I'm lonely, won't you keep me, keep me?
Keep me close to your heart. I'll be yours alone.
'Til another catches my eye and steals me, steals me."

In the front row, a pudgy elf with obvious cybereyes lit up a cig. She ran her index finger down her throat to her chest and stared at him. Ella grinned as his hand shook, and she drew her finger lower. The cig fell from his doughy fingers and struck his pantsleg. He awkwardly patted it out and looked up, but the singer had already moved on to a new target.

She leaned forward, batting her thick lashes and teasing the top of a young dwarf's carefully-trimmed mohawk. He stood next to the footlights, mutely gaping at her. *A newcomer,* she thought, *one who dresses well and smells faintly of White Cristal cologne.* His breath carried a hint of graypuppy, and made her yearn for a slip. *He'll have something to tell the boys in the office tomorrow—if he doesn't think this is all a hallucination.* She coyly winked at him, then pivoted smoothly and returned to the center of the stage.

"Hot passion, let it find you, find you.
Let it burn inside you, 'side you.
Your heart sings a melody, sings you'll be mine alone.
'Til another comes along and steals you, steals you.
'Til another comes and steals you away. . ."

Ella shut her eyes and hummed the last few notes, the alto sax wailing a sad, haunting riff as her voice faded. The spotlight shrank, allowing the shadows of the stage to reach up and envelope her. The crowd responded wildly, clapping, hooting, whistling, and shouting as the curtain closed. Ella hiked her dress up to her knees and strode off.

"Beautiful, beautiful, beautiful, beautiful Ella dear!" gushed Cadi Hamfyst, the hulking, one-tusked troll who owned Cadigal's Corner. He gently patted her shoulder as she glided past. "Beautiful, beautiful, beautiful Ella my sweet. I love that song."

Ella pressed against the wall as a trio of song-and-dance girls tap-tap-tapped past, dressed in silver and blue tights, feathered skirts low around their hips. They were a new act, come up from Canberra, and Ella thought Cadi should have watched their vids closer before signing them. All elven, the tall one in the middle had overdone it with her breast implants, and looked so top heavy that she might fall forward at the slightest shuffle-ball-change. The shortest had fiberoptic hair that was never the same color twice. The third was simply unremarkable, too plain for the live stage. Amateurs.

After they'd passed. Ella headed down a twisting corridor filled with clothes racks and lined with dressing rooms. She was the only entertainer at Cadigal's that commanded her own room—Miss Ella Gance painted above the door. She'd told Cadi to put a star above it, but that hadn't happened yet. Maybe she'd get a star elsewhere someday—if she ever made it into one of Brisbane's top nightclubs. She was always "away with the pixies," thinking about getting out from under this near-constant mana storm, to a place where fate and a random bolt of magic couldn't turn someone walking down the sidewalk into a wombat.

But that would never happen, would it? She'd pay her dues in the Cross—amid its antiquated strip shows, sex parlors, tawdry-houses, and pubs—until she died. The few-square-block area was Sydney's armpit, civilized folk claimed, the neighborhood still clinging to the past and its outdated constructions, right down to the original bricks that made up the streets and sidewalks and the metal keys that opened many of the doors.

Despite the area's backwater vibe, Ella and her friends considered Kings Cross the heart of the city. It pulsed with a rhythm found nowhere else, and everyone of every background and sexual persuasion was welcomed with open arms. The purist Aborigines. The fanatically moral RighteousRight. The wide-eyed tourists. The jaded locals. The zealots of every stripe—from those who embraced the time of Sydney's founding as halcyon days to the ones who held dear more recent years. Even the cyber-addicts, ever searching for new enhancements and attachments, ever drunk on the technology spewing from Sydney's research centers . . . even they came here. The Cross attracted them all like a magnet, enfolded them in its shadowy arms, and hugged them to its big, stormy bosom.

The Cross had welcomed her more than thirty years ago, in an earlier incarnation of herself. And though she wanted to be a star in Brisbane, where the nuyen flowed faster, the weather was kinder, and the audience more sophisticated—thought about picking up stakes and going to Brisbane every day—she knew she'd miss this place terribly if she did. Going somewhere else would just kill her. So she could damn well dream about leaving, but she knew she was staying.

Ella reached her room and nudged the door open. Twenty-five minutes before her next number. Plenty of time. She grabbed her sequined purse and darted to the back door, looking over her shoulder to make sure Cadi wasn't around. The troll discouraged the girls from leaving the building between acts—fearful, she imagined, that they'd get it in their pretty heads to keep going. Satisfied no one was watching, she slipped out the security door and felt the alley's sweltering night air wash over her.

She squatted and groped for the brick, her insurance against getting locked out. There was no handle on the alley side. It was dark behind Cadigal's Corners; the streetlight a half block away was broken—again. Had the neighborhood accepted the hydroposts the rest of the city used, there wouldn't be such problems. But just enough light spilled out from the opened security door and twinkled down from the stars in the rare gap in the cloud so Ella could see a little. At last her hand closed on an empty Toohey's bottle. It would work. She stuffed the neck into the jamb and the door caught against it.

Padding across the alley, she sat on an empty crate and fumbled in her purse, retrieving a small compact that held her slips. Just one, she admonished, as she placed it under her tongue and felt a rush akin to swallowing a few shots of expensive whiskey. She edged her fingers beneath the gold choker and rubbed her Adam's apple. The balmy night, coupled with the slip of graypuppy, made her sweat. No, glow, she corrected.

The heat felt good; she never complained about hot weather.

She let the delicious sensation roll through her, imagining herself by a waterfall eternally cascading over some tropical sun-baked cliff. Then the experience ended all too soon, and she nearly reached for another slip.

"Don't," she whispered. "Too easy." Way the hell too easy to pop one after another and be swept away by the rapture, to lose all track of herself, and miss her next number. She'd done it before.

Ella wasn't sure how much time had passed. She'd put the chrono in her purse, but without the streetlight she wouldn't be able to read it. *Better get back inside to be safe.*

She stood, brushed off her bottom, and started for the door, but stopped when she heard a trash bin fall over behind the Chinese restaurant two doors down. *Cats,* she thought with a smile. Cadi often kidded that the restaurant served Siamese cats with ribs attached.

But then another bin tipped over, and Ella heard something shuffling in the debris. Something much bigger than a cat.

From the shadows, the stranger watched the singer. He sniffed the air, sorting out the smells of beef and lamb and soyjerky, of rotten vegetables and redfish. He was hungry, and his stomach rumbled with the thought of the discarded food. But he also smelled the singer, and the singer was what he'd come here for.

He was pleased; this one was walking slowly in the sparkly high heels, unable to move too quickly over the brick alleyway. The one he'd killed nearly four weeks ago had been a more challenging target, faster in flats, athletic, an elf, almost got away. He was glad this singer wasn't an elf; in another life he'd loved her. That voice. Good thing she was human, wasn't an elf. Hated elves. Most elves were nimble and quick.

He preferred easier targets, and humans fit that bill; took less time to deal with.

The stranger stuck out his tongue, licked his bulbous lips, and started toward his prey.

This one should be easy enough.

This one wasn't an elf.

The regulars knew the girls came out back between acts to grab a smoke or some fresh air. They often waited here to buy some of the girls' services—the ones who were joygirls on the side—or sell them slips, though they didn't usually do either amid the refuse. But it was a good spot to set up arrangements.

Ella peered into the shadows and saw a man, very dark and well over two meters tall.

"Sorry, mate," she said. "Break's over. No time for fun."

The man walked closer, and Ella guessed he was likely a bum or a pug—Lord knew the Cross had enough of them. *Scrounging in the alley for food, no doubt.*

"Try the trash behind Wesley's Diner. The tucker's much better there—Australian-style." When she said 'Australian,' it came out 'Strine' like the Loyalists desperately hanging onto the land's original accent pronounced it. "Grilled redfish. Smell it? Yum."

Ella stepped toward the back of Cadigal's, but the man slid around her even faster. One more large step, and he blocked her from the door. Maybe he was a troll; he was certainly wide enough, and taller than Cadi, maybe 2.4 meters. Ella watched the figure stoop, remove the Toohey's bottle. The door closed, and the light disappeared.

Ella bolted, but she couldn't match the large man's speed. Several long strides and the stranger came even with her, and then shot past, stepping to the center of the alley as he flicked open a long-bladed knife that *thrummed* softly. He slashed the air with it, the *thrum* growing louder and the knife's edge glowing pale red-orange.

A heater. Like some of the bangers carried. Ella felt faint, and nearly toppled off her high heels.

"Please, m-m-mate. Let's not have any trouble here." She started backing up, and the stranger followed. "I'm not even a woman. So if women're what you're interested in, you can look elsewhere." Ella reached down the front of her dress and pulled out a piece of sweat-soaked foam. "See? I'm a false sheila. I'm an impersonator. N-not a joygirl, either."

He took another step forward, and Ella took another one back. The singer was sweating profusely now—from the heat that she'd never minded, from fear, from thinking about how she might get out of this without a scratch on her perfect and oh-so-expensive body with its high-end vocal range enhancers.

"No!" Ella sputtered as her heel caught in a crack between the bricks. She tugged her foot free of the shoe, and then kicked off the other one. Out of the corner of her eye, she saw the stranger lean in, the superheated blade edge glowing in the darkness.

She whirled and ran down the long alley, leaving Cadigal's Corner and the Chinese restaurant behind. She felt her beautiful sequined purse slip from her sweat-slick fingers, heard her bare feet slapping against the bricks, and then heard a louder sound catching up to her from behind—the stranger's pounding feet.

Her heart hammered madly as she took in great gulps of the humid air. Her lungs burned, and her temples throbbed like her head was going to explode. But she willed herself to run even faster. If she could just break out of the alley on the other side, she'd be near the park. There'd be people around the restored El Alamein Fountain, there always were. They'd help her.

Ella grabbed her aching side, then felt herself flying forward, her feet tangled in her long dress. The ground rushed up, and she slammed hard into the bricks.

The stranger bent down and his muscled arm shot out, fingers closing on a slender ankle. Ella flailed, grabbing at the cracks between the bricks and trying to pull herself toward the end of the alley—closer to the park and to the people gathered there, who were always by the fountain late at night, drinking and laughing and wading in the water.

She felt her battered knees, her sore ribs, which were probably cracked because she'd never bothered with bone lacing, had never thought she'd need it. But she also felt like she was making progress. Clawing at the street with all her strength, Ella dragged the man with her, until at last she saw faint light filtering into the end of the alley. The streetlight from the park.

"Help!" she screamed as the stranger tightened his grip. *So strong. Impossibly strong.* Pain shot up her left leg as the bones in her ankle broke, then she felt the stranger's hands on her other leg, squeezing until those bones splintered, too.

Tears spilled from Ella's eyes, and her chest heaved as she was harshly rolled over. Pain stabbed up from her shattered legs, and she stared in mute terror as the stranger placed a heavy foot on her silk-covered stomach.

Ella whimpered, tears slid down her perfectly sculpted face. She felt the heated knife pierce her skin, heard her blood begin to sizzle, and in that instant, she caught a glimpse of an empty Brisbane stage, and knew she'd never see the real thing.